T3-ANT-275

PAT NIXON—
AS ONLY HER MOST INTIMATE FRIENDS
HAVE KNOWN HER

—The story of what her marriage has been like, from the first romance to what it later became

—Her feelings and actions at the time of Watergate and her husband's other political adventures

—The deceptions she was forced to commit in public, and her very different personality in private

—How she feels about her two daughters, and their lives today

—The extraordinary contrast yet strange links between her and Jacqueline Kennedy

—The long-overdue facts about her alleged drinking

—Her life today behind the high walls of San Clemente

This book was written after extensive interviews with those who have known Pat Nixon best from her California girlhood to the present. The result is a tremendously moving human drama—the intimate story of one of the most heroic and tragic women of our time!

THE LONELY LADY OF SAN CLEMENTE
by LESTER DAVID

THE LONELY LADY OF SAN CLEMENTE
THE STORY OF
PAT NIXON

LESTER DAVID

A BERKLEY BOOK
published by
BERKLEY PUBLISHING CORPORATION

Excerpts from the book have appeared in various newspapers, through the services of the United Feature Syndicate, Inc., and in *Good Housekeeping* magazine.

This Berkley book contains the complete text of the original hardcover edition. It has been completely reset in a type face designed for easy reading, and was printed from new film.

THE LONELY LADY OF SAN CLEMENTE

A Berkley Book / published by arrangement with Thomas Y. Crowell Company

PRINTING HISTORY
Thomas Y. Crowell edition published August 1978
3 printings through 1979
Berkley edition / August 1979

ISBN: 0-425-04253-7

A BERKLEY BOOK® TM 757,375
Berkley Books are published by Berkley Publishing Corporation,
200 Madison Avenue, New York, New York 10016.
PRINTED IN THE UNITED STATES OF AMERICA

FOR WILLIAM AND REGINA DAVID

Contents

SECTIONS OF PHOTOGRAPHS FOLLOW PAGES 00

I saw my lady weep,
  And Sorrow proud to be exalted so
In those fair eyes where all perfections keep.
  Her face was full of woe;
But such a woe, believe me, as wins more hearts,
Than Mirth can do with her enticing parts.

—Songs set by John Dowland, 16th century

Upon such sacrifices, my Cordelia,
The gods themselves throw incense.

—William Shakespeare, *King Lear*

1

Behind the Walls

ONE DAY

In mid-1978, nearly four years after she left the White House, one day was much like another for her.

She awakens before seven in the darkened bedroom of her San Clemente home. When the drapes are parted, the Pacific Ocean appears as though through gauze in the July morning haze; by ten or eleven, a commanding view of the coastline will stand out brilliantly as far as Dana Point, eight miles to the north.

In twenty minutes she is at breakfast, brought by Fina Sanchez. Fina and her husband Manolo have been cook, valet, and maid for the Nixons for more than ten years. There are no other servants in the U-shaped house. Breakfast is always light: fresh fruit or fruit juice, toast and coffee. It has not changed in decades, nor has the time she rises, but now there is a difference.

She eats slowly, using her left hand instead of the customary right. The physical therapist has instructed her to use the hand, especially the fingers, as much and as often as possible, to strengthen the muscles affected by the stroke she suffered in July of 1976. The stroke has partially paralyzed her left side, slightly affected her speech, which is still somewhat slurred, and brought on a painful arthritic condition.

1

Her hours are precisely planned. After a lifetime of tightly organized days, she cannot get over the habit. When she was First Lady, her schedule was typed out in advance after consultation with her staff, and she had insisted on following it punctually. Now she has no staff or even a secretary; she plots out in her mind what she will do and when, and does it to the minute, as always.

She knows this is the day for the physical therapist's visit—three each week—to supervise the exercises. But before the therapist's arrival, she has planned some gardening, one of her major delights. Because of the continued weakness of her left side, it is difficult for her to kneel to tend her roses and vegetables. She can manage much better if she gets down on all fours, supporting herself on both knees and one hand. "She puts on dark pants," her daughter Julie confides, "so the stains on her knees won't show." Julie, who knows how hard her mother is fighting to regain her full health and strength, says softly: "I ache for her. . . . It makes me sad to see her growing older because I never think of her as old. She's so young looking and acting."

Despite her illness, she looks extremely well. Her weight has returned to its normal 110 pounds and, with her height of 5 feet, 5¾ inches, she looks straight and slim. She keeps her hair a pale gold, but the lines are deeper now in her face, neck, and forehead, though she hardly looks her age—sixty-six in March of 1978. Lines or no, she still uses only a light beige base to make up, light pink lipstick, and a small amount of eye shadow and mascara. She has never had cosmetic surgery to remove lines or wrinkles.

Doctors cannot predict how quickly a patient can recover from the effects of a stroke, or how completely. Richard Nixon is convinced that his wife will regain her strength completely, but Julie is less optimistic; she feels that while her mother has made remarkable progress because of the vigorous rehabilitation regimen she has followed, she will never make a full recovery. "She tires so easily," Julie says sadly. "She's just not that strong."

For a few months following the stroke, she used a

cane when she walked inside the house and on the grounds. She has since discarded it.

After the gardening, there is a period of rest but not for long. Soon she will be sitting at a card table dealing herself a game of solitaire. But it is not to kill time. This, too, is part of her program to get well. She has been instructed to exercise her fingers by dealing the cards, picking them up, laying them down with her left hand. She does this at least once each day, sometimes more often.

After lunch—usually a small salad or sandwich, sometimes a cup of soup and a hamburger, followed by iced tea, coffee, or a soft drink—she takes a nap. Afternoons, she may talk to close friends on the telephone. Julie and her husband, David Eisenhower, have rented an apartment at Capistrano Beach a few miles away and visit often. Tricia Nixon Cox, her blond, delicate-boned elder daughter, lives in New York. She flew in on July 4, 1977, for Julie's birthday. Julie turned twenty-nine on the fifth and there was a small family dinner party, with gifts and banter. Pat had laughed and enjoyed herself hugely that weekend. Tricia's husband, Edward F. Cox, a gangling, serious young man who towers a full head and neck above his tiny wife, had been unable to break away from work at the law firm of Cravath, Swaine and Moore.

After her session with the therapist, she sits on the shaded terrace which looks out over the Pacific at San Mateo Point and reads. She prefers biographies and historical novels. *Nicholas and Alexandra,* Robert K. Massie's account of the lives and last tragic years of the Russian imperial family, was a special favorite. She also liked Morris L. West's novel *The Ambassador* and Antonia Fraser's *Mary Queen of Scots.* She read with considerable interest Anne Morrow Lindbergh's *Gift from the Sea,* a poetical evocation of the precious values of privacy and solitude. The book was published in the mid-1950s and Pat has taken it from the shelf and reread it several times. She will often listen to music, too, on the stereo; semiclassical pieces and operettas are favorites. She adores such musical comedy recordings as

My Fair Lady, Carousel, Oklahoma and, coincidentally, *Camelot,* which Jacqueline Kennedy played over and over in the White House when she was First Lady.

Although she receives hundreds of letters daily, she can no longer answer each personally or dictate replies, as she did with every message that came to her in the White House. Almost 104,000 pieces of mail, 5,000 telegrams, and hundreds of floral arrangements arrived at San Clemente in the three weeks following her stroke. Since then, she has received more than a million messages from all over the world. A corps of local volunteers, women who have remained loyal to the family and to her, come to San Clemente to sift through the letters, answer some, and pass along to her those that arrive from special people. In groups of six, the volunteers work several hours each day. However, they come to the office complex, which is about a quarter-mile from the main house. They never see her.

When she feels up to it, she will sit on her terrace and write brief replies to close friends like Helen McCain Smith, who was her press secretary up to the time of the resignation and later became an information officer at the American Embassy in London, or to blond, pert Terry L. Ivey, who was Mrs. Smith's assistant. On plain white notepaper headed La Casa Pacifica, she writes chatty little notes in blue ink in a neat, slightly slanted script. She expressed thanks to Terry for remembering her birthday (March 16, 1977); Terry's greeting, she wrote, brought her "joy laced with happy memories," and she added: "David and Julie are living here for a few months so the days are likely to be especially happy."

In late afternoon, her husband returns from the offices, which are outside the white adobe wall of the estate. In 1975, when he was recovering from the phlebitis that almost killed him, he would travel the distance in a golf cart, but now he walks. Every day, when he comes home, the Nixons get into their bathing suits and swim in the tiled outdoor pool. Lounges and folding canvas chairs are ranged around, four of them bearing names on their backs like directors' chairs on a movie set: The President, Mrs. Nixon, Tricia, and Julie.

She enters the water and swims, hard and purposefully, using the breast stroke. She does a lap, rests, and goes at it again. Before her stroke, she could easily do a dozen without tiring. Except for swimming, exercises of the type she must do now are new to her, for she has never performed any formal calisthenics or owned any gym apparatus; neither had she ever subjected herself to the pounding of a masseuse or sat in a sauna or steam bath. She had always preferred hard physical work. She would don slacks and an old windbreaker and strike out along the pathways at Camp David, the presidential retreat at Catoctin Mountain in Maryland, for a brisk walk in the sharp morning air or at twilight. At San Clemente, she used to stride briskly along the water's edge on the beach, breathing deeply, arms moving. Occasionally, the President would walk with her, and bad weather was never a deterrent. The Nixons' three dogs—King Timahoe, an Irish setter; Vicky, a gray French poodle; and Pasha, a black and tan Yorkshire terrier—usually darted around them. Whenever time or her schedule allowed, she would walk for at least two hours each day. In Washington, too, she would frequently join the President and his friends for a bowling evening in the basement alleys and became so expert she regularly outscored her daughters and Charles G. Rebozo, the Florida financier who has been a Nixon crony since the mid-1950s.

Once a bowling ball slipped from her fingers and fell squarely on a presidential toe. Nixon danced around the alley, hopping on one foot and howling with pain. Julie, recalling the story, says he lost his temper; then, remorseful, "couldn't have been more considerate and thoughtful to Mom" all the next week.

After a fifteen- or twenty-minute swim, they dress and Fina and Manolo Sanchez serve them dinner, often on the poolside terrace, sometimes in the dining room. Usually, they dine alone; rarely, there will be guests —Julie and David, and only close personal friends. Rebozo and Robert Abplanalp, another millionaire friend linked to Nixon's financial affairs, telephone frequently and come personally whenever they are on the West Coast. Sometimes people high in official life come to see them, though the visits are not publicized.

Nobody stays late. Everyone watches closely to see if she is tiring. When the signs come, they make their goodbyes.

There are many nights when they sit alone. Often he will go alone to his study, which she decorated in royal blue and which has a magnificent view of the ocean through its arched windows. Here, as a log glowed in the tiled fireplace, he worked on his memoirs. She will read or look at television.

Sometimes they will watch a movie, a print of which has been sent by friends in the industry. A screen is put up at one end of the large living room and a technician operates the equipment. Recently, a friend suggested they see *Network*, a corrosive indictment of the television business written by Paddy Chayefsky. He called Victor Lasky, who knew Chayefsky, to try to obtain a print, but there was a great deal of worried consultation about the profanity in the movie. Wouldn't it upset the Nixon women? Lasky, who relates the story, laughs and shakes his head. A shrewd man, he realizes the illogic of the concern, for Julie and her mother were hardly unaware of the expletives deleted from the Watergate tapes.

They have separate bedrooms toward the rear of the house, each with an ocean view, as they did in the White House and at their Key Biscayne estate, which they no longer own. (At the Florida home, he slept in the office complex, away from the main house.) He goes to bed late, often after midnight, usually taking his work with him and either reading or working for an hour or so.

She retires early, usually by ten, and reads a short while before she falls asleep.

RECLUSE

Patricia Nixon, the country's First Lady from 1969 to

1974, became a virtual recluse after Richard Nixon resigned as the 37th President of the United States. She disappeared from public view, secluded behind the high walls and impenetrable trees and shrubbery of the 5.9-acre estate where they went to live.

Helen Smith explained to me in February of 1978 following a conversation she had with Pat: "She doesn't leave often. She's just not well. Her blood pressure has not stabilized. She gets very tired because the pressure fluctuates, and she cannot stand much excitement."

Jack Brennan, Nixon's aide-de-camp who sees the family daily, told the San Clemente Republic Club in the summer of 1977: "She's not recovering as rapidly as we would like." And Roy O. Day, Nixon's first campaign manager in the race which launched his career in politics, told me sadly: "She's a recluse. It's a damned shame. She's a great lady." Day, now seventy-seven, still lives in the district which elected Nixon to Congress in 1946 and has kept in close touch over the years with the family.

"What does she want to go out for?" Virginia Counts, one of her oldest and closest friends, told me. Mrs. Counts, who lives in Washington, visited Pat during the Thanksgiving holidays in 1977. "She has everything she wants on the estate." Everything, of course, but the outside world in which she once lived, worked hard, and rose to become First Lady of the land—a world which, for the present at least, she apparently no longer wants to face.

There was always something magnificently tough and durable about Pat Nixon. "I do or I die," she once said. "I never cancel out." And, indeed, she never did on anything in her incredibly difficult life. At the time of her greatest trials—the death of her parents when she was still a teenager, her struggles to earn a living as a young girl during the Great Depression, the blows that came as the wife of a hard-charging politician who could arouse a large segment of the population to fury—she was poised, self-possessed, and, above all, rock-hard. One was convinced that Pat Nixon could never give way under any conceivable pressure, for she had taken almost the worst there was and didn't cancel out.

There was a pride, too, in her strength and even a certain forgivable arrogance when she would tell the novelist Jessamyn West, a cousin of her husband: "I'm never tired. I don't get ill."

It was because of this remarkable strength in adversity, this courage and dignity, that readers of *Good Housekeeping* magazine chose her as America's most-admired woman in 1973, 1974, 1975, and 1977; in 1976, she ranked second to Betty Ford. "The unsinkable Pat Nixon," *McCall's* magazine had called her.

It seemed so. When the dam was bursting in 1974, she had been the coolest and most sensible Nixon in the family quarters, the one with the greatest self-discipline. The President had his black moods. Julie was often overly emotional, Tricia was withdrawn. David Eisenhower and Edward Cox, the sons-in-law, were distraught at times. But Pat was granitic. David said it best in the midst of the turmoil: "Mrs. Nixon is always there with a shoulder to lean on."

But the President's downfall cracked the granite and her illness widened the breach.

Following the resignation, it was difficult for her to talk about the presidency without bursting into tears. She remained in seclusion because she did not want to expose herself to questions about her husband and the scandal that led to the first presidential resignation in American history.

She will not talk about Watergate and its aftermath. Even the family does not discuss it now, because they all know how she has been affected.

"She was devastated, and still is," says Earl Mazo, a highly respected Washington journalist who traveled with Nixon on four continents, assisted him with his book *Six Crises,* and wrote the first Nixon biography in 1960. Mazo and his wife, Rita, have been family friends for twenty years.

The anguish she suffered through the ordeal and in the years that followed cannot be measured.

"I would imagine," Mazo told me one evening at his

home in the Chevy Chase section of Washington, "that she must have been hurt even worse than he."

I expressed surprise. "What makes you feel that way?" I asked.

His quiet reply was shattering. "She had the stroke, didn't she?" he said.

Invitations to Las Casa Pacifica are hard to get. One Washington couple who had known the Nixons for years wanted to see them; they sought to be invited again and again, but Pat said no. Once a high official from a foreign country was invited because of his position. Neither the former President nor Pat went to the airport to greet him. They sent emissaries instead, because Pat knew there would be newspeople there and refused to go.

Virginia Counts, who is married to a labor relations executive, is one of her few old friends who has visited her in San Clemente. Pat and Mrs. Counts were classmates at the University of Southern California; the Countses were among the small group who attended the Nixons' wedding; and thereafter they shared many a potluck dinner with them in their struggling days.

Says Mrs. Counts: "She is always glad to see me. We laugh and walk around the estate and talk small talk about old times."

But never about the events that brought Nixon down. Nor does she ever mention any of the individuals involved in the Watergate scandal. "I am certain the hurt still runs deep," Mrs. Counts says. "It will take a long, long while to get over that kind of pain."

She began her withdrawal soon after the Watergate scandal showed signs of involving Richard Nixon, sequestering herself inside the White House, leaving only for walks late at night when she could be certain she would not be seen. On official occasions she was heavily protected by Secret Servicemen and would not talk to newspeople. After Nixon resigned in August, 1974, she vanished with him into their seaside villa at 4100 Calla Isabella.

In June of 1975, on the thirty-fifth anniversary of

their marriage, she emerged for a rare drive around Dana Point with Nixon. He had proposed to her there, on the beach, looking out at the ocean. They drove around Golden Lantern Street, marveling at the changes that had taken place, the new homes and shopping centers built in what they remembered as an uninhabited area. Several times they went to one of his favorite restaurants, El Adobe in San Juan Capistrano, eight miles to the north, a block from the famous mission founded by Father Junipero Serra in 1776. (The restaurant features on its menu a meal called "The President's Choice,"* the dinner served when Nixon gave a party there for some eighty newspeople during his first term.) On New Year's Eve that year, they went to the Victor Hugo Inn, a large restaurant on Cliff Drive in Laguna Beach. She had even gone out to San Clemente, once to a local hardware store to buy things she needed for the house.

Since her stroke in July, 1976, her outside visits have been so rare that even the uniformed guards stationed at the gates night and day can hardly recall them. One, a short and slender man, says: "In fourteen months, I've seen her come out twice." Another, stocky and gray-haired, saw her leave only once in the same period.

Once, in the late spring of 1977, she was driven out in a black limousine, on her way to visit Julie and David at Capistrano Beach. A guard smiled at her and she smiled back. Then she lifted her left arm and waved to him.

It was an impressive act of bravery. Pat Nixon knows that the world knows her left side has been partly paralyzed, and she was demonstrating, even to a lone elderly guard, that she was undefeated.

In June of 1977, she showed even greater courage. Julie had gone to the Beverly Wilshire Hotel on Sunset Boulevard in Beverly Hills to promote a book she had written about famous people she had known, and had invited her mother to lunch. Pat called in a hairdresser,

---

*A combination of chile relleno, Spanish rice, refried beans, and a beef enchilada.

dressed carefully in a beige pants suit, and was driven to Los Angeles.

She spoke briefly to the manager who greeted her and took the elevator to Julie's suite. At the entrance she encountered by accident a lone woman reporter for United Press International who had just completed an interview with Julie. When the reporter, twenty-six-year-old Roberta G. Wax, complimented her on her hairdo, Pat replied, "Thank you very much," and walked by into Julie's room.

"She looked positively beautiful," Ms. Wax told me afterward. "And she walked straight into the suite with a good stride and no limp whatever."

It was a magnificent gesture. Pat had left at home the cane she was still using and literally willed herself to walk with a straight and sturdy stride.

Debilitated as she was, Pat Nixon could not allow herself to be seen as anything but strong and well. "Even if I were dying," she had once said, "I wouldn't let anyone know." Afterward, Julie confided to Helen Smith that it had been a tremendous effort for her mother to make the fifty-mile journey. "She went once," says Mrs. Smith, "and that was kind of it."

Sometimes, though not often, she and Helene Drown, one of her oldest friends, who lives in Rolling Hills, California, will meet and go shopping at Fashion Island in Newport Beach, twenty miles to the north of San Clemente.

She does not venture far on her infrequent trips. In mid-January she was the only First Lady of the past four not present at the memorial service in the Capitol Rotunda for Senator Hubert Humphrey. Rosalynn Carter, Betty Ford, and Lady Bird Johnson were there. Nixon few to Washington with Jack Brennan and Secret Servicemen and attended the services with Tricia, who was staying at San Clemente. It was the first time he had been in the capital since his resignation.

She has received hundreds of invitations—social ones from close friends, bids to officiate at all sorts of civic and charitable functions—but rejected them all.

By the spring of 1978, she was beginning to emerge, but only a little. She flew with Nixon to the Bahamas to visit old friends and then on to New York, where she spent some time with Tricia and her husband. It was the first time she had left California in four years. A few days later, she returned to the shelter of her estate. But wherever she goes, whatever she does, life will never be the same again for Pat Nixon. At the estate or away from it, she will remain a tragic figure, unable to escape the loneliness of exile.

The family tragedy has brought Pat and Richard Nixon closer than they have been in years.

His preoccupation with his drive for power, climaxed by the scandal, had driven them apart. They had not seen much of each other; he would sit alone a great deal, wrapped in moodiness, or go off to Camp David without her. His treatment of her in the last years of his presidency had been so indifferent that her personal staff and members of the astute women's press corps assigned to cover her activities were shocked.

After the resignation, there was a change. He became more protective. He would fly into a rage when he felt she had been hurt by media comments he said were untrue. When he was alone inside La Casa Pacifica he apparently remembered how strong she had been throughout his career and how valuable to him. And he could see once more the devotion she showed him.

It had struck him full force the first morning he awoke inside the San Clemente estate after the resignation. She had gone to his bedroom in the White House the day before when the family was packing and had personally chosen a number of objects she knew he liked, familiar things he had collected over the years. She had put them in a special crate and, after their arrival at San Clemente, unpacked them and placed them herself around his bedchamber so that, when he awoke in the morning, the change would not seem so stark and abrupt.

Once again, as she had done all her married life, Pat Nixon was devoting herself to the next phase of Richard Nixon's career, and he had understood that.

* * *

I went to see how the famous San Clemente estate, which once held world attention as the Western White House, appeared after the tragic events that convulsed the country. The Nixons are as heavily protected as royalty—or a President.

Going there and trying to gain entrance is an astonishing experience. There are private roads, a maze of gates within gates, 1,900 feet of concrete walls, hedges, towering palms and cypresses, and constant patrols of Secret Servicemen who are alert to signals emitted by remote-control sensors hidden in the walls. Intruders bring them on the run, shotguns cradled.

On February 26, 1978, as part of San Clemente's fiftieth birthday celebration, 7,000 visitors paid $2.50 a head to be herded into buses and taken for a seven-minute ride around the former Western White House. They listened to an announcer's recording of a brief description of the estate, based on information Pat had provided. Nobody was permitted to leave the buses. All proceeds from the tours went to the city's Chamber of Commerce to help pay for the city's birthday party.

To reach the gates, a visitor drives down the Avenida del Presidente to its terminus at the south end of the city. The street is actually a frontage road, orginally called, simply enough, Front Street; after the Nixons moved in, the City Council promptly bestowed upon it the more imposing name. Just before the ramp leading to the freeway, one turns sharply to the right and stares at tall iron gates in front of which stands a sign: NO SIGHT SEERS BEYOND THIS POINT.

There is a space between the "sight" and the "seers," which has given rise to a local joke among the young Marines stationed at the huge Camp Pendleton base to the east, that the sleepy, sun-splashed city has always been somewhat spaced out anyway, and that there was more fun to be had in San Diego to the south or Los Angeles to the north, each about fifty miles away. The gate is actually the entrance not just to the Nixon estate, but the Cyprus Shores community of seventy-five exclusive seaside homes, one of which belongs to Jim

Arness, the Marshal Dillon of the *Gunsmoke* television series. The others are owned by retired service and government officials who held major posts, and wealthy business and professional people. The Nixon estate is separated from Cyprus Shores by an eight-foot concrete wall and thus most of the wealthy residents there, like everyone else, are unable to see inside the Nixons' yard.

Once a visitor has been screened by the guardians of the gate, he proceeds along the Avenida de las Palmeras to Calla Isabella, and halts before another gate—this one electronically controlled—the entrance to the estate. From here, a quarter-mile of roadway leads to the mansion.

Members of the Nixon family, and the former President himself, rarely use the Cyprus Shores entrance. There is an alternate one to the left of the gateway which leads to a Coast Guard loran station. A block-long street leads to another electronically controlled gate where a visitor picks up a direct-phone line to the Secret Service headquarters inside. If one is approved, the gate swings open. A roadway leads to the office complex, Nixon's center of operations now as it was when he was President. Adjacent to the offices is the helipad he once used as Chief Executive, but no helicopters land there now. Once there, a visitor is still outside the walls of the estate. Another gate opens onto a roadway that swings in a wide arc toward the white stucco mansion with the red-tiled roof which sits majestically on a bluff with the best view of the Pacific of any of its neighbors.

Whichever entrance is used, anyone entering or leaving the estate must drive in front of the ornate Cyprus Shores gateway and be seen by the guards. Five of them work in shifts so that the gate is covered at all times. They see Nixon driving out two and three times each week with Jack Brennan for golf at the Estrella Country Club at the north end of the city. But they rarely see Pat leave.

The house itself is secluded behind still another high concrete wall, unseen even by visitors on the grounds. The main entrance is through an arched doorway of heavy oak, framed in sculptured wrought iron and topped by a picture of a pink-gowned senorita and a Spanish vaquero on a white mount, done in tile.

You walk through the door and step into an open patio, decorated with hand-made Mexican tiles, a fountain in the center. Surrounding it is the house, classically Spanish in its architecture and unchanged in appearance since it was built in 1926 by Henry Hamilton Cotton, a wealthy real estate developer who also served for a while as the Democratic Party's national finance chairman. In 1935, Ham Cotton had given a barbecue party for 4,000 guests here, among them President Franklin D. Roosevelt, then serving his first term.

The building, which is completely air-conditioned, is one-story high except for three towers, and has four main bedrooms and seven baths. All the rooms are large and open onto the sheltered patio; the living room is 42 by 24 feet, with a fireplace and three tall arched windows overlooking the ocean. The floors are tile laid by Mexican artisans, the furniture is massive, the doors thick and wood-pegged. The hand-hewn ceiling beams in the living room and dining room are painted off-white. Both rooms are decorated in Pat's favorite color, a golden yellow. On the floor of the dining room is an elaborately patterned Oriental carpet which Pat has called "my cookie rug." The family has had it since their two daughters were small girls. "It doesn't show cookie crumbs," Pat explained.

There is a stereo set in Nixon's study and a large library of classical recordings which he often plays. The view of the Pacific from the window is so breathtaking that Nixon has placed his reclining chair with the back to the window so that he will not be distracted by the glory of the seascape while he works or reads.

On one wall is a shelf where a red telephone once stood, the phone that was used only for communicating with world heads of state. It is gone now. But still standing there, is an eight-by-ten-inch frame, is a poem his daughter Julie wrote about him on ruled paper when she was eight years old. It is called "My Dad," and it reads, misspellings and all:

Handsome and kind,
Handsome and kind,
Always on time,
Loving and Good.
Does things he should,
Humerous, funny
Makes the day seem sunny,
Helping others to live,
Willing to give, his life,
For his belovd country.
That's my dad.

Love, Julie

The grounds are not kept as well as they were during Nixon's presidency, but neither are they run down. The Nixons have a full-time gardener, Brigidio Garcia, whose family lives on the estate, but there is more work than he can handle. The area close to the house is well maintained but the outer reaches are not. The three-hole golf course, for example, is no longer usable. The greens have become overgrown and the fairways are lush with grass and weeds.

Unless reminded by some special occasion, San Clemente's 17,000 residents appear to have lost interest in their most famous resident.

Just after the resignation, tourist traffic backed up far onto the Avenida del Presidente: thousands of "sight seers" came daily, keeping the police busy from dawn until late evening. They would stop at the gate, takes pictures of the cops and the guards and the sign, and leave. Every week, too, numbers of them were caught trying to sneak into the grounds. One man, collared inside the estate, explained that he wanted Nixon's permission to castrate himself and, to prove he meant it, showed police some surgical tools. He was hustled to a mental ward.

But the number of tourists rapidly dwindled. There is no longer any need to call in city policemen to handle traffic. Cars still come at the height of the vacation season, but the roads and the gates are deserted at other times.

The most visible members of the household are Fina and Manolo, who do the family's shopping at the Alpha Beta supermarket on El Camino Real, the city's main street. They move quickly through the aisles, choose their foods, and depart, answering no questions. They make no more special requests, as they once did when Nixon was President: macadamia nut ice cream was a favorite of his but the store did not stock it. The market quickly put it in a special order and always had it ready when the Sanchezes asked for it.

There is little spontaneous talk about the Nixons. The people in the restaurants, the motels, and the modern boutiques in the town center go about their business as though they were not a presence anymore.

Once, in 1969, Pat Nixon began planning the things that would go into a future Nixon museum and library. It would be in California and would house not only the presidential papers but also the vast collection of dolls she and Nixon bought for their daughters during their foreign visits. There is no library and no plans for one, and the San Clemente public library now has only a few folders filled with newspaper clippings about him. Few readers ask to see them.

Even the city's newspaper, *The Daily Sun-Post*, has almost given up on them because they have shut themselves away so completely. Only a few articles appear from time to time.

Occasionally visitors will stroll down the beach to stare at the estate. They can see only the embankment and a gazebo where Secret Servicemen are stationed. The agents sit there and look disinterestedly at the visitors.

2

Country Girl

UNDERCURRENTS

One day in early fall, when she was sixteen years old, Pat Ryan and Myrtle Raine, who lived next door, "stole" a car.

It wasn't the first time. "Hooking" an older brother's automobile was a frequent pastime of the teenage set in Artesia, a farming and dairy community in California where she lived, worked, and played as a young girl.

Usually the incidents ended happily enough: the boys got angry, walloped their sisters if they could catch them, and forgot about the incident until the next time. On this occasion, though, Pat and her friends almost got themselves into serious trouble.

Myrtle, her sister Louise, a girl named Teresa Galvers, and Pat wanted to go to a dance at Excelsior Union High School in Norwalk, where they were classmates, but they had neither dates nor transportation. The school was six miles away, too far for walking and certainly for returning late at night. The only logical way to go, it seemed to Pat, was in her brother Bill's Model T Ford, which stood at the side of the house, alone, unused at the moment, and practically waiting to be swiped.

18

So she got in and drove off with Myrtle and Louise, picked up Teresa, and headed up South Street toward the school. Ironically, it was Bill who had taught his sister to drive. Pat was a fully licensed driver, though not an officially tested one: all she had to do was show up at the Artesia City Hall, write her name, address, and age on a form (fourteen was the minimum), and walk out with a permit. Myrtle remembers that the man she later married got his license at twelve because he lived with his grandmother and was the oldest able-bodied person in the household.

In front of the school another car was parked in the middle of the roadway, its lights out, probably stalled. Unable to see it in time, Pat slammed into it and the Model T flipped on its back, its wheels spinning. Myrtle's chin and lip were cut and she suffered a deep knee wound. She still bears some of the scars. Teresa, Myrtle remembers, "got a hole on top of her head," but Pat and Louise escaped with minor scrapes.

Pat exhibited even then the coolness and control that, years later, would become a hallmark of her character. Calmly, she crawled from the wreckage, shed no tears, showed no hysteria. The car had been bashed into a total wreck. The girls, giggling by now, were rushed to a hospital by a passing car and patched up. Then, one by one, they were dropped off at home.

She caught modified hell from Bill and her parents, their anger tempered by relief that neither she nor the others had been seriously hurt.

As this and other incidents of her childhood and young adult years reveal, Pat Nixon was hardly the perfect child, showing few signs of growing up to be the "perfect political wife."

In her late twenties, she married Richard Nixon. Once she did so and became aware of his single-tracked passion for the power that high office can confer, she consciously and deliberately programmed herself to help him achieve his political ambitions. She became committed to his ego and aspirations, submerging her own self and her own desires, pleasures, and ambitions.

It was an awesome decision because it was to alter her

life almost completely. Julie Nixon Eisenhower admitted to me, "Mother made many sacrifices," but the full extent of what she did can only be seen by looking closely at the entire life from its beginning to the tragic turn it took in its seventh decade—to see how the personality began to flower and how the self that could have developed was allowed to wither while she set about making herself into what she thought was the best helpmate any political man could possibly have.

Pat Nixon did this willingly, even eagerly, in spite of her own feelings and yearnings. She believed in the simple axiom—whose validity, if it ever had much, is now being seriously questioned—that a husband leads and a wife follows. This was conventional behavior in the pre-feminist years when she married him, bred into her not only by the culture of the times but by the example of her parents. For her mother had willingly followed where her husband had gone, guiding and chiding and advising at times, but there had been no real question about whose decision counted.

Success in politics was Nixon's goal and he was her husband, and so she made herself into the very model of the dutiful political wife—standing behind him, shoring him up, shaking the hands he missed in the long reception lines, defending him. Whither he went, she went too. And she became an almost classic example of the woman who can become a victim of a man's single-minded drive for power.

She became known pejoratively as "plastic Pat," "antiseptic Pat," "Pat the robot," "Pat the pluperfect," because of the permanent-press smile that stretched her lips but did not light up her eyes, the hair that was always in place, the shining face that never showed a bead of perspiration or a smudge of soot, the creaseless and spotless dresses and suits, her absolute tirelessness. She would remain for hours at state dinners, the smile constant, never excusing herself to go to the ladies' room. Since Washington protocol decrees that at these functions nobody goes to the powder room or men's room unless the First Lady or the President goes first, there were many high-ranking women guests who wore pained faces and tightened their thighs as the evenings progressed.

She worked hard to project this image of perfection. She felt it was the way she could best help her husband. For most of her years in politics, she said as little as she could in public because she was terrified of making mistakes. While great events were happening in the nation and the world, she would make only small talk with people of all levels, taking care to express no views of substance lest they turn a single voter against Richard Nixon. Only in the last years did she dare speak out in public on some issues. But privately, she was not plastic at all. There were deep emotional currents in her that went undetected by the media, which knew little and perhaps cared less about the woman's human side. At home or with friends she trusted, she was a wholly different Pat Nixon from the one who appeared in public. Privately, too, the tight rein she imposed upon herself would sometimes slip, and then even outsiders could see her fears, tears, anger, and—though it was hard to believe—the true lightness of her spirit. Julie put it best: "Nobody really understands Mother. I feel that she kind of lost faith that journalists would interpret things as they really are, and just didn't want to reveal herself at all."

The young Pat Ryan had a temper, and a good one. She was stubborn and rebellious. And she was aggressive. These traits remained and would surface now and then over the years, though she honed the talent of hiding them exquisitely fine.

Even as a growing girl, she could mask her feelings, but not so well as she would later, and not so well that her close friends, and certainly her father, could not tell what was going on inside.

Myrtle Raine says it plainly: "Pat had a pretty good temper once in a while, but she never showed much of it." Nor did she get over her anger quickly. "When she was provoked," Myrtle recalls, "she was provoked for a while." And at such moments, Will Ryan would look at her darkening face and, though she said nothing, laugh and exclaim: "You stubborn Irishman!"

George Gortikov, a high school classmate, got a good taste of Pat's aggressiveness and remembers it vividly. He was president of the student body and she was the secretary. Gortikov, who now lives in Glendale, California, recalls her as "very quiet" but with a "strong personality," though he adds that "she wasn't the kind to give that impression at first. It was only after I worked with her for a while that I understood what she was doing. And I still feel that she had a big hand in the governing of the entire United States. She's that strong."

But she was subtle in her aggressiveness, he says. "That's why you wouldn't know what was hitting you because it hit so suddenly. . . . I know we'd be conducting meetings [of the student body] and I was supposed to be conducting them but it wound up that she was taking over."

The streaks of anger, rebellion, and aggression would surface from time to time during some of the most critical stages in her husband's political life. And forcefully. Though her dedication to him was total, she could, and did, tease him with a sharp needle and even give him plainspoken hell at times. She was adamantly opposed to his accepting the vice presidential nomination in 1952 as Dwight Eisenhower's running mate, and made it perfectly clear to him how she felt.

However, once he made the decision, she backed him unwaveringly and worked hard to help him win it. She could become furious with him when she felt he had tripped up. One example: During the 1956 campaign, when he was running for re-election as President Eisenhower's running mate, he had rewritten an important speech many times and dictated the final draft on a recorder. But one of his staff assistants had forgotten to push the correct button and the tape was blank. Disheartened, he delivered an earlier draft he had not liked, written by Father John Cronin, a theologian who was a member of his "brain trust." Disliking the speech, he did it badly. Afterward, Father Cronin says, "Pat chewed the hell out of him in front of the staff."

Although she had more political savvy than people

thought and was more critical of her husband in private than many imagined, none of this meant that Pat Nixon was Richard Nixon's political partner, as Lady Bird Johnson was to Lyndon, as Rosalynn Carter is to Jimmy, or as Bess Truman was to Harry. Truman called his wife "the Boss" and she was: she was consulted on every problem of importance and her opinion counted heavily with him. Bess was not only Truman's supporter but his close counselor during his senatorial campaign in 1934 and later worked on his Senate staff; no important report was ever issued from his office, Truman admitted, without going through Bess's hands. She continued to perform in this important role all through his brief vice presidency. During the 1948 presidential campaign, she blue-penciled every one of his speeches.

Lady Bird Johnson, well trained in politics, advised the President and he, too, admitted her importance: she urged him to run in 1964, and he did; she urged him not to run for re-election in 1968, and he did not.

Pat operated on a different level. Her role was supportive but not consultative. He turned to others for substantive advice, and she never offered any. (Never? Only once. Later, as the story of their lives unfolds, we will find out that one time she did make a suggestion, a crucial one, and it was ignored.) He made the decisions and she accepted them. If he said he would run, she would run with him as hard as she could. Nixon singled out Mrs. Charles de Gaulle as "a marvelous woman" who, he was certain, was never consulted about a political problem by the Grand Charles.

This was the kind of woman Nixon admired, and as far as he was concerned, it was the kind he had married.

ST. PATRICK'S BABE IN THE MORN

A visitor going back into Pat Nixon's life heads toward South Street in the city of Cerritos, twenty miles southeast of Los Angeles. It is a broad, clean, multi-lane thoroughfare running east and west past housing developments, stores, gasoline stations, and, not far away, one of the swankiest motels in the entire area.

It was different when she grew up here in a small house which still stands facing South Street. In 1914, when Pat's father moved his growing family here, South Street was a narrow, rutted dirt road, dusty in dry summer heat, muddy and pocked with treacherous water-filled holes after the rains. In the fall, when the hard Santa Ana winds came, the dust would swirl into eyes and throats, tumble trees, lift unsecured objects and toss them around. The children of the farmers and dairymen would then hide fearfully in their homes and their parents would hope that the damage this time would not be great.

The area was called Artesia* then—an unincorporated town, a poor town, its main street unpaved even in the business center. The largest structure was the two-story Scott and Frampton Building, which housed the Scott and Frampton General Merchandise Store (founded by Arthur Frampton and C. B. Scott shortly after the turn of the century) and the Scott and Frampton Bank. Parker's Hardware Store carried an excellent supply of milking equipment, needed by the area's dairy farmers. There was also a drugstore, a barber, two blacksmith shops, two garages for cars, two churches, a small hospital which had the only X-ray machine in the whole area, and nothing much else.

William Ryan, Pat's father, was a transplanted Easterner, a man who early in life had developed an itch for travel and adventure and responded, as though conditioned for it, to the lure of riches from wherever it beckoned. He spent years seeking the rainbow, had more adventures than most people, and ended his days as a poor farming man.

Born in Ridgefield, Connecticut, on January 7, 1866, Ryan had little formal schooling. He would travel to the waterfront along Long Island Sound, not far from his home, and spend much of his time watching the boats come and go. At New London, to the east, a great

---

*In 1956, the town of Artesia joined with neighboring Dairy Valley to become an incorporated city. Eleven years later, the citizens elected to change their city's name to Cerritos.

whaling port at the time, he saw the fat whaling ships steam in and out and was fascinated by the sight of the huge catches tied to their sterns. Like many small boys of those years, he dreamed of manning the powerful new harpoon guns which had changed old-fashioned whaling completely. Men no longer were going out in tiny whaleboats from the mother ship to hurl harpoons into the big mammals; now harpoons were loaded into the muzzles of cannons mounted on the whalers, aimed and fired at the whales. Grenade heads in the harpoon would explode, set off by a time fuse, after the whale was struck. In his teens, young Ryan signed onto a whaling ship as a deckhand and spent the next few years on the high seas.

In his twenties, he became a surveyor in the Philippines, and then the itch for adventure and the lure of riches returned. In August, 1898, there had been another discovery of gold in Alaska, this time the biggest of all— the Klondike strike—followed by other finds in the Yukon River basin at Nome. Excitement gripped the area, spread to gold-seekers everywhere, and hit Bill Ryan full force in the Philippines. He dropped his surveying and trekked up to the Yukon country to find his fortune, discovered none, and after a few fruitless years moved southward again, across the Canadian wilderness and down to southwestern South Dakota, where one of his brothers was a miner, working to extract gold, silver, and other metals from the Black Hills.

William Ryan's search for riches was as unsuccessful here as it had been in the Yukon, but he learned more than he had ever known about mining techniques. And he wound up with a wife. It was here that, in 1909, he met and married Kate Halberstadt Bender, a widow with two children.

Kate had come to the United States as a child of ten from Hesse in west-central Germany, where she had been born. She had married a shop foreman in South Dakota before her twenty-first birthday and borne him two children, Matthew and Neva. While she was still pregnant with Neva, her husband perished in a flooded mine after an accident, and young Kate, short, stocky, and sweetfaced, caught the eye of William Ryan. He was then forty-three years old, tall and lanky with a moustache across his sun-leathered face. Kate was only twenty-nine.

They had not been married long when the lure called again. Word was seeping north that there was money to be made to the southwest in the city of Ely, State of Nevada, due east of Virginia City, where the fabulous wealth of the Comstock Lode had been discovered a half-century before. There was more gold, silver, and copper there, the stories said, and other valuable minerals too, like zinc and lead. Ryan packed up his family, his few possessions, and set out across the country in an old car for new fields.

In Ely the family set up housekeeping under canvas in a tent city near the mines, where Ryan, thanks to the techniques he had learned in South Dakota, got a job as a silver-mining engineer. Kate cooked and cleaned as best she could, working almost constantly. Eventually they moved into more substantial surroundings. Three more children were born to them: first William Jr., then Thomas, and finally, on March 16, 1912, a little girl Kate named Thelma Catherine. Will Ryan was working in the mines when the baby arrived. When he came home after midnight and learned he had a daughter born so close to St. Patrick's Day, he whooped, added the name Patricia to the other two, and called her his "St. Patrick's babe in the morn." Although he never called her anything else but Pat, she herself was not to use the name until she entered Whittier College years later. Through grade and high school, she was Thelma to her friends, who would also call her by her nickname, Buddy.

Kate, who hated and feared mining, pleaded with her husband to give up the perilous business. Safety measures were still rudimentary, if they existed at all, and accidents were frequent and awesome in the tolls they took. Farming would be a great deal safer, she told him, and finally he was convinced.

In 1914, when Pat was two, Ryan packed up his

family once again and took them to a small truck farm, barely 11 acres of flat ground, in Artesia, about twenty miles southeast of Los Angeles. He proudly called it a "ranch," and from that time he described himself as a "rancher."

There was a small house on the property which Will Ryan set about improving when he wasn't busy growing corn, potatoes, grapes, cauliflower, and watermelons. Pat spent her childhood here, in the five-room house which consisted of a "front room," kitchen, and three other rooms used as bedrooms. There was no electricity, nor was there an indoor bathroom. The tiny kitchen in the rear hadn't room for a sink; that was on the back porch. Water was pumped from a water tower some 100 feet from the back of the house. Will acquired from somewhere a large piano which he installed in the "front" room, dwarfing the 14-by-11-foot chamber, though he didn't play and neither did anyone else in the house. Louise Raine doesn't remember anybody in the house making any use of the huge instrument.

In December, 1974, after years of planning and work, this childhood home of Pat's was converted into a museum and youth center and part of the farm became Pat Nixon Park.* Children play on the swings now, and there is a bike rack near the rear door. Young people come daily to use a large addition to the house, built after the Ryans moved out, as a recreation room. A basketball hoop hangs near the top of the water tower, and its base has been paved.

Much has changed, yet enough remains to evoke strongly the presence of the young Pat Nixon here. Small things are there, unnoticed perhaps by many, yet there are powerful links to the past. The original number of the house is still there at the left, below the large window of the front room; it is 12364 in three-inch-high metal letters. The "2" has long since gone, but the imprint remains, uncovered by the coats of white paint.

*On January 16, 1978, the interior of the house was seriously damaged by a fire which, officials said, was started by a homemade firebomb. Lacking the funds needed for restoration of the building, the city of Cerritos had it torn down in June.

After the Ryans had lived there a while, electricity came. A single naked bulb atop a shutter near the front entrance illuminated the front door at night, and still does. The door is a slab of wood with an old-fashioned latch lock, unchanged from that day.

At one side of the house there is a California walnut tree, its trunk growing almost parallel to the ground. Still alive, it has been propped up by metal bars to keep it from falling prone. Pat Nixon planted this tree there. One night in October, a vicious Santa Ana wind struck violently at Artesia. Pat, then about fourteen, cowered beneath the covers, listening to the shrieking of the storm and the shuddering of the house. In the morning, her walnut tree had blown down but its roots took hold again and it grew once more in its odd way.

Making the soil in Artesia provide a living was a little easier than it had been in the other places where Will Ryan had lived—but not very much. Some years the crops were poor; other times the prices he received were so low that the margin between costs and profits was paper thin. Then there was the problem of water. When the hot, dry summers came, neighboring farmers would pump so much from their wells that Will couldn't get enough for his needs. So he would rouse the entire brood in the middle of the night, when everyone else had finished. Then Pat, along with her brothers and mother, would pump almost the entire night through so that the water tank could be filled.

"It was very primitive," Pat Nixon recalls. "It was a hard life, that's true. I didn't know what it was not to work hard."

Until her late teens, when she left home to earn a living and later to attend college, Pat occupied a small room at the rear of the house. It was actually not a room at all but a wide hall off the living room; and it had no door, just a dark curtain hung on a rod to separate it and give her privacy. There was just enough space for a wooden clothes cupboard, a dresser in a corner, and a simple single bed. There was a window, though, that looked out upon the fields and had gaily colored curtains upon it.

She also made room for some of the "souvenirs" she would "hook" and carry away—a city "stop" sign, a "slow" sign, a construction horse that she somehow picked up and lugged home. Marietta Malcolmson Baron, a high school classmate, says: "We were all so envious that she had the nerve to do it." One day, Marietta and another friend decided that what Pat needed to supplement her collection was one of the metal containers in which the local newspaper, the *Long Beach Press-Telegram*, was inserted each day for subscribers. They waited until evening and drove down Artesia Boulevard, hunting for one.

"There was one," Marietta says, "close to the street, and it was the easiest thing in the world to get. So we stopped and pulled it up by its roots, post and all, and put it in the car. All of a sudden the lights of the house turned on. People had been sitting on their porch. Well, of course, I was panic-stricken because they were going to take the license of the car and my parents were going to know about it. You know, to have stolen something was terrible! So we drove around again, and threw it back in the yard. We didn't dare go on with it."

Pat never added a newspaper box to her collection.

She attended Artesia's sole grade school, a small red-brick building across the street from a Methodist church. Like the homes of its pupils, the school had no water supply of its own: a huge tank stood in the backyard, near the slides, swings, and athletic field, a bumpy, scrub-grass area cleared out after a fashion, upon which the boys would play, no matter the season, a form of soccer. School was a mile from her house and Pat walked in all but the very worst weather down the dirt road upon which, in prolonged drought, farmers would sprinkle used crankcase oil to keep the dust down. Only if it rained very hard would Will Ryan or a neighbor pile the kids into ancient cars and drive them.

The school day was intensive—it was no-nonsense work from the beginning. Officials knew the children had no time for lengthy homework assignments, for their afterhours had to be spent in farm chores. And the education was nothing if not practical. The boys received sound instruction in woodworking and the use of tools in preparation for home fix-it chores most would need to perform on the farms; and from the early grades, the girls were taught to sew and cook.

Pat loved school and was good at it—so good that, before long, she was skipping grades and catching up to her older brothers. Even though she was two years younger than Tom and three years younger than Bill, she soon overtook them both. She graduated grade school the same year as Bill and a year ahead of Tom. Later, Tom caught up and the three Ryans got their high school diplomas in the same class.*

As a child, Pat rarely played with dolls nor was she interested in the play-house types of games that traditionally have occupied little girls growing up. Being a tomboy was more her style.

She wore jeans long before they were fashionable for girls, jeans and bib overalls. So did her girlfriends, and none minded the general disapproval of the older folks in town who thought that girls should look like girls. They were not the ubiquitous, girl-tailored, buttocks-hugging jeans worn today but baggy ones, droopy in the seat, taken, with or without permission, from their brothers' wardrobes. "All the neighbors talked about us wearing our brothers' jeans," Louise Raine recalls. "And their shirts. They didn't think it was the type of thing to do." But, she adds, youthful rebelliousness existed then as in all other times: "We wore them anyway." But not in school, where the rules called for dresses. Later, in high school, Pat and her friends put on the required white long-sleeved middies with navy blue collar and the navy blue skirts. In her last year, the rules were relaxed: the girls were allowed to roll up the sleeves, or cut them off and hem them.

After school and work, Pat raised some hell with her

---

*Let us not assume the boys were slow. Because of the irregularity of their farm duties, the boys had to stay out of school for extended periods.

friends. When she was ten, she led a raid on a beehive near a "haunted house" across the road—a home that stood empty, its roof sagging, the wind whining through its broken windows. "I'll hit the hive, drive the bees away, and then we'll take the honey," she told them. Followed by a small gang of fearful girls, she tiptoed to the hive, smacked it hard with a stick, and got, for herself and her entire patrol, not the honey but painful bee stings.

Play was limited to things that cost little or no money. On some Saturday afternoons, when someone's father could take them, she and her friends would go to the beach at Cherry Avenue, not far from Long Beach, where most of the youngsters of the area gathered. Once in a while, they would ride the streetcar which ran hourly all the way into Los Angeles twenty miles away. The fare was 70 cents, saved penny by penny. They would walk the streets, look in the shops and, if there was money enough, go to a movie.

More frequently, though, when transportation was needed, it was "hooked." When the Ryan brothers' car was being used, or watched too carefully, Pat would help Myrtle and Louise hook the Raine family buggy. The girls would wait until Mr. and Mrs. Raine had gone to town or were visiting on a Sunday, then would lead one of the two old workhorses from its corral, hitch it to the buggy, and cluck off for several hours. They would always have the horse back in the corral and the buggy standing behind the house before the folks returned, a feat requiring equal measures of intuition and sheer luck, but they were never caught.

They'd hook bicycles, too. Pat never had one as a child, and neither did the Raine girls, though their brothers did. Once, when the three girls wanted to go to the Artesia business section a mile and a half away, they waited until the boys were inside the houses, then mounted their bikes and pedaled swiftly off. The boys heard, rushed out, and hollered after them to stop. They didn't.

Pat would occasionally attend the local Christian Science church but was not, on the whole, a religious child. Her father was a Catholic who rarely went to church; on Sundays, he would say, he became a Seventh-Day Adventist because he had to work that day to get his crops ready for market.

Will Ryan was the disciplinarian in the family, running as tight a ship as he could, considering the time he had to spend in the fields away from his family. Kate was too gentle to do much more than scold now and then, but Will's face could darken when the kids got out of line and his voice would thunder commands. When Will said something had to be done, and the menace had crept into his tone, it got done and no questions were asked. Pat, who got into as much trouble as the boys, was not spared the looks or the voice, though she was never spanked as a child.

Pat's mother was a warm-hearted woman who still spoke with a soft German-accented English and whose tiny kitchen always smelled of baking bread, pies, and especially the cinnamon rolls which drew the kids of the area as though magnetized. She began feeling ill in the summer of 1924, when Pat was twelve and still in grade school. As Mrs. Ryan's health declined, Pat was called upon increasingly to nurse her mother and take care of the household.

By the time she entered Excelsior Union High School in September of 1925, Pat—still Thelma to her friends and teachers—had grown into a somewhat plump, altogether adorable girl. Her eyes were dark, her hair brown with red highlights, and her round cheeks were sprinkled lightly with freckles.

On June 18, 1926, with her family at her bedside, Kate Ryan died in the early morning hours of stomach cancer. She was only forty-six years old. Services were held at the Bellflower Undertaking Company's small chapel in Bellflower, a few miles from Artesia. Afterward, a group of Pat's classmates stood awkwardly outside, wondering what to do or say. Pat emerged smiling and walked directly to them. "Didn't she look beautiful?" she said.

Pat at fourteen—not twelve, as most accounts of her early life have stated—took over the household duties.

She rose at dawn to prepare breakfast, raced to catch the high school bus, returned after school to clean, wash, sew, iron, and prepare supper. There had to be time, too, to help her father pack corn and tomatoes, help him irrigate the farm from the deep well Will Ryan had dug, pick the melons and cantaloupes, and scuttle around doing sundry other chores. (And, once in a while, hide a few choice melons in a haystack for consumption later in the evening with friends.)

She was an excellent little cook and housekeeper and about all the problems that anyone could recall of those hard days were the constant feuding between Pat and Tom over the ironing of his white shirts. He insisted they be done without any wrinkles, especially in the collars and cuffs—difficult for an experienced ironer and almost impossible for a young girl with limited time at her disposal. Louise and Myrtle, sorry for their friend who seemed unable to please the fastidious Tom, would help her iron.

Though she had much to think about and occupy her days, she was as anxious as any other freshman girl to receive an invitation to the class prom in spring. When none was forthcoming at once, or even several weeks after the dance was announced, she was as distressed as any other dateless classmate. Finally an invitation came (the person has long since been forgotten), and the search for "the dress" began. The prom was to be a "formal," and Pat had no dress in her closet that would even remotely do.

She asked a friend, Marietta Malcolmson, who lived in Fullerton, to help her pick one out in Los Angeles. Marietta agreed and the two girls rode the streetcar to the city and spent the day hunting for something that Pat could buy with the few dollars she had been saving for months. The city with its tall buildings and fine stores scared them; it was one of the first times either of the country girls had gone there. Finally, they found the perfect dress—a green formal gown with a filmy net overskirt. "She looked like a picture in it with her coloring," Marietta remembers.

She was a superior student in high school. She joined

the debating team; was a member of the Filibuster Club, a group of students interested in public speaking; was secretary of the entire student body in her senior year and vice-president of her class; and she barely missed being chosen valedictorian. The school's yearbook for 1929, the year she graduated, provides an intimate glimpse of a pixyish nature:

> Pseudonym: Buddy
> Intention—To run a boarding house
> Liability—My two brothers
> Occupation—Watching (brother) Tom
> Talent—Watching (brother) Bill

Her social life was limited to school activities. Pat would have a date for a special dance or event, but, like most of her friends, was part of a group. She rarely went out with one boy more than once or twice. And the boy she dated was carefully scrutinized by brothers Tom and Bill, who issued stern warnings to their sister that they expected impeccable behavior. Howard Frampton, a classmate, remembers "they wanted things to be kept up and aboveboard at all times."

Of all her interests as a young girl, dramatics overshadowed the others. Coincidentally, the youthful Richard Nixon, growing up in Yorba Linda and Whittier, a few miles away, was also attracted to amateur theatricals. In 1937, the mutual interest was to bring them together.

Even as grade-schoolers, Pat and the Raine girls would "put on shows" in the Raines' tankhouse, a large room beneath the water tank where they fashioned a small stage, made up their own plays, costumed them, and acted them out. At Excelsior High, she joined Les Marionettes, a drama group conducted by Madeline Thomas, and was acting in its plays almost at the same time that Nixon, at Whittier College, was collaborating in writing a play called *The Trysting Place,* in which he acted the male lead. (Years later, Dr. Albert Upton, drama and English professor at Whittier, saw photographs of Richard Nixon at the Wheeling, West

Virginia, airport, awaiting the arrival of General Eisenhower after the "Checkers" speech. Nixon's head was cradled on the shoulder of Senator William Knowland of California, and he was weeping. "I taught him how to cry," Professor Upton said, recalling that he had trained Nixon to weep during a production of John Drinkwater's *Bird in Hand*. By performance time, Dr. Upton said, "tears just ran right out of his eyes. It was beautifully done.")

Pat had the leading role in her junior class play, *The Romantic Age*, and the next year played the eldest daughter in a dramatization of William Dean Howells's *The Rise of Silas Lapham*, winning accolades for both performances. Says Ms. Thomas: "She was a good actress, far better than run-of-the-mill." Marcia Elliot Wray, a classmate who now lives in Whittier, calls her "the unchallenged actress of the class."

On Graduation Day, she came home with her diploma and sat alone in her room, contemplating her future. She could not know that the next few years were to be bleak, sad, and even harder than the first seventeen.

3

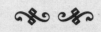

On Her Own

SATURDAY'S CHILD

On a hot fall afternoon, Pat Ryan, then eighteen years old, was bending over her accounts at the First National Bank of Artesia when a young man thrust a note through the slot of her cage. She looked up and found herself staring into the muzzle of a gun.

Calmly, though her heart was beating hard, she read the note, which demanded all the cash in the drawer. She was standing next to Frances Potter, another teller. Wordlessly, the two young women emptied the drawer and pushed the money through their slots. The man took the cash, which amounted to several thousand dollars, and ran from the building.

A short while later, he was caught by the sheriff and his deputies, and Pat, who had seen his face and memorized the features despite the gun pointed at her, was brought to court to identify him. Her testimony helped to convict the robber.

It was 1930 and Pat had added another job to an already impossible schedule, though she had scarcely counted on facing a bank robber. She had walked into the office of the Artesia Bank on Pioneer Street soon after graduation and been hired as a part-time cleaning girl and teller.

Her days were endless: She shopped, cooked the meals, did the laundry, cleaned the house, and studied—for she had enrolled at Fullerton Junior College a few miles away and was taking a full schedule of classes. On top of it all, she had to squeeze still another task into her day—nursing her father.

Will Ryan had not been well for a year; he coughed a great deal and tired easily. Young Bill and Tom were shouldering most of the farmwork, and Pat did what she could as she cared for her father.

In the morning, before the bank opened, she would drive to Artesia and clean up the lobby floor of the bank. Then she would rush off to classes, returning at 1 P.M. to the bank to work as a teller. Her job was to "post" the checks—go through all that had come in and enter them into the account books. If there was time when she was finished, she would be given bookkeeping assignments.

In the spring of 1930, on May 5, Will Ryan died at Dore Sanitorium in Monrovia at the age of sixty-four. The death certificate, signed by a Dr. J. M. Furstman, put the cause of death as pulmonary tuberculosis, but it was silicosis, brought on by the inhalation of metallic dust, that had caused his lungs to become tubercular.

On the day of his death, Will's daughter decided to change her name to the one he loved best—henceforth, in his memory, she would be called Patricia.

With their parents gone, the three young Ryans had to reshape their lives. After holding jobs in town for a while, the boys decided to go off to Los Angeles and work their way through the University of Southern California. Soon, Pat was left alone in the little house on South Street, going to school and supporting herself with her job and whatever money the farm could produce. From time to time, the boys returned to do what they could with the chores.

She had grown to her full height, wore her hair cropped short in the fashion of the times, and was still a plumpish 138 pounds, though her cheeks had lost the roundness of early adolescence. She had little money but always appeared at the bank and at school dressed remarkably well, with flair and style. The girls with whom she worked were impressed and complimented her continually. There was no special secret: she made all her own clothes. (According to Blanche Potter Holmes, whose sister Frances worked with Pat at the bank: "She had little to work with but she made every cent count.")

At Fullerton, Pat studied English, history, and drama, still her favorite. Despite her full schedule of work and study, she joined the Nightwalkers Club, which presented most of the school's plays, and somehow found the time to play the leading role in one of its productions, *Broken Dishes*.

In 1931, she seized a chance for a free trip to New York. An elderly couple, friends of her family, had been visiting in California and were preparing to drive back to Connecticut, where they lived, in their large Packard touring car. Pat made the couple an offer: she would drive them back, all 3,000 miles of the way, without a fee. Since superhighways were only distant visions in those years and a transcontinental automobile trip, mostly over local roads, was a hazardous adventure, the couple readily accepted. And threw in a bonus: they would give her bus fare back to California.

The car, Pat remembers, was "huge and ancient" and did not look as though it could make it to the California border much less all the way across deserts, mountains, and plains to New York City in all the kinds of weather they would doubtless encounter. But she packed her few belongings and started on the journey.

Loaded to its canvas top with the couple's possessions, the old Packard trundled over the highways and performed remarkably well. There were problems, but not as many as Pat had expected. In the 120-degree heat of the Arizona desert country, the car's cooling system gave out and caused a long delay. In mountain country, Pat had a terrifying experience when the brakes (nonhydraulic in those days) suddenly wouldn't work. The car careened down a steep grade, lurching frighteningly from side to side. Pat, her right foot pressed to the floorboard, gripped the wheel and kept the car steady. Finally, the dip ended and a rise in the road slowed the automobile down and then stopped it.

She lost count of the number of flat tires they got. Each time, she would sigh, get out, jack the car up, replace the flat with the spare and move out again. "I was eighteen," she says, "driver, nurse, mechanic—and scared."

For most of the trip, the woman she was driving sat in the rear seat, bundled in blankets, looking like a sack of clothes. Her husband was with Pat in front. Hour after hour as she drove, he would make a clicking sound with his teeth that was clearly audible above the sound of the wheezing motor. It was the one thing about the journey that unnerved her: she did not mind the hardships or the risks, but the teeth-clicking of her companion was a sound she would remember with shudders for the rest of her life.

Finally, she reached New York City.

Once there, she began looking for work. She heard of an opening for a secretary at Seton Hospital, a Catholic institution run by the Sisters of Charity of New York in the Spuyten Duyvil section of the Bronx, then an undeveloped, almost rural area. Pat went up there by subway and saw a four-story building built of Hudson River red brick, set in a large parklike setting. After only one interview with the superintendent, she was hired and went to work at this 231-bed hospital for the treatment of tuberculosis patients, which had a small but highly regarded medical staff.

Within weeks, she had made up her mind to try to advance herself. She enrolled in Columbia University for an intensive summer course in radiology, and at the conclusion received certification as a technician trained to assist the hospital's radiologists and other doctors in operating X-ray equipment and in preparing patients for diagnostic X-rays.

The two years she spent there were the most "haunting" of her life, she remembers. "The patients were so young, most of them, so eager to live." Some would slip out of the hospital grounds in winter and go careening down the nearby slopes on sleds. Pat, in violation of the rules, would go too, racing with them, laughing, tumbling in the snow, afterward trudging back to the hospital, red-cheeked and happy. She sensed that her being with them gave the patients a link to the world of people and movement outside their hospital. "I wanted to reach out and help them," she says. "That is what gives me the deepest pleasure in the world —helping someone."

She lived spartanly in a room nearby, saving her money. She was not lonely. She had slimmed down and, with her reddish hair, dark eyes, and fine-boned oval face, had become a strikingly beautiful young woman and was receiving considerable attention from the hospital's young interns and doctors. There were plenty of dates and parties in her active social life.

But nobody special entered her life. She was seeking not marriage, at this time, but a career and she had settled on what kind: she would earn a college degree and become a department store buyer. Finally, in 1933, she resigned from the hospital* and headed back to California and college. She returned by bus with the ticket promised her by the couple she had driven out, stopping off, free, to see Niagara Falls on the way back.

HOLLYWOOD AND HAIR SPRAYS

Back on the West Coast, Pat moved in with her brothers Bill and Tom, somehow squeezing an extra bed and a measure of privacy into their tiny apartment in a bungalow court near the university. She enrolled, majoring in merchandising; but first, before books and studies, she had to find work. Tom went with her to the school's job placement office and told an official: "This is my kid sister. Can she work her way through college?"

She could and she did. Before long, she was working more than forty hours a week at anything she could

---

* Seton Hospital closed its doors in the 1940s because of the decline in the number of tuberculosis cases. It has since been torn down. On the site is a housing project and a recreation area called Sexton Park.

find: in the cafeteria, in the library, as a phone switchboard girl, at the Bullock-Wilshire department store and, occasionally, as a dental assistant. She also earned a fair amount of money as a movie extra.

The college placement office often received calls from the Hollywood movie studios, which were then grinding out hundreds of films a year. Pat and a new friend, Virginia Shugart, a beautiful blonde, signed up with the bureau for any extra roles that came along. They were hired frequently to be co-eds in college movies—in a cheering section during the Big Game, on the campus during a rally, in a classroom. For a day's work, each would receive $7. Once Virginia's little red Ford was also hired. She and Pat rode in it in a scene depicting a pre-game parade.

Sometimes, members of the USC football squad would tip off the girls about a new movie and they would rush down to apply. Sometimes, too, they would make the rounds of the studios themselves.

Their striking beauty landed them plenty of jobs. During her three years of extra work, Pat even had a walk-on role in *Becky Sharp*, the first full-length all-Technicolor picture ever made, which, *The New York Times* correctly said, became "a prophecy of the future of color on the screen." Pat Ryan was nowhere to be seen nor was her single line heard in the finished film; her part was snipped prior to release. But she received $25 for the job, which was all she wanted anyway.

Pat also was an extra in *The Great Ziegfeld*, a musical biography of the producer which starred Luise Rainer, Myrna Loy, and William Powell, and she had a walk-on in *Small Town Girl*, starring Janet Gaynor and Robert Taylor. Along with millions of other young women, Pat developed a big crush on Mr. Taylor. "I really eyed him," she says.

"I was a good student," Pat recalls, "so I was able to miss classes and do this extra work. I made quite a bit of extra money that way. To earn the regular $7, you would have to stay out there for the whole day."

Twice she was noticed by directors and offered a contract to be trained as a studio actress, but she refused.

"I never thought of movies as a career," she says, "because it seemed so very boring." She saw famous stars play one scene again and again—"going over and over and over about three words until you almost went mad."

One of the oddest jobs she and Virginia had was to have their hair washed almost daily for weeks. Virginia (now Mrs. J. Curtis Counts) recalls:

"There was a lawsuit between two rival cosmetic firms involving the packaging of a hair spray. Pat and I were hired by one of them to travel all around the area, go into beauty parlors, and have our hair done. Then we'd watch carefully to note the packaging on the spray. We'd have to rush home, wash out the spray carefully, and then go out again. The job was rough on our hair, but it helped get us through school."

Jobs notwithstanding, Pat did remarkably well with her studies, though the long hours took their toll. Dr. Frank Baxter, the Shakespearean expert who was on the UCLA faculty during her years there, remembered her well: "She was a quiet girl," he said years later, "and pretty. And it always used to disturb me how tired her face was in repose.

"There seemed to have been plenty of reason for it. As I recall it, if you went into the cafeteria, there was Pat Nixon at the serving counter. An hour later, if you went to the library, there was Pat Nixon, checking out books. And if you came back to the campus that evening, there was Pat Nixon working on some student research program. Yet with it all, she was a good student, alert and interested. She stood out from the empty-headed, overdressed little sorority girls of that era like a good piece of literature on a shelf of cheap paperbacks."

She graduated in 1937 and was handed a Bachelor of Science degree in merchandising *cum laude*, with teaching credentials as well. Her off-campus business experience and some education courses had earned her the certificate. She was ready for a job as a buyer or a teacher, whichever came along first.

Teaching did. The Whittier Union High School had an opening in its commercial division for a business education teacher in the fall. She went to Whittier for an interview and got the job. The pay would be $180 a month, or $1,800 for the school year.

In late August, she packed and went off to Whittier on the southwestern slopes of the Puente Hills, about fifteen miles east of downtown Los Angeles, to teach in the high school from which Richard Nixon had graduated seven years before and in the town where he had just begun the practice of law.

NEW TEACHER IN TOWN

When Pat Ryan arrived in Whittier, she saw a small city not unlike the one where she had been raised. It was larger, with more people and a bit more bustle, but it was essentially an agricultural community. A large mushroom farm was nudging up close to the heart of the business district. There were orange and lemon orchards, truck gardens, avocado farms, and so many walnut trees that the region was producing more of the nuts than anyplace else in the world.

The center of town was the intersection of Greenleaf Avenue and Philadelphia Street. Steetcars used to run through it; almost thirty years before, the motorman on one of the trolleys had been Frank Nixon, father of Richard. By the time Pat arrived, the cars had gone but the tracks remained; it would be years before they were removed and the road repaved.

The Bank of America Building, a white stone structure, is on the corner here. It was the tallest in the city then and still is. On her first days in town, Pat Ryan passed by the building several times. Upstairs, the law firm of Wingert & Bewley, oldest in Whittier, occupied a five-room suite. One of the smallest rooms had just been assigned to twenty-seven-year-old Richard Nixon, who had come back to the city where he grew up with a law degree from Duke University.

A quiet community of about 15,000 residents, Whittier was a Los Angeles suburb dozing under the hot sun. Founded as a Quaker colony in 1887, it had a no-nonsense air about it, and newcomers were beginning to outnumber the original settlers. The people worked hard, played quietly, and would not tolerate any type of establishment that, as the Chamber of Commerce put it, "may be an invitation to hoodlumism." That included bars and liquor stores; no alcoholic beverages could be obtained anywhere within the city limits. Only wine could be purchased with meals in a restaurant. If a resident wanted a bottle of higher-proof stuff—and not many did—he or she had to travel outside and bring it home discreetly wrapped so that neighbors would not suspect.

There was only one movie house in town, and it was closed on Sundays; a second would open soon. Going to Los Angeles was an event for most residents, and few made the trip except at Christmastime to see the window displays and shop at Bullock's, the May Company, and the Broadway, the largest stores there. Theatrical road companies offering such fare as *Blossom Time* and *The Merry Widow*—nothing racier—would come to town and pack them in at the Biltmore Theater. Most of the young people in the community would attend Christian Endeavor meetings on Sunday nights, after Sunday school and church. Politically, Whittier was an arch-conservative Republican stronghold.

The little city where Pat met and married Richard Nixon and began the climb with him to the highest office in the country is still essentially small-town America, though its population has swelled to 70,000. The mushroom farm is gone now, along with most of the other agricultural lands. In their places are hundred of manufacturing plants producing sewer pipes, swimming pool equipment, drilling tools, knitwear, and bullets. There are ten banks and four savings and loan associations, three major shopping centers, two community swimming pools, two colleges, two major hospitals, 168 physicians, 83 dentists, and a zoo.

The high school was (and still is) located on Whittier

Avenue, a few blocks from the heart of town. The only secondary school in the district at the time (there are now seven), it had a student body of 1,000. It is now a complex of 13 beige stucco buildings in one of which, called Commercial, Pat Ryan began her teaching career.

With Robert Hodel, the school's assistant principal for curriculum, I visited the building to see, at first hand, what it had been like for her. Almost nothing has been changed in forty years.

The massive doors are, perhaps, a little more battered than they had been then, but not much. The dark brown linoleum tiles on the floor of the broad corridor are the same tiles. In Room 120, where Pat taught, one wall has been removed to enlarge it. But everything else is the same as on that September morning, shortly before 8 A.M., when she walked in to meet her students.

She saw a classroom 30 feet square. Across the room, opposite the door, four tall windows looked out on a large, well-kept lawn. To her left as she entered were the blackboards, which stretched along the entire wall. In front of them, in a corner, was her green-painted steel desk and behind it a closet for her supplies. Near the door was a small sink, above it a clock. And in the room were rows of tables with typewriters on them. She would teach typing, shorthand, and bookkeeping.

The students adored her at once. She was young, snappy, modern, a welcome relief from the other teachers, most of whom were older, rather dour, and far stricter.

Ellen Holt Waer, one of her first students and sixteen when she sat in Pat's class, recalls: "She looked so young to us. She was very attractive, red hair, a very slim face. We were fascinated with her. She was soft-spoken, firm, and quite a good teacher." Mrs. Waer, who now edits a weekly shopping guide for Whittier Quad Shopping Center, says: "I am using now what she taught me then."

With her deep-pleated, brightly colored skirts and sweaters and blouses, all in the latest fashion, she was a glittering figure to the girls, many of them reared in strict Quaker families. And more than one adolescent boy developed a secret crush on the new teacher.

Each morning and before each class, she would stand at the door and greet the students by name as they arrived. "She treated us warmly," says Jean Lippiatt, another of her students who still lives in Whittier, "but she insisted on results. By the same token she expected clockwork punctuality from us and we absorbed the gentle hint that questions to her should be prefaced by her name. . . . Miss Ryan followed the book. She allowed no compromises, no errors, no second-rate job. Perfection and high standards were the only things she accepted." Her typing students ruefully discovered that she had a hawk's eye for erasures, spotting them instantly no matter how carefully they tried to camouflage them. And then she would insist that the entire page be redone.

Chewing gum in her class was taboo; so was sloppiness in dress. "We found ourselves being very careful to comb our hair, to tie our shoelaces, and to straighten our skirts before greeting her at the door," says Ms. Lippiatt. "We even adopted her very proper way of sitting and her erect posture during assemblies."

Next door was young Robert C. Pierpoint, a junior whose family had moved to Whittier from Redondo Beach. Room 122 was his home room, where he reported for attendance check before going off to classes. He became friendly with his home room teacher, who was close to Pat Ryan; he, too, came to know Pat well. Years later, their paths were to cross—and then collide when Pierpoint, as White House correspondent for CBS, reported daily on the Watergate scandals. Pat, whose mistrust of the media matched the President's, became frosty and tight-lipped in her attitude toward him. And Pierpoint was witness to the sharp changes that Nixon's political ascendancy brought about in Pat's personality and behavior. But all that was a quarter-century in the future.

Pierpoint recalls the youthful Pat: "She was a different person entirely from the woman who was the wife of the President. She was approachable, friendly, and outgoing. She was happy, enthusiastic, sprightly. Her disposition was sunny, not intermittently but all the time. She was a happy young woman.

"We liked her enormously because she never talked down to the students, always meeting them on an adult level, never intimidating them. Nor was she, as some teachers are, intimidated *by* them. She enjoyed her life and her work."

At Whittier High, Pat met Helene Colesie, a young woman who taught remedial reading, history, and English, with whom she was to form a friendship that still endures. (Miss Colesie later married Jack Drown, a magazine distributor, with whom she lives in the exclusive Rolling Hills suburb of Los Angeles.) Helene worried about Pat's future at the school. "You take a woman as young and beautiful as Pat was then, put her in with a faculty of older women, and you've got almost certain trouble," she says.

Helene admits that her prediction did not materialize, mostly because Pat diplomatically made certain that she would not outshine the older teachers at faculty and PTA functions. "When they were out in front of the audience," Mrs. Drown says, "Pat would be serving the coffee or out in the kitchen doing the dishes."

Because of her outgoing personality and rapport with the students, Pat was chosen as faculty adviser to the Pep Committee, which was assigned the all-important task of rousing school spirit for all athletic games, especially football and basketball. Pierpoint, a committee member, says that the group chose its own adviser and Pat had no competition.

She plunged happily into the job. A prime function was to arrange for the half-time entertainment at the football matches. Home games were held at the stadium on Hadley Street adjacent to the school. She would go by bus with the committee to the schools away from home—Alhambra, El Monte, Glendale, Fullerton. There were no elaborate drills and marching bands then, just clever skits and stunts which Pat helped write and create. She also planned and helped to make the costumes and rehearsed the performers.

Pat conducted noontime rallies on the school campus

and in the auditorium on Fridays before the games, and one skit she devised had the students roaring with delight. She had scoured the campus for the shortest boys she could find, had them dressed in the uniforms of the rival team and spread them out on the lawn in football formation. Then, with piercing yells, out rushed another group consisting of the school's biggest and heaviest guys, who easily mowed down the opposition. She was in charge of the yell squad too, training them and even helping to write the songs and cheers.*

Her energy unflagged by a day's teaching and work with the pep group, Pat took on still another job to earn extra money—night classes for adults several evenings a week. Enrolled in one of her shorthand classes was Elizabeth A. Cloes, a young woman who taught in an elementary school in Lowell, an adjoining community. It was she who was to introduce Pat Ryan to the new young lawyer at Wingert & Bewley.

THE NIXON BOY

There are still a few people in Whittier who remember the young Richard Nixon. Evelyn Dorn, a handsome, gray-haired woman who was his first secretary, is one of them. Mrs. Dorn lives in a sunny apartment a few miles from the town center; her closets are filled chest-high with cartons of Nixon mementos—photos by the hundreds, menus of dinners, old leaflets, newspaper clippings, campaign literature. She remained active for many years at Wingert & Bewley and later worked on Nixon's congressional races.

I visited Mrs. Dorn for a close-up look at the young Richard Nixon, who nailed his new law degree on the wall of his small office in the Bank of America Building in November of 1937.

She recalls the first day Nixon came to work for

---

*Only boys were permitted to be yell leaders. Girl cheerleaders, with their short skirts and pom-poms, had not yet come to Whittier, though some other schools had them. In Pat's day, the girls were song leaders.

Wingert & Bewley in Suite 607 of the Bank of America Building. He arrived early on a November morning in a carefully pressed dark blue suit, and his initial act was nonlegal. The law firm had a small room which housed its library, but neither the lawbooks nor the shelves had been cleaned in years. Nixon, removing his suit jacket, took down every one of the hundreds of volumes, dusted them carefully, cleaned and polished the shelves, and replaced the books, rearranging them chronologically as he put them back.

Nixon put in sixteen-hour days, working from early morning until long after dark. He rarely went out to lunch, but would send Mrs. Dorn to a local coffee shop for hamburgers and a pineapple malt. Often he would be so preoccupied with his work that he passed her in a corridor without a hint of recognition. Afterward, he would be surprised she was in the office.

The cases Nixon was given to handle were hardly earth-shaking. Tom Bewley, head of the firm, who was also the city attorney, assigned him to "a few drunks, some parking problems, traffic stuff"; yet Nixon worked on them as though the fate of the nation was at stake. Later, he would get divorce and tax and estate cases.

Tom Bewley liked the young lawyer's style: "He was thorough," Bewley once said. "He bored right into the heart of a question. And he had courtroom psychology. He could talk so that butter wouldn't melt in his mouth, or he could take hold of a cantankerous witness and shake him like a dog."

Nixon never relaxed. During the dinner hour, he would make speeches to organizations or have conferences with clients. "Even when we attended a football game," Bewley has recalled, "and that was very infrequently, he'd get so excited you'd hardly call it relaxation. Another thing, in the five years we worked together I never once went to lunch with him just for the pleasure of it."

Born on a lemon orchard in Yorba Linda, California, about thirty miles east of Los Angeles, Nixon was reared in a Quaker household in the strict tradition of hard work and serious-minded, disciplined living. While the family, five sons in all, did not live on the edge of poverty as some accounts have stated, there was never an excess of money either.

His father, Francis Anthony Nixon, was born in 1879 of Scotch-Irish parents on a farm close to McArthur, Ohio; in the course of his life, he had twice as many trades as he had children. After the early death of his mother, he migrated westward with his family. Frank left school in the fourth grade for his first job—as a farmhand for 75 cents a day and his keep. Later, he became a painter, potter, glassworker, telephone lineman, oil field roustabout, carpenter, sheep rancher, and potato farmer. When he met Hannah Milhous one winter's day in 1908, he was driving a trolley car on the streets of Whittier.

Four months later, they were married. Soon Frank, reared as a Methodist, adopted Hannah's Quaker faith. Richard was their second son; the first, Harold Samuel, died of tuberculosis in childhood; the fourth, Arthur Burdy Nixon, also died young. The other brothers were Francis Donald, called Donald by the family, and Edward Calvert.

With a little bit of luck, Frank Nixon could have become a millionaire and Richard's life would have been totally changed; but twice in his life, chances came and fortune wouldn't smile upon him.

When Richard was seven, the lemon orchard from which Frank barely made a living finally failed completely and he sold out to begin another period of itinerant employment. Had he hung onto the grove, the family would have become wealthy because some years afterward, oil was discovered in the ground beneath the lemon trees.

After a new turn as oil field worker, foreman on a citrus ranch, and some other odd jobs, the elder Nixon scraped together enough money to buy a filling station in East Whittier, three miles from the town center. The family's fortunes began to improve from that time, but once again Frank's luck was bad. He had a choice of two locations for the station—the one on East Whittier

Boulevard and another in Sante Fe Springs, south of the city. He checked both with the utmost care, remaining at each for hours as he counted the passing cars and studying the growth potential of each. Finally he decided on East Whittier.

One year later, oil was discovered on the other place.

The gas station did make money, though; and within three years Frank had enough to buy an old Quaker church not far away which was for sale after a new one had been constructed. House movers picked it up and moved it next to the filling station, and Frank put up a sign, NIXON'S MARKET. The country store flourished, but the money it made was immediately drained away by the costs of his two sons' illnesses.

Hannah Nixon, born in Butlerville, Indiana, of Irish Quaker parents, was a young girl when her father, an orchard grower, heard of the Quaker colony in Whittier. In 1897, he took his entire family of eight girls and two boys, his nursery stock, and lumber for building a new house out to the West Coast. He built a house on Whittier Boulevard which Richard would later remember as the scene of family reunions in summer and at Christmas.

"My grandmother set the standards for the whole family," he once said. "Honesty, hard work, do your best at all times—humanitarian ideals. She was always taking care of every tramp that came along the road, just like my own mother too."

Hannah, tiny but strong-willed, hard-working and pious, left a deep imprint on Richard. A number of times during his career he referred to her as a "saint" and would say it one more time in public in his pathetic, rambling farewell speech to 250 White House employees and guests in the East Room.

It was Hannah who instilled, by practice and precept, piety and discipline in the young Richard Nixon. The family lived across the street from the Friends church; whenever she heard the bell, which was often, she would go to church. Nixon would attend, too, several times during the week and four times on Sundays.

Richard worked a long day. The store would be open

until 10 P.M. most nights and there was no hired help, so the brothers did what was necessary. Richard pumped gas, sold groceries, delivered orders, took violin and piano lessons, and studied until the small hours. He graduated from Whittier High and, in 1934, from Whittier College, where his achievements were impressive: president of his freshman class, president of the student body in his senior year, winner of more than two dozen intercollegiate debates, Southern California Intercollegiate Extemporaneous Speaking champion and, at commencement, second in his class. He was awarded a full-tuition scholarship to the Duke University Law School, which opened that year, and in September left for Durham, North Carolina, to spend the next three years in hard work to support himself and hard study to learn the law.

By 1938, a year after he graduated from law school, the Whittier Alumni Association had elected him president and the following year, at the age of twenty-six, he was named to the college's board of trustees,* the youngest ever selected. By any measurement, he was an exemplary young man. He was boyishly handsome—the chipmunklike cheeks had not yet appeared. He wasn't earning much money, as new lawyers were plentiful; he started at $50 a month and the raises came slowly. But his prospects for the future were good. If he was almost entirely humorless (he had been nicknamed Gloomy Gus at Duke and everyone who knew him at Whittier called him "serious"), he was intelligent, alert, ambitious, and one hell of a catch for any girl in those hard times.

Everyone, it seems, thought so except Pat Ryan.

---

*Although it produced Richard Nixon, the city may be trying to forget it. Forty years later, the college bookstore did not have a single book about Nixon or his family. "We seem to be out of them at the moment," a clerk reported. A canvass of bookstores on Philadelphia Street revealed a similar paucity of Nixon literature. The Whittier College library has a limited collection of books in a small room and some folders of clippings, most of them unsorted.

4

Dutch Treat Honeymoon

THE MEETING

Casting had just begun for the opening performance of the 1938 season of the Whittier Community Players, an amateur little theatre group which put on five or six plays each year. The first production was to be *The Dark Tower* by Alexander Woollcott and George S. Kaufman, a dreadful mystery melodrama which survived only fifty-seven performances on Broadway. (Woollcott was so ashamed of it that he omitted the play from his list of published works in *Who's Who*.) Its only claim to fame now may be the fact that it brought together Richard Nixon and Pat Ryan.

The community theater struggled for existence and barely made it each year. An untiring and dedicated woman named Louise Baldwin was the director; almost everything else was done by her husband, Clyde, who built the sets, painted them, collected the props, fixed and worked the lights, arranged for the costumes, prompted and, when there was time, hustled program ads. Money from these advertisements, plus the small admission charge, earned a little money for expenses, but it was always a struggle to keep afloat.

Elizabeth Cloes, the young teacher who was studying shorthand in Pat Ryan's night classes, was an active

53

member of the group. One day in late summer, Mrs. Baldwin told her she needed a pretty girl for a small part in *The Dark Tower*. Did she know anybody in town who would do? Elizabeth thought of Pat. "Fine," Louise Baldwin said. "Go ask her."

Elizabeth invited Pat for dinner at her hotel, the Hoover, and over coffee made her recruiting pitch. Pat was dubious. Though her interest in the theatre had not dimmed, she wondered if she could squeeze in enough time for rehearsals. But she also knew the school board encouraged young teachers to participate in local events, so a few evenings later she went to a small building on the property of St. Mathias Church, which was used as a rehearsal hall, read for the role, and got it.

The story of how the romance began has by now been layered over by sentiment and apocrypha. According to the version in most biographies, Nixon heard of a "smashing" new teacher in town and went down to the little theatre group to look her over. Not true, Hortense Behrens and Elizabeth Cloes, who were in the cast, told me. Nixon had been invited to join the players, had consented, and had already been chosen for the part of Barry Jones in *The Dark Tower* when Pat came to read.

Another and more romantic part of the legend is that Nixon blurted out a proposal on their first date. The story has not escaped the psychohistorians, who have seized upon the "impulsive" act as a key to the labyrinths of Nixon's mind. Bruce Mazlish, professor of history at the Massachusetts Institute of Technology, postulates that the proposal was not "out of character but part of a 'plan,' though perhaps an unconscious one, concerning the girl he wished to marry." Having cited Nixon's propensity to "daydream," Mazlish writes: "I suspect plan and dream came together in the person of Pat Ryan, and Nixon acted accordingly."

The trouble is that it just didn't happen that way.

Pat's recollection, as related by Earl Mazo in the first full-scale biography of Richard Nixon, is that Nixon asked her to marry him the first night he met her. "I thought he was nuts or something," he reported her as saying. "I guess I just looked at him. I couldn't imagine anyone ever saying anything like that so suddenly. Now that I know Dick much better, I can't imagine that he would ever say that, because he is very much the opposite; he's more reserved.''

It may be that, over the years, Pat has sentimentalized what was actually said, or that she took too literally a ''line'' that a young man, reserved or not, might hand a very pretty girl. The ''proposal,'' such as it was, came on the third evening after they met and, since it was made in the presence of Miss Cloes and in a somewhat jocular mood, may hardly have been intended quite so seriously as Nixon's biographers seem to believe.

Miss Cloes, who now lives in Los Angeles, says that Nixon hovered around Pat all that first evening and when the rehearsal ended, offered to drive the two girls home. They accepted. He drove them home a second time and a third.

''We got into his Model A Ford,'' Miss Cloes recalls. ''I sat in the middle, Pat sat on the outside. And he said to her, 'I'd like to have a date with you.'

''She said, 'Oh, I'm too busy.' So he laughed and drove us home. The next rehearsal, he picked us up, took us to the rehearsal and drove us home. As we were coming out to go home from the third rehearsal, I said, 'Pat, you sit next to him. He doesn't want to sit next to me.' She said, 'I don't want to sit next to him!' So I was again in the middle and he leaned across me and said to her, 'When are you going to give me that date?'

''She laughed. He said, 'Don't laugh. Someday I'm going to marry you.' He pointed his finger at her and she laughed again.''

A few nights later, she consented to go out with him.

A curious incident occurred during rehearsals.

In one scene Barry Jones, played by Nixon, sits at a piano and goes into the opening bars of ''Stormy Weather.'' Daphne Martin, played by Pat, begins to hum along and then, according to the script, starts to sing the words. But at rehearsals Pat Ryan suffered a block: she could hum but stopped when she had to sing the words. ''Pat,'' director Baldwin exhorted, ''sing,

sing!'' But Pat stood on the stage, helplessly silent. Even at the performance, she could not sing the words. She spoke them instead.

HIS EARLIER ROMANCE

Two years before he met Pat Ryan, Richard Nixon had received a "Dear John" letter at law school from the girl he had asked to be his wife.

He had dated her for seven years, gone steady with her for most of that time ("off and on" steady, the woman told me). The romance, which had begun in high school and continued all through college and for a year afterward, had developed into a serious one.

Everyone in their circle expected them to get married. "It was a foregone conclusion," says Richard Thomson, a Whittier '34 classmate of the pair. But Nixon was jilted, losing out to the handsome manager of the campus store.

The young woman was Ola-Florence Welch, the vivacious dark-haired daughter of Whittier's police chief. Oddly, amateur theatricals brought them together, too. Their Latin class at Whittier High, honoring the 2000th anniversary of the birth of the Roman poet Virgil, presented a version of his *Aeneid*. Richard was cast as the Trojan hero Aeneas and Ola-Florence was Dido, the queen of Carthage who killed herself for love of him.

That began it. "Dick was a marvelous actor," Ola-Florence recalls, "quick, perceptive, responsive, industrious." Looking back, she is not certain why she found Nixon so "fascinating and interesting," but she adds candidly: "I am not counting out sex appeal, which, as a subject, believe me, we didn't discuss in those days."

When Dr. David Abrahamsen* interviewed Ola-Florence in April, 1975, he asked if Nixon ever told her he liked her. Ola-Florence replied that she did not

*Author of the psychobiography *Nixon vs. Nixon: An Emotional Tragedy.*

remember, though to the question "Did he like you?" she answered: "I guess so."

Two years later, when I talked to Ola-Florence (she lives in retirement in Sidonia, Arizona, with her husband, Gail Jobe) she shed additional light on their relationship.

She and Nixon, she said, talked about marriage. Confirming her classmates' views, she told me: "There was a tacit agreement that we would be married some day."

Q. Did he ask you to marry him?
A. Yes (laughing). I should think so.
Q. Was a marriage planned, a date set?
A. No.
Q. Why did the romance break up? Was there any particular reason?
A. No . . . no. It was a general drifting apart.
Q. Was he badly affected by the breakup?
A. I really don't know. (A pause.) Who knows about him?
Q. Were you ever in touch with him afterward?
A. No.

I asked Ola-Florence a blunt, perhaps impertinent question, but important, I felt, because Nixon's sexuality has come into question. (The subject will be discussed in greater detail later in this book.)

"Was Richard Nixon sexually aggressive as a young man?" I asked her.

"It was an entirely different time," she said. When I suggested that young people did not behave then as many do now, she replied: "I guess some people did, but the general group did not."

"Was Nixon a perfectly normal young man?" I asked.

"I would say so," she answered.

During their dating years Ola-Florence's friends wondered what she saw in the dour, funless young Nixon. "He's so *stuffy*," they would tell her, But Ola-Florence was fascinated. "You have no idea," she has said, "how tremendously interesting and engrossing he was to me, the daughter of a small-town police chief. I considered myself provincial and him worldly." For his part, Nixon was attracted by Ola-Florence's pert prettiness and joyous personality. He even consented, grudgingly, to take dancing lessons because she loved to whirl out on a floor. But he couldn't learn then and never did.

The course of the six-year romance was rocky at times. Once he drove her to a college party where they quarreled sharply. Nixon, in ungentlemanly fashion, stalked out, got into his car and left her. "I had to call my folks to come get me," she recalls, a fact that hardly endeared Nixon to them. Another time, in their senior year at Whittier, Richard made a date with another girl. "I didn't like that," Ola-Florence says, "because we were supposed to be going steady. The Metaphonian formal was coming up. I always hated it because you were supposed to ask a boy." Nevertheless, in revenge, she invited Gail Jobe, who lost little time telling Nixon. Richard fumed and retaliated—he invited another girl to the senior prom.

However, the rift was patched up and the romance continued through graduation and Dick's first year at law school. Then came another blowup. Nixon, returning from Durham, called Ola-Florence and announced he was coming over to see her. She told him not to, and for a good enough reason. Gail Jobe was in her living room.

Nixon, of course, didn't know. He exploded at the refusal. "Don't worry," he shouted into the telephone, "you'll never hear from me again!"

She did, though. They corresponded during his second year at school but the romance had cooled. Then her letter arrived.

Ola-Florence was to meet Pat only once. Years later, Nixon invited the entire Whittier class of 1934 to the White House for a reunion. She was introduced to Pat, who gave no sign that she knew Ola-Florence had come so close to being Mrs. Nixon.

THE PRESIDENTIAL SUITE

A few weeks after they met, while rehearsals for *The Dark Tower* were still continuing, Pat began to go out with Richard, though she continued to date other men. He would call for her in his battered Model A, take her to the movies and an ice cream parlor afterward. On Sundays, they would drive to the beach or go hiking in the woods. Invariably, they would be accompanied on these walks by Pat's Irish setter, who adored Pat and was loved in return. She would nuzzle and fondle the dog, prompting Nixon to observe ruefully that she liked the animal more than she liked him, a fact which, early in their relationship, might well have been the case.

When *The Dark Tower* was performed, Frank and Hannah Nixon sat in the front row. Afterward, Richard took Pat home to introduce her to his parents. They had coffee and sandwiches and, in less than an hour, Nixon drove her home. When he returned, he asked Hannah what she thought of her. Hannah made a classic noncommittal reply: "I told him she did her part nicely."

Years later, Hannah explained: "Since we had only just met, it was too early for me to form an opinion."

But clearly he was smitten from the start. One member of Pat's circle was blunt about it: "He chased her but she was a little rat. She had Dick dating her roommate and all he did when he took the roommate out was talk about Pat." Years later, after Nixon had been elected President, Pat offered an explanation which defies logic: "I thought so much of him that I got him a date with my best friend." Clearly, Pat was very sure of herself, and of her ardent suitor whom, she felt, she could have at any time she wished.

She did something else that demonstrated her confidence and would be dismaying, if not outright infuriating, to many young men. She had other boyfriends back in Los Angeles, men she had known since USC days, who would call her for dates. She would go to meet them. So much in love was Dick Nixon that he would not permit her to take the long trolley ride but would drive her to her dates himself. He would then wait in the city, walking aimlessly, dropping into a movie, sitting in a hotel lobby and reading, until it was time to chauffeur her back home.

Pat admits that these unique acts of fidelity and perseverance indeed occurred. "It's true," she says, adding: "But it's mean to report it."

He would do anything to please Pat. He tried once again to learn to dance, and again failed. He even bloodied himself at the artificial ice skating rink that had just opened in nearby Artesia, falling hard two or three times but keeping doggedly at it, as persistently as he pursued her.

Despite all this, Hannah Nixon always felt that Pat was the aggressor in the courtship. In 1960, she confided this to Flora Rheta Schreiber (author of the best-selling book *Sybil*). Ms. Schreiber, who lived with Hannah for a month and became a close friend, told me: "Hannah was convinced Pat was chasing Dick."

At first look, one might tend to dismiss this as an attitude not uncommon for mothers of sons, but Hannah was an exceptionally truthful and perceptive woman. And indeed, Pat was not as cool to her Richard as the biographies of the former President have indicated. She would, for example, show up at the store from time to time to help out behind the counter. On many mornings, she would arrive at dawn and help Hannah bake her cakes and pies before going on to school.

As many young women have done and doubtless will continue to do, Pat was apparently hedging her bets—dating other men but, at the same time, making certain that she kept Richard Nixon in reserve just in case.

By the spring of 1940, Nixon's two years of total devotion paid off. Pat agreed to become his wife.

Why did she finally accept the man who, quite obviously, did not impress her overmuch at the start? ("He's a bit unusual," she had told a friend soon after he began his courtship.) The possibility has been suggested that Nixon might have won Pat on the rebound from a broken love affair, that she had been hurt or disillusioned, or perhaps both, by one of the dates to which Nixon had driven her in Los Angeles. Pat has never talked publicly of those years and probably never will.

Whether or not the rebound story has any merit, she was quite obviously ready for marriage. She was twenty-eight years old, past the age when most women of that era married. She was not a "career" woman or, at least, had not entered into the career for which she had primarily aimed. Apparently she had had enough of the independent life and, after her years of almost incredible toil, the bright promise of eventual security which Richard Nixon was offering looked good. "He was making $50 a month. I knew he was going to get places, though," she said later. "He was vital, and ambitious—not ambitious for anything in particular, and certainly not for money—but he had drive. . . ."

This, added to his obvious devotion to her, made him ideal husband material.

There were more plusses. Nixon had family all around Whittier, while she had only Tom and Bill, whom she could not see too often, and her half-sister and brother, whom she rarely saw. (Hannah Nixon said in 1960: "We have so many relatives, we have a standing joke that if they all voted for Richard, he'd surely be elected.") Family meant stability, roots. She had often told friends that she wanted time to "travel and see the world," but travel was a distant wish, hard to do on a small salary, and Nixon was the bird in hand. Love, too, was a reason, but the probability is that at twenty-eight Pat came to marriage with level-headed objectivity, was serious about it, and, viewing marriage as a lifelong partnership, intended to do all she could to make it succeed.

With the same diligence he pursued everything else, Nixon spent days researching rings. He talked for hours with a jeweler friend, a fellow member of the Whittier 20-30 Club, a men's service organization of which he was president, discussing size, setting, and quality. His brother Don still remembers that, on a business trip to Northern California, Richard kept him up until almost morning weighing the advantages of one ring over another. "A man," Richard pointed out, "only buys a ring once in his lifetime, and that should be a ring his wife would always be proud to wear."

Actually, the subject appeared to be academic because Nixon's bank balance was too small to buy any but the tiniest ring. He was contributing part of his income to his parents and there were still some college debts to pay. But Pat, who had carefully saved her money, chipped in to buy her own ring, which Nixon presented to her inside a basket of spring flowers. She also agreed to adopt her husband's Quaker faith and to have a Quaker ceremony, a fact that made Hannah very happy.

By that time, Richard's old Model A had sputtered its last. He traveled to Lansing, Michigan, to buy a new car, after paper-and-pencil calculating that it would be less expensive to pay bus fare and drive one back than to buy the car locally with the delivery costs tacked on. He bought an Oldsmobile—with Pat's money.

It was a small wedding in one of the most unique settings in California. Though by custom the bride chooses the wedding place, Nixon suggested theirs, and Pat agreed. They selected the Mission Inn in Riverside, then an eighty-year-old Spanish-style hotel covering a city block. A California showplace, it had bell towers, altars, balconies, fountains, paintings, and hundreds of historical objects. Stained glass windows had been installed in the baronial-style music rooms. There was a tower patterned after the Mission Carmel, and in the hotel's center was a magnificent rotunda with a spiral staircase, colonnades of arches, wrought iron grilles, and tile shields of many nations imbedded in the concrete walls.

Most weddings at the Mission Inn were held in the Chapel of St. Francis of Assisi, with its centuries-old wood-carved altar from Guanajuato, Mexico, exquisite mosaics, and Tiffany windows. Nixon, however, with Pat's approval, wanted a Quaker ceremony someplace else in the hotel. He chose (and the reader is invited to speculate on this coincidence) VIP rooms which, even then, were called the Presidential Suite. Many noted personages had stayed there, including Presidents Harrison, McKinley, Theodore Roosevelt, Taft, and Hoover. The suite was on two levels: the first was a 24-square-foot living room with arches, windows, thirteenth-century wood carvings, and a heavy beamed ceiling; on the second was a bedroom and bath.

Nixon had frugally rented the suite for only a few hours that 21st day of June in 1940. He drove into the circular driveway and escorted Pat inside. She wore a light blue dress with fitted bodice and full gathered skirt which fell to the ankles, and a small hat. He was wearing a new dark suit.

With only about a half-dozen members of their families and a few friends as guests, they stood on a red Oriental rug in front of a large grand piano and were married in a Quaker ceremony. Afterward, there was a reception with punch and small cakes served. The wedding party then drove to his father's home at 6799 Worsham Drive in Whittier for a more substantial wedding meal.

By five that afternoon, Pat and her new husband were embarked on their honeymoon. They were going to Mexico for two weeks, Nixon had about $200 in his wallet to pay for the trip—half of it Pat's.

Years later, the Presidential Suite was turned into a cocktail lounge. In 1963, the two Nixon daughters, Tricia and Julie, then teenagers, were invited to a party at the Mission Inn and joined a group of tourists who were being guided through the famous inn. The girls had never seen where their parents had been married and were anxious for their first look. They were accompanied by Janet Goeske, who had worked on many Republican campaigns in California and is now president of the Riverside Republican Women Federated.

When the touring party reached the Presidential Suite, the woman guide swept her hand around the room and announced: "And here is where Richard and Pat Nixon were married." The girls stared at the long bar, the banquettes, and the cocktail waitresses serving drinks. Mrs. Goeske was horrified and at once challenged the guide. "I beg to differ with you," she said, "they were married in here, but then it was a *Presidential* Suite." She turned to the two girls and assured them: "Your mother and father were not married in *this* place." Recalling the incident, Mrs. Goeske has a final word: "The lady guide was a staunch Democrat."

"We didn't have a honeymoon trip outlined," Pat says. "We just went." Mexico City was their ultimate destination, but they zigzagged their way. If a side road looked inviting, they took it. If they saw something they liked, they stopped to examine it. They visited temples, ruins, churches; they walked through old towns, marveled at the artisans at work, edged off narrow roads to let ox-carts transporting crops to market go by, haggled at marketplace stalls for tiles, pottery, and blankets.

Their money dwindled. Sometimes they would drive all night to save the price of a hotel, one at the wheel while the other slept.

They also saved the price of restaurant meals. The trunk of the car was loaded with a supply of canned goods, mostly from the Nixon store. But while the wedding luncheon was going on, someone in the party had slipped out and removed the labels from most of the cans, so it became an adventure each time they opened a can to eat. They had one breakfast of peas and carrots, another of baked beans, a third of spaghetti and meatballs.

On their way home, they counted the meager cash left over from the $200 they had started out with. They had spent $178 on their honeymoon.

They drove into Whittier to the accompaniment of exploding firecrackers. "Some welcome," Pat grinned. It was the Fourth of July.

5

Wartime Wife

On their return they were able to scrape together another $200, barely enough for the deposit and rental on the first apartment they didn't yet have. They spent two weeks hunting for a place, finally finding one in a small cluster of bungalows on East Beverly Boulevard, about two miles from his office and her school.

In mid-July, they moved into a rear apartment at number 12326, a stucco house with a small lawn and some scraggly shrubs pathetically trying to dress up the entrance, and a backyard Pat could cross with three giant steps. There was a living room, bedroom, kitchen, and bath.

The newlyweds scoured the city for secondhand chairs, tables, cabinets, an easy chair, and a couch. Pat quickly bought yards of colorful material and covered the scars and tears of some of the pieces with slipcovers, often sewing far into the night. They moved in practically penniless; and her beloved Irish setter, who had been boarded by a friend during their honeymoon, moved in with them. Shortly after, the dog died and Pat was grief-stricken. Nixon went out and spent $25 for a burnished metal plaque of a setter in bas-relief. "It was our first major extravagance," she recalls; she has kept the plaque through the years.

Despite her years of hard experience in money-stretching, their joint income of about $65 a week just about got them through. Pat shopped, cooked, cleaned, washed, sewed her own clothes, and pressed his. Years later, when Nixon won high office, the pants pressing got to be something of a national joke and even aroused skepticism on the part of women who simply didn't believe she was doing it. But she did in the early years, and the later ones too.

They rose early to get to their jobs, and often, close to paydays, they went with just a few coins in their pockets. Richard would come home most evenings but leave again for the office soon after. Their friends were young marrieds like themselves, couples struggling to make their way. Closest to them were Helene Drown, who still taught at Whittier High, and her husband, Jack, then in law school at USC. Drown was to enter the law but soon afterward would become a successful newspaper and magazine distributor in the Los Angeles area. Helene Drown is still one of Pat's most devoted friends.

Once in a long while, Pat and Dick and the Drowns would buy seats for the Los Angeles Opera Company performances, sitting so high in the gallery that the singers were barely visible or even audible. On some weekends, they would pack lunch and drive down to Capistrano Beach, an hour away. Once or twice, Pat got Dick to go to the Ambassador Hotel in Los Angeles, where the Cocoanut Grove attracted the younger set. He was reluctant because he lacked two of the requisites—money (it was expensive) and the ability to dance. They got around the first by sipping one drink, purchased at the bar, all evening long, and he sweated through the second.

Mostly, the young couples in their set entertained each other at home. Evelyn Dorn and her husband remember the first dinner party the Nixons gave. Pat made a huge pot of spaghetti and meat sauce and Nixon mixed the drinks and the salad.

In June, one year after their wedding, with money still tight, they decided to celebrate their anniversary with a two-week sea trip to New Orleans by way of the

Panama Canal. In Mexico, the sight of many feeble old people "tottering around" had left a strong impression on Nixon. The years, he told Pat, will pass all too quickly; he convinced her that they should take vacations while they were still youthful enough to enjoy them, even if they had to borrow to pay for them. Ironically, before long he would become too busy to take his own advice.

Pat was dubious. She would have preferred building up a savings cushion first, but he convinced her and they bought passage on a United Fruit Company vessel, the *Ulua.* Having paid the lowest fare, they were assigned to the worst cabin, down in the hold. In their dreary, poorly ventilated little room, they could hear the noisy throbbing of the engines and smell the oily wastes. It was hardly luxury travel.

In New Orleans, they ate frugally but, on their last day in the city, decided to have at least one memorable meal. At Antoine's on St. Louis Street, one of the most famous restaurants in the country, they split one order of Oysters Rockefeller, Antoine's world-renowned dish, and an order of the almost equally famed Pompano Papillote. They returned to Whittier with some memories, and the oily smell of the ship's engines still in their nostrils.

Six months later, the Japanese attacked Pearl Harbor and the lives of all the young people in their set began to change drastically. Some of the men went into the armed services, others into war work. There were many hours of talk in the Nixon bungalow during which they discussed options. Finally, a few weeks after Pearl Harbor, he decided on Washington. As usual, she agreed.

She packed his suitcase and drove him to Los Angeles, where he boarded a train for the capital. On January 9, 1942, a bitingly cold day, he barged into the office of Thomas I. Emerson, associate general counsel of the Office of Emergency Management, with a portfolio of his credentials under his arm.

Professor Emerson, on leave from the Yale Law

School, was bemused by the brash young man who, without an appointment or letter of introduction, was asking to be put to work. "He just walked in and said he wanted to help in the war effort," Emerson says. Emerson liked his appearance—"nice-looking young fellow, clearly intelligent and without a doubt a man we could use." He hired Nixon on the spot and put him to work developing rules and regulations governing the rationing of automobile tires. His salary was $62 a week.

That night, Nixon telephoned Pat and told her to give up her job and their apartment, sell what she could, put the rest in storage, pack, and come to Washington to live. She did it all, quickly and efficiently, and by March she was on a train to join him in the capital.

Pat found a small apartment and she and Dick lived for about a half-year in wartime Washington, making few friends and wrestling with a dual problem. Nixon hated his job with the OPA because of the bureaucratic time-wasting and began to think of military service. But pacifism was a strong tenet in the Society of Friends who, through the centuries, worked to heal the wounds of war through relief and other work, not to create more wounds. As a Quaker, Nixon could have asked to be exempt from active military service. With Pat, he probed his beliefs and, after lengthy introspection which continued night after night for months, decided to apply for a Navy commission to which, as an attorney, he was entitled. On September 2, 1942, he was commissioned a lieutenant, junior grade.

Pat joined the millions of other wartime wives in America during those years. Starting at Quonset, Rhode Island, where Nixon took his basic training for two months, her life during the next four years was a series of moves from bases to cities, often on a few days' notice.

"A woman," she has said, "must first and foremost be a homemaker." So she set about making a home out of every tiny apartment in every old house in which they lived. Her sewing machine and slipcover materials were indispensable accompaniments wherever she went with her husband. Almost the first chore she undertook in every place they had to call home was to slipcover the battered furniture, hang up curtains or drapes, and do what she could to brighten a drab set of rooms.

Only then would she buy the newspapers, scout the classified ads, and go job hunting. With her formidable list of marketable skills, she always found one—as stenographer, store clerk, bookkeeper, bank teller. After work, she shopped and cooked dinner, an easy enough task because Nixon was never a choosy eater.

Soon after basic training, Nixon was assigned to Ottumwa, Iowa. Pat looked it up on a map. It was in the southeastern part of the state in the midst of corn-growing country, and the only body of water nearby was the Des Moines River which, she was certain, couldn't float a naval vessel. Why on earth was Dick going to Iowa? He soon found out. On his arrival, he discovered he would sail a desk at an uncompleted air base near the city. Pat joined him soon after and got a job in a local bank.

Finally Nixon, who had put in for sea duty, got his orders for an overseas assignment. In May, 1943, he shipped out to serve with the South Pacific Combat Air Transport Command (SCAT) as operations officer. His job was to supervise the creation of temporary bases in the islands upon which the Air Force DC-3s could land cargo destined for the war zones. He served in this capacity at Guadalcanal, Bougainville, Vella Lavella, and, finally, at Green Islands.

Meanwhile, Pat went back to Washington to live alone and work as a price analyst for the OPA. Soon, she was transferred to a San Francisco OPA office, where she lived in a boarding house for fourteen months, saving every dollar she could.

At the same time, Nixon had discovered a way, strange for him, to acquire some money. Although the Friends condemned gambling as a sin,* he watched his

---

*In 1960, William Costello wrote in his biographical work *The Facts About Nixon:* "... although Quakerism may remain the wellspring of his beliefs, his personal code of behavior no longer reflects the orthodoxy of his forebears. ... In war he took up arms; in the service he took up cards." He also began smoking, downed drinks occasionally, and developed a formidable vocabulary of obscenities which, years later, were to shock the nation.

fellow officers play poker (totally unknown to him until then except by name) and decided that (a) this was a game he could learn to play and (b) he could learn well enough to put together a nest egg of some considerable size. He did both on Green Islands in the South Pacific during the long and lonely days and nights, sitting impassively at the table, analyzing every hand for where the percentage lay, playing conservatively and shrewdly. In the recollection of Lester Wroble, a Chicago businessman who served and played with him, Nixon never had a losing day. Nixon took no notice of rank: he would win indiscriminately from enlisted men and officers. While he never revealed his total winnings, officers who served with him agree he must have raked in, and kept, between $3,000 and $4,000, a sum which, with Pat's savings, became the financial foundation of Nixon's career in politics.

In long letters to Richard, Pat often wrote of returning to Whittier when the war ended—he to resume the practice of law and she to raise their family. Politics as a career was as far from her mind in the 1940s as galactic travel; nor, indeed, did it occur to him.

When he returned home in July, 1944, as lieutenant commander, their nomadic life continued. She lived with him in Alameda, California, where he worked for Fleet Air Wing 8; then after a few months, they traveled across the country to live, successively, in Philadelphia, New York City, and finally in Middle River, Maryland, near Baltimore, where he wrote terminating contracts between the Navy and aircraft companies, and she kept their apartment shining, his uniforms pressed, and their budget in line.

It was in Middle River that Pat told Richard she was pregnant. With a family now on the way, they were anxious to return to Whittier as soon as he could get out of uniform.

Then, on a brilliant afternoon in September, 1945, a telegram arrived from California that stunned them both and changed their lives forever.

6

Her First Hurrah

"I WOULD DO WHAT HE LIKED"

Politics had never entered her mind during the six years of their marriage and the two of their courtship. Now, however, it exploded all around them. The wire was from Herman L. Perry, manager of the Bank of America branch in Whittier. A candidate was needed in the 12th Congressional District to oppose the Democratic incumbent, Jerry Voorhis. Republican leaders, scouting for one, had been told about the promising young lawyer who was on his way out of the Navy.

The telegram asked Nixon if he was interested in making the race against the popular and formidable Voorhis, a legislator of national reputation, who would be seeking his sixth term. The Nixons had company that night. Incredulous, he read the wire aloud several times. After the guests had gone, Nixon couldn't stop talking about the offer.

Pat listened. Knowing nothing about politics, she had no questions but one: "Wouldn't a congressional campaign cost money," and where would it come from? Nixon guessed that the Republican committee would provide some funds, but he wasn't sure how much. He pointed out that they had about $10,000 in the bank—her savings and his poker winnings. They had

71

counted on half that sum to make a down payment on a small house where they could raise their family but they agreed to put aside $5,000 for the house and gamble the rest on the campaign.

At this point, Pat did not feel strongly about the new career one way or the other, but his eagerness was plain. "I could see it was the life he wanted," she said, "so I told him that it was his decision and I would do what he liked."

Neither slept much that night. The next morning he called Perry and said he was available. Within two weeks, he had flown out to California with $300 sent him by the Committee of One Hundred, the GOP group seeking a Voorhis challenger.

After conferences with political leaders, he returned to Baltimore and impatiently awaited his discharge. It came early in January. Within a few days, still in uniform, he was westward bound to launch his campaign while Pat, expecting her first child in six weeks, lumbered about the apartment, packing and getting ready to join him.

From the beginning, Pat worried about the effects politics would have upon their family life. Back in Whittier, she told Dick she would work hard for his candidacy, as hard as she ever had for anything, but he must agree to two ground rules: First, on no account would she make any political speeches. And second, her home must always remain a quiet refuge where she could raise her children peacefully and normally. This was most important to her. She had had time to think after the bombshell dropped into their Baltimore living room and, though politically naive, she reasoned quite correctly that much bitterness could enter the life of a politician. She wanted none of it to seep into her home.

Both rules eventually would be broken. She had to make political speeches; and neither of them could have known in those innocent years the extent to which her home, her children, her sons-in-law, and her entire life would be sucked into the political whirlpool.

Richard gave his word and Pat Nixon went into

politics with the same energy she tackled everything else.

Headquarters was a Whittier storefront at the corner of Philadelphia Street and Bright Avenue, rent for which was paid out of the Nixon nest egg earmarked for the campaign. Pat, Dick's brother Don, and a high school classmate named Marion Budlong scurried around town borrowing furniture, Hannah offered them an old sofa she had in her basement; one morning, Don loaded it onto his grocery truck and lugged it into the office. A desk arrived from somewhere; chairs, ludicrously mismatched, were scrounged up; somebody heard of a desk they could have and they went and got it.

Some other money came in, but not much. The State GOP's finance committee wasn't opening its purse strings very wide to them because it didn't believe Nixon had a chance against the veteran Voorhis. Roy Day, Nixon's campaign manager and a member of the GOP County Central Committee, told me that a total of $24,000 was spent on the campaign. "The only one who got paid," he said, "was Murray M. Chotiner, who got $500 a month for three months." Chotiner, a lawyer from Beverly Hills who ran a public relations firm, knew his way around California politics; it was he who had been largely responsible for the selection of Earl Warren as governor in 1942, and he was Senator William J. Knowland's campaign manager for Southern California. Chotiner, a wily strategist, and Nixon were to be closely allied through the years.

Nixon pledged a "fighting, rocking, socking campaign," and Chotiner helped provide the ammunition, creating the leaflets which called the young veteran a "clean, forthright young American who fought in defense of his country in the stinking mud and jungles of the Solomons." Meanwhile, the incumbent, said the literature, "stayed safely behind the front in Washington."

Pat was his entire full-time office staff. Marion Budlong, Evelyn Dorn, and a few others came in for a few hours when they had time. Pat typed all the campaign literature, took it to the printer, and then lugged stuffed envelopes to the post office. Those that were not mailed were distributed by hand. She would walk with them for hours from store to store and house to house.

As the days went on, she became increasingly, tensely involved, and here a trait emerged that is central to the understanding of Pat Nixon. A close friend put it this way: "She gritted her teeth and did it because she felt it was her duty to do it." Through the years, she would be called upon to undergo punishing ordeals in campaigns. She would "grit her teeth and do it" because it would be unthinkable to her to avoid doing it. Once involved, she would become part of the battle, her own basic feeling subsumed, and would react strongly to victory or defeat. Once, for example, a large batch of circulars was ready for mailing. When she discovered there was no money left for stamps, she burst into tears and sobbed uncontrollably. Another time, she was furious when she learned that she had been fooled by an old trick; the opposition had sent a band of its own volunteers to the Nixon office to pick up pamphlets which, of course, were torn up and thrown away as soon as they got out of sight. New circulars were printed. (According to one story, reported by Henry D. Spalding, director of publicity for the 1952 Draft Eisenhower League, funds were so low that Nixon sold one of his two suits to help pay for the new leaflets.) When they arrived, Pat was more careful. While Nixon spoke on street corners and in meeting halls, she circulated among the throng or walked up and down the aisles and handed them out one at a time.

More than 3,000 miles away, the lanky, boyish John F. Kennedy, also fresh out of the Navy, was also running for the first time, seeking a congressional seat from the 11th District in Boston. Without realizing it, Dick and Pat and the man Nixon would oppose for the presidency fourteen years later were all hustling votes with a similar technique.

The Kennedys were beginning to use a campaign tactic that they would perfect over the years and that would be responsible in no small measure for the success of John, and later Ted, in Massachusetts elections. This consisted of carefully arranged and coordinated tea and coffee parties. In each community, a Kennedy representative would call a friendly neighbor and ask if the house would be available for an afternoon get-together. The Kennedy organization would send gallons of coffee, pounds of cookies, and dozens of paper cups and napkins with the Kennedy name and the candidate's photo on them. Meanwhile, the host would round up a few dozen people to greet the Kennedy women and, if he were available, the candidate himself. An hour would be spent in neighborly chit-chat intended to endear the candidate and his family to the voters. The technique was repeated with greater intensity in John Kennedy's successful Senate race against Henry Cabot Lodge in 1952. Afterward, the Lodge forces ruefully admitted that their candidate had been drowned in 75,000 cups of tea, which may not have been far from the truth: Kennedy won by a majority of 70,727 votes, just about the same number of women who had attended the parties they gave.

Roy Day had no notion of what the Kennedys were doing. "I'd never heard of John Kennedy," he says. Now seventy-seven and living in Pomona, he recalls how he would set up "coffee klatches" around the district, "little get-togethers" where the neighbors could meet the candidate and his wife. But the neighbors provided their own coffee and cake.

Pat would come along, standing uneasily beside her husband, saying very little, never making speeches. Residents still living who attended these small parties remember her tight little smile, her whispered "Hello, I'm so pleased to meet you," her warm handshake. Roy Day says: "She was nervous, uptight, and tense. It was all so new to her."

She was no more comfortable on visits she would make to hospitals, colleges, homes for the elderly, children's centers, and meetings of women's civic groups, arranged for her by Day. Though her nervousness was painfully apparent, her sincerity shone through. "She was a hell of an asset," Day says. "She won a lot of brownie points for Dick with those appearances."*

Pat continued to work until a few days before her baby was expected. On February 21, she gave birth to Patricia, who soon became known as Tricia, at Whittier Hospital. Helene Drown accompanied Pat to the hospital, and Jack Drown paced the waiting room floor until the baby arrived. Only three weeks later, Pat was back in the office and making her campaign rounds. Each morning, before going to work, she took Tricia to Hannah's house and picked her up at the end of her long day.

MRS. NIXON GOES TO WASHINGTON

Voorhis remained in Washington, playing it cool, refusing to lock horns with the newcomer. It was smart politics. Tangling with Nixon would give him status; ignoring him diminished the opponent. Meanwhile, the Nixons campaigned up and down the district all through winter and spring until the primary vote in June.

It was not encouraging. At the time, California permitted cross-filing, which has since been outlawed. Democratic and Republican candidates could run in each other's primaries. Voorhis had no trouble taking the Democratic nomination and he got a sizable GOP vote as well, 49,994 to Nixon's 65,586. When all the votes cast for the candidates in both primaries were counted, Voorhis had beaten Nixon by more than 7,000.

To his supporters, the young candidate was brisk, businesslike, and optimistic. "We'll take him in November," he told them confidently. He cited the analysis of a Los Angeles political newsman who pointed out that

---

*Day remembers: "Nixon was still so shy in those years that he couldn't look women in the eye. When he talked to them, he would avert his eyes. I gave him hell for that. I told him he had to get over that shyness and look straight at the ladies. I also gave him hell for wearing wild neckties. He thought it looked sporting. But I told him that when people met him, all they would remember was that he wore a crazy tie and not what he said."

Voorhis's total vote was 6.5 percent lower than it had been two years before.

Privately, Nixon was far less certain. He paced the floor of their deserted headquarters late at night, worrying and wondering, as Pat sat and watched. She encouraged him, told him he could go on to win. He wasn't so sure now; Voorhis's total vote was larger than he had expected. Over the days, she helped him gain new confidence and he believed her.

It was a pattern that would be repeated at other times in other crises—Nixon doubting himself, yielding to dark pessimism, Pat bolstering his sagging sense of self-worth.

By a curious turn of circumstance, little Tricia played a role in helping to start her father's political career.

After Tricia was born, Voorhis sent the Nixons a booklet called *Infant Care* which had been published by the U.S. Children's Bureau since 1914 and had been updated periodically. For years Voorhis had been mailing a copy to all new parents in his district. On the cover of the copy he sent to the Nixons, he wrote: "Congratulations. I look forward to meeting you in public."

The pamphlet was valuable to both Nixons. Pat learned all about feeding, baby clothing, and toilet training; and Richard seized upon Voorhis's little note as a pretext to challenge the incumbent to a series of debates.

It was a clever move. Voorhis was trapped. He was forced to abandon his aloof tactics and confront the newcomer, or face the charge that he had thrown down the gauntlet and was running away when his opponent picked it up.

They met in a series of encounters that summer and early fall, debating in schools, community centers, and missions in the district. Pat was always in the audience, her hands in her lap, eyes unwaveringly on her husband, her face pale, her lips pressed together, her body tense. Louise Voorhis, the congressman's wife and herself a seasoned campaigner, noted that Pat had appeared timid the few times their paths had crossed and then saw how exceptionally nervous she was as the debates progressed.

Nixon had found his issue. The CIO's Political Action Committee had voted to endorse Voorhis, though the congressman had neither sought nor wanted it. Nixon had been hammering away at the theme that the PAC was Communist-dominated and had a "gigantic slush fund" at the disposal of candidates who saw things its way. In pamphlets and newspaper ads, he was charging that the PAC "looks after the interests of Russia, against the interests of America." Nixon began claiming that Voorhis's voting record "is more Socialistic and Communistic than Democratic."

His timing was perfect. Four years later, an obscure Senator from Wisconsin, Joseph R. McCarthy, was to hang an infamous career upon the same issue, but Nixon had it first. The extent of the "Communist conspiracy" has long since been deflated but the American public, mystified by the Russian monolith, was ripe at this time for terrorization. Nixon would never attain McCarthy's enormous power to frighten the public and to cow not only the Congress but two Presidents, Harry S. Truman and Dwight D. Eisenhower, but like McCarthy, he was a skillful manipulator of public opinion. And he rode the issue for all it was worth from then on.

Nixon's assault on Voorhis at their first encounter, held in a junior high school, was virulent. Even his supporters were astounded by his slashing, blustering attack. In the audience, Louise Voorhis was shocked; Pat sat quietly.

The first debate drew much attention in the press, the second even more. Crowds grew. The fifth and last, held at the San Gabriel Mission near Los Angeles, was jammed. Since many could not get inside, amplifiers were placed outside so they could hear.

Jerry Voorhis, who still lives in Claremont with his wife, looks back upon that blistering campaign and is happy he got out of the rough congressional waters. "I got a better job," he told me with a laugh. Voorhis went into the public relations business and, in late 1977, past eighty years old, he was still active in it. After he lost, he saw Nixon only once. "He came to my office and asked me for my mailing list. I didn't give it to him and I never saw him again."

About Pat, he says: "I felt she was as shocked as I was by some of the things he said." This view is not shared by Pat's close friends or by any of the Nixon campaign advisers. Everything she was ever to say, privately to her family and friends and publicly to newspeople, points the other way. Pat Nixon believed. From the moment she became a political wife, she supported her husband in everything he did or said, to the last day of his political career and beyond.

On January 3, 1947, she sat proudly in the special relatives gallery of the House of Representatives and watched her husband sworn as a United States Congressman.

Her own political life, which spanned twenty-seven years, had begun, and she was to loathe most of it.

In the same gallery, watching John Kennedy being sworn, sat most of the Kennedy clan, up from Florida and in from the Riviera. Pat looked at them with interest and curiosity—even then their robustiousness drew attention—never suspecting that their political lives would converge later in a presidential battle.

Contrasting Nixon and Kennedy as freshmen congressmen is irresistible and even significant.

John arrived in the capital from Palm Beach, where his father, Joseph P. Kennedy, owned a seven-bedroom white stucco home on North Ocean Boulevard, the resort's swankiest street. He rented a house in Georgetown, a few minutes' ride from downtown Washington, to which his family sent Margaret Ambrose, who had been cook and housekeeper ever since John Kennedy was a small boy, to care for his needs.

The Nixons, with their ten-month-old baby, went from their small apartment on Walnut Street in Whittier into an inexpensive hotel room, where they lived crowded together while Pat scoured the ads and trudged the streets, hunting for a permanent place. She finally found an $80-a-month unfurnished two-bedroom apartment in an area called Park Fairfax, Virginia, six miles from the Old House Office Building. There she cooked, cleaned, did the laundry, shopped, and cared for Tricia. Since Nixon had always been inept at household chores, she also stopped faucets from leaking, hung pictures, unstuck doors, put up shelves, and performed any other handywoman jobs that came up.

Nixon met Kennedy early in his freshman days; both were assigned to the House Education and Labor Committee. But they never socialized. Kennedy was handsome, wide-grinning, Harvard-educated, sought-after by Washington hostesses; Nixon was quickly dubbed "the greenest congressman in town" by the *Washington Post* and looked it; he owned two suits, not fashionably cut, obviously off the rack and inexpensive, and had the wide-eyed, eager look of a provincial congressman overwhelmed by the power center of the world, which he was.

After John Kennedy was elected senator in 1952 and married Jacqueline Lee Bouvier a year later, the contrast sharpened. The Kennedys bought a beautiful Georgian house on six and a half acres of prime rolling land in McLean, Virginia. The estate, Hickory Hill, cost $130,000.*

The differences were not inconsequential in helping to explain how Nixon would come to feel about the subject of money. At this stage in his life, Nixon developed a hunger for wealth, whereas earlier his drives were centered on accomplishments rather than things. Jessamyn West speculates that his early exposure to the Kennedys reminded him strongly of his "underprivileged youth," and certainly from that time on, his bitterness and resentment at his early life and hard times began emerging with increasing frequency in his speeches. He would talk of wearing an older brother's hand-me-down shoes, of his mother who rose at dawn to bake the cakes

---

*After Jacqueline's baby was stillborn in August, 1956, her second unsuccessful pregnancy, she could no longer bear to live in the house, where a nursery had been made ready for the infant's arrival. The Kennedys sold Hickory Hill to Robert and Ethel Kennedy, who needed the space for their rapidly enlarging family. Ethel still lives there.

and pies so the family could earn a living, of Pat, too, who had worked hard all her life.

Miss West may be right when she says that "perhaps it is politically expedient to put on your log cabin clothes when you run for office," but Nixon, it soon became clear, was not merely making political capital of his early deprivations. It would not be long before he made friends with people who had done extremely well financially, like Charles G. (Bebe) Rebozo and Robert Abplanalp. Eventually he would acquire magnificent mansions in San Clemente and Key Biscayne and a 12-room cooperative apartment on New York's Fifth Avenue. He would also buy expensive furniture, get his suits made to measure, have a chauffeur-driven limousine while he was a private citizen, and surround himself with the other accoutrements of wealth. He would become less and less willing to part with money, for contributions to charity (negligible) or for taxes.

"While no recent American President has been lacking in luxury," writes Dr. Eli S. Chesen, a psychiatrist, "Nixon extended the personal perquisites of the nation's chief executive to an unprecedented degree." *Fortune* magazine counted up the private offices he had installed and completely furnished: nine across the country. Just to secure his San Clemente residence alone cost $6.1 million. He would give himself the splendid luxury of turning up the air-conditioning in mid-summer, making a room cold enough so that he could enjoy logs burning in the fireplace.

But Pat, who saw the contrast in those early days as clearly as he did—not only with the Kennedys but with other wealthy persons in official Washington whom she met and whose homes she visited—was not affected in the same way. She asked for so little that Nixon always had to trick her into revealing what she would like as presents. For example, on the trips they made to Central America and the Far East when he was Vice President, he told the escort officer to let him know if she admired anything in the stores. That was how he discovered that she wanted a silver vase, a clock, and other gifts she otherwise would never have mentioned.

It may seem strange that two people, each reared in economic uncertainty, each a product of the Great Depression, would come to maturity with such divergent attitudes toward the acquisition of wealth. Yet is it so strange after all? Each sought security: Richard Nixon in money and power, Pat in a home and family. He was to achieve both and fall harder than any President in history; she, committed to him, would find peace only for a few brief years.

The full extent of that commitment and how much she yielded up was staggering.

7

Politics and Pat

"I'VE GIVEN UP EVERYTHING . . ."

Pat fooled everybody who did not know her intimately, never letting on that most of the time she hated the whole thing.

Her closest friends knew. But the voters who watched her on a platform—her brown eyes fixed adoringly upon Richard, her head nodding approval as he spoke—never suspected. For outwardly she put on a wonderful show, pretending to enjoy her role as the wife of a politician, giving interviews in which she said how thrilled and enthusiastic she was about the "rewarding and interesting life."

Her true feelings were summed up in a profoundly sad remark she made to a close friend in February, 1960, a few months before her husband was nominated for the presidency:

"I've given up everything I've ever loved."

It was one of the few times she allowed her emotions to overflow. Tears filled her eyes. She could not speak for a moment and she turned away. When she had once again regained control, she continued: "The people who lose out are the children. Any of the glamor or reward in it comes to the grown-ups. It's the children who really suffer."

83

It was conventional wisdom in Washington all through Nixon's political career to hold up Pat as the paradigm of the uncomplaining wife. Wives who were becoming restive in their roles*—like Mieke Tunney, Phyllis Dole, and Ellen Proxmire, all of whom divorced their senator-husbands—were compared with Pat. When Angelina Alioto disappeared in the midst of her husband's campaign for the governorship of California, the pundits pointed out that political marriages aren't what they used to be. Joan Kennedy's marriage suffered severe strains, mostly because of her fears that harm would come to Edward, the last remaining Kennedy brother. Sharon Rockefeller, the daughter of Senator Charles H. Percy of Illinois and wife of Jay Rockefeller, governor of West Virginia, once remarked that in a campaign year she responds to her husband's eighteen-hour days as follows: "I cry and I get angry. He can count on one major blowup a month. People forget that just because you grew up in politics, you're just as human as anyone else."

"There are no more Pat Nixons around in the wives division," wrote one Washington correspondent.

The writer must have been unaware that Pat was as unhappy as the others, not with her husband but with the game of politics.

Nixon's 1950 campaign for the Senate in California against Helen Gahagan Douglas, one of the most vicious in years, was the turning point. From that time on, politics was anathema to Pat. Through the years that were to follow, she made this luminously clear to persons she knew and trusted.

Earl Mazo knew. "She didn't want politics ever," he told me. "Her friends were never political friends. She hated the idea of ever facing another campaign. Every time Nixon entered one, she was in despair. In 1962,

---

*Domestic flare-ups and crack-ups among political couples accelerated throughout the 1970s. The latest, early in 1978, was the separation of President Carter's chief assistant, Hamilton Jordan, and his wife, Nancy, after seven years of marriage. A White House source, predicting other failures will follow, said: "The demands of life here, the in-fighting for position, put terrific strain on marriages."

when he decided to run for governor of California, Christ, she could have just gone through the floor.''

She had been happy that year, out of politics for good, she thought. "Look at this," Nixon told Mazo and other friends one day on the terrace of his California home, following his defeat in the 1960 elections. "I'm earning more money the first year out of politics than I made in fourteen years in it." Pat threw her hands in the air and exclaimed joyfully: "Hallelujah!"

Flora Schreiber knew. Pat told her that she never wanted Nixon to run for the presidency in 1968, confiding that she had been through a great deal of "horror" and that she did not want to go into what she called a "whirlwind."

William P. Rogers, Secretary of State in Nixon's Cabinet, and his wife, Adele, knew. (Rogers has been one of Nixon's closest friends ever since they met during the Hiss-Chambers case. Rogers was chief counsel to the Senate Internal Security Subcommittee.) In 1963, after the disastrous defeat for the California governorship, the Nixons and the Rogerses went to dinner at New York's "21" restaurant. They discussed Nixon's political career and even Nixon agreed with Rogers that, after seventeen years, it had ended once and for all. Reports William Safire, a Nixon insider who later was to join his White House staff: "They all got a little high, and the happiest was Pat—glad to be rid of politics where not even the victories were sweet."

Richard Nixon himself knew her feelings only too well. In 1954, only eight years after they had gone to Washington, her loathing for politics had become so intense that she had a long talk with her husband about what it was doing to them and the children. He was then Vice President, but despite the high office and the promise of a higher one, she wanted no more. She pleaded with him to leave, and he yielded to her wishes.

Near the end of his term, two years thence, he promised he would, once and for all time, divorce himself from politics. He even offered to put the pledge in writing. On a sheet of paper she brought to him one evening in their Washington home, he wrote: "I promise to Patricia Ryan Nixon that I will not again seek public office." He wrote the date, folded the paper, and placed the promise in his wallet.

It was, of course, broken.

His explanation: "Once you get into this great stream of history you can't get out. You can drown. Or you can be pulled ashore by the tide. But it is awfully hard to get out when you are in the middle of the stream—if it is intended that you stay there."

At first, it didn't seem so bad. Nixon's first term, only two years, flew by and his re-election in 1948 was easy. He was unopposed in the Republican primary and, having entered the Democratic primary under the cross-filing system, he defeated his opponent, Stephen Zetterberg, by 3,000 votes.

There was no need to do much campaigning either, and for that Pat was grateful. Nixon was already making a name for himself as a subversive-hunting member of the House Committee on UnAmerican Activities. He had been co-author of the Mundt-Nixon Bill,* which required Communist-front organizations to register with the Attorney General and he had begun to go after Alger Hiss, a former State Department official under President Roosevelt and then president of the Carnegie Endowment for International Peace. The Hiss case, begun in August of 1948, splashed Nixon's name across the front pages. Hiss was being accused of passing government secrets to a Russian espionage ring in this country through Whittaker Chambers, a confessed former Communist and an editor of *Time* magazine.

The Hiss case was absorbing most of Nixon's time and attention. He left early, often before breakfast, and arrived home long after Pat had gone to sleep.

On July 5, 1948, Pat gave birth to Julie at Garfield Hospital. With an infant and a toddler in a small apart-

---

*Introduced during Nixon's first term in Congress, the bill was passed by the House but altered in the Senate, emerging as the McCarran Act and no longer bearing Nixon's name.

ment, life became hectic. She worked a sixteen-hour day and still managed to find time to attend some of the official functions required of a congressman's wife. Accustomed as she was to hard work, the pace was punishing and she began to look tired. She was obviously in need of a vacation and Nixon promised that "soon" they would take one. There had been no holiday for either of them since they arrived in Washington, and long before that.

Finally, after the 1948 elections, he came home triumphantly with two tickets—reservations aboard the S.S. *Panama* sailing December 2 for a Caribbean cruise. This one, he told her, would be nothing like that smelly room aboard the *Ulua*; this would be a first-class trip. Pat was excited but said she'd withhold her enthusiasm until she was safely aboard.

On December 2, they ascended the gangplank, unpacked in their cabin, and as the vessel got under way, she watched the disappearing shoreline and breathed a sigh of relief.

Two days later, a Coast Guard amphibian landed in the Caribbean. The Nixons entered a lifeboat and winches lowered them to the water. Crewmen took them to the plane, which roared off to Miami. A few hours later, he was back in Washington and Pat was back in their apartment.

Bert Andrews, chief Washington correspondent for the *New York Herald-Tribune*, had cabled Nixon aboard the *Panama:* "INFORMATION HERE IS THAT HISS-CHAMBERS HAS PRODUCED BOMB-SHELL STOP INDICATIONS ARE THAT CHAMBERS HAS OFFERED NEW EVIDENCE. . . ." The next day Andrews sent another cable: "DOCUMENTS INCREDIBLY HOT . . . FACTS ARE FACTS AND THESE FACTS ARE DYNAMITE." Secretary of Defense James V. Forrestal had signed an order dispatching the Coast Guard plane for Nixon, and Pat's vacation was still far in the future.

By 1950, Alger Hiss had been convicted of perjury in a federal court and Nixon set his sights on a seat in the U.S. Senate, opposing Helen Gahagan Douglas, a New

Deal Democrat who had served three terms in the House. He won and, with their savings and increased salary, then $12,500, they finally were able to move into a modest two-story white brick house with blue-green shutters in the northwest corner of Washington. The home, on the corner of Tilden Street in Spring Valley, cost $41,000; they paid half down and mortgaged the rest.

There was no acreage, just a small backyard and a screened porch in front, but it was the first home with real space they had had since they were married. As usual, Pat made all the curtains, draperies, and slipcovers. And somehow she found time to attend a sewing class in the community where she learned quilting, so she made a blue quilted spread for the double bed she shared with Dick.

She looked after the children, did her own housework, cooked the meals, sprinkled the grass in the yard, made hats, and answered the phone, which seemed to ring almost constantly. Once in a while, she went to Richard's office and helped the secretarial staff.

Her wardrobe was skimpy. The "respectable Republican cloth coat" which Nixon later would tell the nation she owned was black and slightly worn. She had four evening dresses to wear at official functions, several light summer dresses, and some sweaters and skirts. At receptions, the respectable coat was usually the only cloth one among a forest of furs in the cloakrooms. She also owned three suits, thanks to a half-dozen ladies in Whittier, friends from her teaching days, who decided during the 1950 campaign that Pat did not have enough clothes. They knitted the three suits for her and presented them when Pat came to Los Angeles. Martha Russell, now living in retirement at Capistrano, says: "She accepted them gratefully."

Before moving forward with Pat Nixon's life story, we should pause to examine why, at this early point in her husband's career, she had come to abhor the business of politics that magnetized her husband so powerfully.

The long absences from home, and the feelings of guilt they produced in her, probably represented the most significant reason.

Wives of congressmen are deluged with invitations to teas, official receptions, and private parties. A woman who thrives on the glitter can be kept hopping from breakfast to midnight, beginning with the Women's National Press Club's "welcome to Congress" dinner on opening day and continuing throughout the session. Ellen Proxmire, the former wife of the Democratic senator from Wisconsin, found when she arrived in the capital in 1959 that "the social whirl can keep you on the run all day every day if you let it."

Pat cut it as thinly as she could. She had been feeling the weight of guilt ever since Tricia was born because she had to be away from the baby while she campaigned; when Julie arrived, she wanted even more to stay home. But there were some functions she could not avoid, so she hired baby-sitters, left precise instructions, and rushed off, returning home as quickly as she could.

Both girls grew up knowing about their mother's feelings of guilt: Pat told them, Tricia says. Pat, bred in a home where family closeness had been stressed, apparently felt it was wrong to be away from her children so much and so often.

But things were not about to improve. Nixon's political star was rising and she was expected to be away from home for longer and longer periods without the children. Her feelings of guilt were bound to worsen.

When Julie and Tricia were small, they would both start to cry as they watched their parents pack for what they knew would be a long trip. Pat would hug them as she said goodbye. They would still be crying as she shut the door and left.

Once when Tricia was five, she came into her parents' bedroom in the middle of the night. She woke them, saying she was afraid. Pat put her into bed between them. Obviously, their frequent absences had given the child insecurity feelings which were being manifested by apprehensiveness. The incident did not ease the pain of

Pat's guilt; she knew there would be more absences from home.

In the fall of 1953 when Pat and Dick were about to leave as President Eisenhower's emissaries on a ten-week, 45,000-mile goodwill tour of the Far East, five-year-old Julie threw herself on the floor, screaming uncontrollably. Hannah Nixon, who was to stay with the children, watched helplessly. Nixon begged her: "Mother, take her in your arms, or something." Hannah picked up Julie, and Pat left with her husband.

When the girls were older, she took them with her on some campaign trips. They were adorable, and adorable children win as many votes for politicians as dogs do. The Nixons, like many politicians, had both.

But Pat liked taking them even less than leaving them at home. Once, during a campaign, she was in a corridor of a high school just before the family was scheduled to appear at a rally in the gym. She tried to fix their clothing so they would look their best. "These girls simply have no clothes," she said to nobody in particular, "because there's so little time to buy them any."

Another time, in San Antonio, Texas, Julie, then almost out of her teens, came down with a throat infection and a 102-degree fever. Pat led her into the airport's VIP lounge where she took her in her arms. She sat there motionless, not saying anything. On her face was a look of great sadness.

The other factor that was probably responsible for turning Pat against politics was its sheer brutality. It astounded and horrified her. She was deeply shocked by the vilification of her husband that she was forced to see and hear, and which filtered down to affect her children.

The 1950 campaign for the Senate in California was a landmark for political savagery. Mazo calls it "the most hateful one California had experienced in many years." Bruce L. Felknor, then executive director of the Fair Campaign Practices Committee, termed it "a dirty campaign in a dirty year."

Pat Nixon was there every step of the way and heard it all. Whatever one's political views may be, this must be understood: Pat Nixon believed in her husband, was at this point truly in love with him. Every obscenity hurled at him, and there were many she was forced to hear, added to her horror. Every scornful epithet she read in the newspapers, and there were scores, made her quiver and blanch. She heard Mrs. Douglas denounce her husband as a "pipsqueak" for whom, like Senator McCarthy, she had "utter scorn." On September 29, she picked up the *Independent Review* and read an editorial in which her husband was described as "Tricky Dick." It was the first time the phrase was used and it would follow him for the rest of his political career and beyond.

She supported him totally. Once in San Francisco he stood up on an opened tailgate of a station wagon and began making a speech when one of Mrs. Douglas's sound trucks passed. Every time Nixon began a sentence, the occupants would blast interruptions over their loudspeaker.

"Even when he tried to answer them," she remembers, "he could not be heard above the din." Nixon raised his voice to a scream but he was no competition for the amplifier. Pat was distraught as she watched. "Please, Dick," she implored him, "don't answer them." Nixon waited it out and eventually the truck left.

Nixon whaled away at Mrs. Douglas in a sound truck of his own, speaking more than a dozen times daily, starting early in the morning and stopping only when too few people were left on the streets to form a crowd. In sixteen weeks, he racked up more than a thousand speeches. Pat heard them all: assaults on Mrs. Douglas as the "Pink Lady"; attacks upon her as a "member of a small clique which joins the notorious party-liner, Vito Marcantonio of New York, in voting time after time against measures that are for the security of this country."*

Perhaps the lowest point of the campaign came when

*The late Representative Marcantonio of New York was openly pro-Communist.

anti-Semitism was introduced. Mrs. Douglas, who was Irish herself, was wed to the actor Melvyn Douglas, of half-Jewish descent. "Help Richard Nixon get rid of the Jew-Communist," thundered Gerald L. K. Smith, a notorious anti-Semite. Nixon disavowed the support of Smith's Christian Nationalists, and the B'nai B'rith Anti-Defamation League exonerated him of any association with anti-Semitism.

Pat Nixon heard all this too, and it chipped away still more at her estimation of the political game.

During the 1956 campaign, when Nixon was running for Vice President, Mrs. Eleanor Roosevelt went on *Meet the Press* and, in her deceptively gentle, high-pitched voice, dropped lethal charges against Nixon. In reply to a question, Mrs. Roosevelt said: "I have no respect for the way in which he [Nixon] accused Helen Gahagan Douglas of being a Communist because he knew that was how he would be elected, and I have no respect for the kind of character that takes advantage and does something they know is not true. He knew that she might be a Liberal but he knew quite well, having known her and worked with her, that she was not a Communist. I have always felt that anyone who wanted an election so much that they would use those means did not have the character that I really admire in public life." Pat was upset by the remarks, but Nixon told her to pay no attention because it was just politics.

If she was horrified by the vilification of Nixon, she was even more shocked to discover that her children were seeing and hearing it too. "Okay," she once said to Rita Mazo, Earl's wife, with whom she had become quite friendly, "maybe Dick is a public servant and maybe he is fair game, but why do they hurt our little girls." Herblock, the political cartoonist, often caricatured Nixon as dark-bearded and menacing. Each time a cartoon appeared, Tricia and Julie would come home from school in tears, having been teased and tormented by their classmates about their "monkey father." Nixon ordered his subscription to the *Washington Post* stopped so that his daughters would not see the Herblock drawings. "It's no fun," Julie said later, "to have kids tell you your father stinks."

All their lives, Julie and Tricia heard their father excoriated. For Julie, it began early. When she was four years old, she overheard a woman remark how much she despised that (expletive deleted) Nixon. Pat knew and she was wounded as much as the girls.

Afterward, Pat would say that the vituperation directed at Nixon hurt her so much that she stopped reading critical comments. But she could not turn off every radio and television set or avoid all the crowds during and in between campaigns.

It would not be long before the criticism, some of it cruel, would be directed at Pat too. She was especially upset when Drew Pearson, the late columnist, wrote that she wore costly dresses because her neck was too long and her shoulders too bony to fit into cheaper models. Nixon, who had learned to control his temper, exploded at this. "I thought that was the height of viciousness," he told writer Eleanor Harris. "It was the meanest, lowest thing a guy could say about a woman. In the first place, it wasn't true about Pat. In the second place, it would be a mean thing to say about any woman if it were true. The air around me was blue for some time after I read that."

When the Nixon-Douglas campaign finally ended, Nixon, worn out, said he would not stay home to hear the returns. He wanted to go to the beach but there was a bleak chill in the air. He got into his car and drove off alone, southward from Los Angeles, where his headquarters were, toward Long Beach, through the factory section there, and back. Pat remembers that he came back in a dark mood, "sure that we were licked."

He wasn't. He won by more than 680,000 votes—2,183,454 to 1,502,507. He even ran seven percent ahead of the Republican congressional slate.

His mood changed abruptly, reports Ralph de Toledano. "He spent the rest of the night going from party to victory party, rattling off his own stilted piano rendition of 'Happy Days Are Here Again.'"

Pat was delighted over his victory, but she was not at all sure that happy days were ahead.

When Nixon was nominated for the vice presidency in July of 1952 in Chicago, Pat was with him, as usual. She had left their daughters, then five and three years old, in the care of a trusted sitter. At the Stockyards Inn, where the Nixons were staying, Pat had argued with Nixon, pleading with him not to accept if he was named as Eisenhower's running mate. Murray Chotiner, called to Nixon's room at four in the morning, saw plainly that there was a tenseness between them.

"If this vice presidential thing is offered to me," Nixon asked Chotiner, "do you think I shoud take it?" When Chotiner replied that he should indeed accept, Nixon wanted to know why. Chotiner was in a spot. He, too, had known of Pat's attitude toward continuing in the game, that she wanted—at this point desperately—to be left alone to raise her family in peace. But Chotiner was as ambitious for Nixon as Nixon was for himself. He explained that if Nxon did not accept, he would probably remain California's junior senator and "you'll never amount to much in politics as a junior senator. For you it's a question of going up or out—there are no other alternatives."

Nixon said he'd think it over. Several hours later, having barely slept, Nixon was summoned by a phone call to the Blackstone Hotel, where Ike's chieftains were in the process of winnowing out candidates for the number-two position. Pat bid him goodbye, sure that she had won and that he would refuse an offered bid.

She went down to the restaurant for a sandwich and, when the waitress brought it over, began watching an old movie that had just begun on television. She picked up the sandwich and took a bite. Suddenly the movie was interrupted by a news bulletin. Eisenhower had chosen Nixon. "That bite of sandwich popped right out of my mouth," she says. Quickly she rushed from the restaurant into a cab and to the convention hall, remaining backstage until the balloting ended.

She had lost, but the game now had to be continued. She must be at his side, smiling and gracious and cool. That evening, Nixon was nominated. Later, Pat joined him on the platform. She was answering another call.

Back in Washington, she learned later, news photographers who had been waiting in front of their home rang the bell, rushed past the frightened sitter, and woke up the little girls. They instructed them to pose for pictures. The flashbulbs and the sudden awakening terrified the children, who broke into tears. Julie, four years old, sobbed, "I want my mommy."

CAMPAIGNER

Despite her dislike of politicking, Pat was a magnificent campaigner—a paradox explainable only when one understands how completely she was able to submerge her own ideas, feelings, and goals. By the necromancy of a remarkable will, she became on the surface a mirror image of Richard Nixon, with his goals her goals, his wishes her wishes. She did this so well that countless articles appeared over the years commenting in surprising fashion on how much Pat Nixon resembled her husband.

She was an enormous asset to him because he arrived on the scene long before feminism had been transformed from underground rumblings into a militant movement. Betty Friedan was still writing articles on "Teenage Girls in Trouble" for *Coronet* magazine and "The Coming Ice Age" for *Harper's*. Marriage patterns were changing and many, if not most, American women were dissatisfied to varying degrees, but the roles of husband and wife were still clearly marked. He was the provider and she the housewife; the ability to bake the best pie on the block and keep the nicest home was still being given high points by society.

Pat exemplified to many American women —especially to Middle American women, where the Nixons pulled strongest—the type of wife and mother they still believed was the best kind to be: a woman with all her chores done, perfectly of course, yet still looking fresh, poised, and squeaky clean. But much more important, she communicated a signal that women detected with little trouble—that Pat Nixon really ruled the roost but was doing it quietly and raising no fuss about it. For America, women knew, was a matriarchy. Despite a man's titular position as "head of the house," it was the woman who was the glue that held the nuclear family together. And they suspected, quite correctly, that without Pat the Nixons would soon become unstuck.

When she disclosed that she was still pressing the vice presidential trousers because only she could do it really well and that she did all the packing herself, many women grimaced because that was a bit much. Few wives felt shamed by Pat's expertise at pants pressing, but the very ingenuousness of the confession was endearing; it came across as simple eagerness to show what a good wife she was.

Men, too, were impressed by her for special, male-oriented reasons. She was helpful but never came on strong; she was in no way domineering. Warren Rogers, Jr., pointed out in the *New York Herald-Tribune* during the presidential campaign against John F. Kennedy: "She is a good listener and a trustworthy confidante." Nor was it only the average man who felt drawn to Pat. President Eisenhower himself and John Foster Dulles, his Secretary of State, sought her out on many serious social occasions—and, observed Rogers, "doted on her company." She listened well, she was a good backboard against whom to bounce their views, and she had a way about her that inspired confidence. To Henry Kissinger, Nixon's Secretary of State, she was "a silent patriot . . . a loyal and uninterfering female in man's world of politics, speaking only when spoken to, and not sullying the cigar smoke with her personal opinions." It was an evaluation that would cause even a mild feminist to grind his/her teeth in anger, but it worked in those years for Richard Nixon.

She was also one of the first of the political wives to become aware of the immense power of television to win or lose votes. As early as the famous "Checkers" speech in 1952, she discovered that the camera's lens could reveal to millions the *personae* of the politician *and* his wife—everything the voter wanted to know about their characters, temperaments, personalities, and even idiosyncrasies but never had the chance to observe so clearly or so closely.

When Nixon made that incredible sentimental defense against charges that California supporters had raised an $18,000 slush fund for his personal use, Pat stared unwaveringly at him, worry about his future and her utter devotion to him unmistakably mirrored in her face. Those who watched and were touched outnumbered by far those who watched and scoffed. Nixon knew what he was doing—he told the Radio and Television Executives Society only three years later that he had "staged" the entire speech! He did not say, and neither has ever said since, that Pat had been briefed on how to act. But, briefed or not, her performance was superb, and she apparently learned a great deal from it.

Thereafter, her performances on the campaign trail, on camera or just before live audiences, were excellent. I am using the word "performance" here as in acting; it must be recalled that both Pat and Dick were well trained in the histrionic arts, and both performed together with remarkable effectiveness for more than a quarter of a century. It was a great act, and it worked. Pat would know by heart every word of her husband's speeches, could recite them from start to finish if she were awakened from a deep sleep. Yet she always gave the impression in public of hearing them for the first time, her face lighting up at precisely the correct moment when he made his points. She was a marvelous prop.

And he knew it very well. Constantly, he would remind audiences how great she was. ("Whatever you think of me, I'm sure you'll agree that Pat will make an excellent First Lady." . . . "Whatever you think of me, everybody admires the job Pat had done." . . . "One of her great assets is a sensitivity about people.") His political weather vane was telling him that women would be playing a decisive role in the political life of the country from 1960 on, and he needed her and his daughters as a campaign tool. He used them fully.

Her energy was inexhaustible; Nixon would often give

out before she did. At one time during the 1960 presidential campaign, a line of thousands shuffled past them for a handshake and a few words of greeting. Finally, as the afternoon sun cast long shadows over the speaker's rostrum, a weary and finger-sore Nixon whispered sidelong to his wife: "Let's break for a few minutes." The line halted while the Nixons retreated for a breather. Pat, however, could have kept going, a fact Nixon admitted in recalling the incident. "Her physical stamina had been even greater than mine," he said. "It was I, rather than she, who would first have to ask for a break in the line."

Nor was Nixon the only one who cried uncle before her boundless energy. Often she outlasted women reporters assigned to cover her. And in Moscow in May of 1972, Mrs. Leonid I. Brezhnev, wife of the Communist Party chief, returned to the Kremlin halfway through the First Lady's tour of the city.

The demands made on her were horrendous. There were nine campaigns in all, seven of them covering wide areas. Each meant almost constant travel for her, often awakening before dawn and whirling through days that rarely ended before midnight.

When Nixon traveled by plane, she slept curled into a seat, and emerged fresh and ready to go whenever called. When he was barnstorming by train, she would wait inside the rear car until she heard her introduction; then, like a special guest star, would come out smiling and perfectly groomed. She never looked tired. On receiving lines, she would focus her attention on every individual, eschewing the tactic of the "Irish handshake" developed by John F. (Honey Fitz) Fitzgerald, Rose Kennedy's father, and inherited by the Kennedys. Honey Fitz, a former mayor of Boston and a consummate politician, would shake hands with one person on line and pull him or her gently along as he turned his smile on the next; meanwhile, he would extend his left hand to the one following as he transferred his right from the first individual to the third person coming along. It was complex but it got the people through the line fast. And experienced politicians are keenly aware that spending as little as a minute with one person means that only 180 will be greeted in three hours; and when a thousand or more are on a receiving line, as often happens, the ordeal could be endless. But Pat would not only speak personally to each one but have individual pictures taken with as many as 250 in a single evening. In just a single day's campaigning in Detroit in 1960, one aide took count: during a 17-hour round of receptions, press conferences, talks, lunches and dinners, she had shaken 3,650 hands. After she left a city, she would write thank-you notes to her hosts and hostesses.

Her self-discipline was a rare advantage in campaigning. Politicians, and politicians' wives as well, have lost elections and careers because they have not been able to control their emotions or their mouths. One thinks of Edmund Muskie in New Hampshire, destroyed because he cried as he defended his wife against scurrilous charges. Or George Romney, who admitted to having been "brainwashed" in Vietnam. Or Nixon himself who, in 1962, virtually self-destructed when he exposed his raw emotions before the nation in that remarkable "You won't have Nixon to kick around any more" farewell to the press. (Nixon's return to power six years after that episode was one of the most remarkable comeback stories in American political history.)

Pat Nixon, who had faced dozens of hecklers in her first campaign and saw firsthand thousands more as the years progressed, learned that there was nothing to be gained politically by replying in kind; that turning the other cheek won sympathy—and votes; that pleasing all was better than alienating some.

This she knew well: "It is always the person about whom you care most who is the center of your life, whom you will help or hurt by your words and deeds." It was the core credo of all her campaigning.

So she developed to a high art the knack of giving nonanswers to questions. She gave full replies in clichés that hurt nobody and revealed nothing. A few illustrations from an interview with Warren Rogers, Jr., in the *New York Herald-Tribune* during the 1960 presidential campaign against John Kennedy:

Q. Do your daughters mind being left alone so much when you and the Vice President are traveling? Do they complain about their father's job keeping him away from home?

A. "No, they are very good about it. They know it is important to go on trips, and they understand the importance more now than when they were younger. They are optimistic about the campaign, far more than we are. Tricia went down to headquarters the other day to do volunteer work, folding literature for envelopes and things like that."

Q. You had it pretty rough as a child, didn't you?

A. "I wouldn't say that. My father was a miner in Ely, Nev., where I was born. But there were accidents in the mines so we moved out to California. . . . In a lot of ways I was a lot more fortunate than children growing up in a city. There was always lots to do on the farm. Our parents made fun for us and we played games like 'run, sheep, run' and my father gave us all a peanut patch for our very own. No one asked for anything and we were grateful for what we got.

"I remember I used to ride to town with my father in the buggy to go sell his produce and hope that he would have enough left over for an ice cream cone. I'd sit there in the buggy. I wouldn't get out. And I'd watch to see if he went into the drug store. If he did it meant I'd get a cone. Strawberry. I loved it. Some days he didn't bring it."

Q. Has your life changed you in any way that you don't like? Doesn't it get wearing to be always in the public gaze, living a life in a fishbowl? Would you do it all over again?

A. "Well, I don't daydream, and I don't look back. I think what is to be will be, and I take each day as it comes. I never cared much for frivolous things. Frivolous things have never meant much to me.

"I like the idea of doing public service, no matter how small. And I like to meet people. It is kind of hard to get around sometimes because people recognize you and come up and start talking. Like the other day, I went shopping downtown for some shoes and a hat. It took forever because people kept coming up. But I love it."

The foreign press also took note of the facade she erected. Late in 1958, she and the Vice President paid a four-day visit to London to represent President Eisenhower at the dedication of the chapel in St. Paul's honoring the U.S. war dead. "Nattie Pattie," as the British journalists called her, presided at a tea for women reporters at the official residence of the American ambassador. Later, the prestigious London publication *The Spectator* published a devastating portrait:

> She chatters, answers questions, smiles and smiles, all with a doll's terrifying poise. There is too little comprehension. Like a doll she would still be smiling while the world broke. Only her eyes, dark, darting and strained, signal that inside the black suit and pearls there is a human being, probably content not to get out.

She appeared so *perfect*. She *never* worried about politics, *never* minded all those dreadful things people said about Richard. Her political duties *never* affected her family life, and she didn't *in the least* mind being considered the perfect wife of a politician. The account concluded: "One grey hair, one hint of fear, one golden tea-cup overturned on the Persian carpet and one could have loved her."

When pressed by frustrated newspeople to explain why she was not speaking out, she explained: "I have always campaigned this way. You see, I'll always be the same person. I would never change and try to pattern myself after someone else."

CBS White House correspondent Robert Pierpoint was in a unique position to note the sharp change that politics wrought in Pat's personality, having been a student at Whittier High when Pat was a teacher there. As a member of the Pep Committee, he had been impressed by her vivacity and enthusiasm.

Pierpoint: "After I graduated, I did not see her for twelve years. When we met again, she was the wife of the Vice President of the United States. She had changed drastically. She was extremely uptight, difficult to talk to, very nervous and not at all the happy, outgoing personality I had remembered from high school days.

"By that time, I had become a reporter for CBS News. I had been based in Tokyo and was sent to cover their arrival in the Philippines, where they had been sent by President Eisenhower to visit the newly elected president, Ramón Magsaysay. Magsaysay took the Nixons on a sightseeing trip to Corregidor Island off Bataan Peninsula of Luzon. I went along on the presidential yacht with a number of other newspeople.

"On the sail out, I mentioned to Bill Henry, then Nixon's press secretary, that I had known Mrs. Nixon back in high school days and I'd like to say hello. He said, fine, and took me up to where she was seated with Mrs. Magsaysay. I greeted the two ladies and tried to talk with Pat and was astonished at the reception I got.

"Look, the natural thing for anyone to do would be to open up, smile, ask about what I've done, if I had been married, had any children, seen the other kids—all those things you'd expect a former teacher to ask a student. But she became stiff and wooden and acted as though she didn't want to talk to me or hear of the other students and teachers.

"I sensed this in a couple of minutes, then quickly thanked her and left."

A few times the crust she had laid over her emotions would crack and she would reveal, fleetingly, the feelings inside. Once a reporter asked her a question routinely asked of all political wives: Would she want one of her daughters to marry a politician? She answered: "I'd feel sorry for her if she ever married anyone in politics." In 1970, during a tour of a training school for delinquent boys, she told the youths: "I want you to be something great. One of you can even be President." She turned away and, in an aside audible only to a few people standing closest to her, added: "I wouldn't want to wish it on them."

The feminist leader Gloria Steinem penetrated deeper than most into her defenses. During the 1968 campaign, Ms. Steinem sat with Mrs. Nixon during part of a two-hour flight from Denver, Colorado, to St. Louis, talking to her about her own girlhood which, she explained, was not unlike that of Pat Nixon. She had been seeking, she explained later, to make "human contact" with her but didn't succeed. Finally, after questions about the dreams and hopes she may have had as a child, Pat Nixon let some of the bitterness she had bottled up pour out:

"I never had time to think about things like that," she said in a low, accusatory voice—"who I wanted to be, or who I admired or to have ideas. I never had time to dream about being anyone else. I had to work.

"I haven't just sat back and thought of myself or my ideas or what I wanted to do . . . I've kept working. I don't have time to worry about who I admire or who I identify with. I never had it easy. I'm not like all you . . . all those people who had it easy."

Quickly she sealed the opening and there were no similar spillouts of public anger for the next six years. But what she said that day in the plane revealed only too clearly the resentments that had been building up within Pat Nixon during her more than two decades as a political wife.

8

Second Lady

"CHECKERS" WITH TEARS

Pat Nixon was weeping. "Why," she asked a close friend over and over, "why should we keep taking this?" Her friend tried to comfort her but Pat was inconsolable. She could barely touch food; she slept little.

It was September 24, 1952, the day after Nixon had delivered his "Checkers" speech. Pat had been confident that her husband had been vindicated and that Eisenhower would be fully satisfied.

But he hadn't been at all. The General was still keeping them dangling, not saying whether he would allow Nixon to remain on the ticket as his running mate or dump him. There had been suspenseful moments in Pat's life but none so far like this one; there would not be one to match it for another twenty-two years. "Mrs. Nixon never regained her taste for politics after that," Earl Mazo wrote.

The nightmare, a brief but terrible one for Pat, had begun in mid-September that year. Nixon had been nominated for the vice presidency and the campaign had been in full swing when the slush-fund story came to light. Whispered around since July, it was revived in September. Peter Edson of the Newspaper Enterprise Association had interviewed Nixon on *Meet the Press* and later, though not on the air, had asked him about the fund story.

Nixon said the rumor that he had profited personally was entirely wrong and that a full account could be obtained from Dana C. Smith, a California lawyer who was managing the fund. Smith told Edson that there was indeed a fund, that one hundred Republican businessmen were contributing $500 a year each but that the money was being used to help defray Nixon's transportation costs between Washington and California.

A full-blown scandal erupted when the *New York Post* published a story on September 18 with a headline that occupied all of the front page: SECRET NIXON FUND. Inside was another headline: SECRET RICH MEN'S TRUST FUND KEEPS NIXON IN STYLE FAR BEYOND HIS SALARY. Even Nixon-haters now agree that the story was vastly overplayed and exaggerated—actually it was soon discovered that Governor Adlai Stevenson of Illinois, the Democratic candidate, had a private fund, far larger, that was used to supplement the salaries of his staff employees who had given up higher-paying jobs to work for him in his administration.

The Nixons had been whistle-stopping by train in California when the news hit them. Speaking to crowds in Northern California, he was treating the fund charge as another political assault, but as the hours passed, the Nixons realized it was much more than that. They learned that the GOP had been thrown into a panic, that the National Committee was being flooded with calls and wires, and that Eisenhower himself had been stunned.

The issue quickly became a raging controversy. The *Washington Post* and the *New York Herald-Tribune* called on Nixon to resign from the ticket. Eisenhower, stern-faced, told reporters that everyone involved in his campaign must be "clean as a hound's tooth." The Nixons heard that General Lucius Clay, who had fought with Eisenhower in Europe and whose opinion he respected, had called Ike and urged him to dump his running mate. (Afterward, Clay denied making the call, but Nixon did not know this at the time.)

Nixon now wavered. Perhaps he should quit, he felt; but Pat dissuaded him. "Maybe I am looking at this too much from my own standpoint," he had said. "If the judgment of more objective people around Eisenhower is that my resignation would help him to win, maybe I ought to resign."

She could have kept silent, or agreed that leaving the race was advisable and got what she wanted most—a life of privacy. But she had already submerged herself so deeply into his career, wanting what he wanted despite the sacrifices she knew would be required of her, that she argued him out of his doubts.

"You can't think of resigning," she told him, pointing out that if he left the race the General would almost surely lose the election. "He can put you off the ticket if he wants to," she said, "but if you, in the face of attack, do not fight back but simply crawl away, you will destroy yourself. Your life will be marred forever and the same will be true of your family, and particularly, your daughters."

Pat became furious when rumors reached her that she had spent $10,000 of the fund to decorate her Spring Valley home. She knew who had decorated her home and how much it had cost. "Why are they doing this to us?" she asked him. He didn't reply, but knew that his political career was now on the line.

Five days after the story broke, the GOP had raised $75,000 and called Nixon in Portland, Oregon, to fly to Los Angeles and defend himself on national television. On the plane, Nixon fished some picture postcards from his pocket and began making notes for the most crucial speech of his political career to that point. Later he would call it one of his six crises.

On board the plane, Nixon told Pat that their only hope was to bare their private financial lives before a nationwide audience to prove they had not profited from the fund. "We'll need to tell them everything about ourselves," he said.

Pat was appalled. "But why do we have to parade how little we have and how much we owe in front of all those millions of people?'' she asked.

"All candidates' lives are public," Nixon replied briefly and went back to his notes.

Pat broke in. "It seems to me," she said, "that we are entitled to at least some privacy."

He replied that she must understand that the situation was not a normal one. "Right now," he said, "we're living in a fishbowl. If I don't itemize everything we've earned and everything we spent, the broadcast won't convince the public. I just don't have a choice."

At 3 P.M. on September 22, the plane arrived at Los Angeles and the Nixons went to the Ambassador Hotel, occupying separate suites across the hall from each other. He needed isolation to pace the floor as he refined his thinking about the speech. There would be no written text; he would speak only from notes.

At 5:30 the next day, he went to Pat's room. She was ready. They walked silently down the corridor to the elevator and into a waiting car, reaching the El Capitan theater in Hollywood, an NBC studio, less than a half-hour before air time. They spent most of the waiting time in a dressing room offstage. She said nothing as he shuffled through his five pages of notes.

The speech was to be televised on a hookup of 258 NBC and CBS stations and 560 Mutual Broadcasting System radio stations; there would be 60 million viewers and listeners, until then the largest audience ever to watch and hear a political broadcast.

At 5:57, Nixon almost cracked. In the dressing room he turned to Pat with a distraught look and spoke to her for the first time: "I just don't think I can go through with this one." "Of course you can," she answered. There was no more time for talk. A studio aide escorted them to the stage in the empty theater. Nixon sat behind a desk and Pat took her place in an armchair at the side. The red light on the TV camera flashed on and he was on the air.

The speech was pure soap opera, even for those less sophisticated times, but it worked. Ike and Mamie watched it, along with some thirty aides crowded into the small manager's office at the Cleveland Public Auditorium, where the General had been scheduled to make a campaign address. Downstairs, 17,000 persons listened to it over loudspeakers. Ike, pencil poised over a large yellow pad, sat in front of a small television set.

The General was stone-faced but Mamie cried a little when Nixon spoke of how little he and Pat really had, that a man in Texas had heard that their two little girls would like to have a dog, and that a day later a package arrived at Union Station in Baltimore and, folks, it was a little cocker spaniel in a crate sent all the way from Texas. "Black and white and spotted," Nixon had said. "And our little girl—Tricia, the six-year-old—named it Checkers. And you know the kids love that dog and I just want to say this right now, that regardless of what they say about it, we're going to keep it. . . ."

Nixon was incredibly cloying but undeniably effective as he bared every detail of his personal financial life. He owed $20,000 on his house, had only $4,000 in life insurance, plus his GI policy, owned a 1950 Oldsmobile, had no stocks or bonds and no direct or indirect interest in any business. He also owed $4,500 to a Washington bank, another $3,500 to his parents, and had borrowed $500 on his life insurance. Then came the imperishable remark: "I should say this, that Pat doesn't have a mink coat but she does have a respectable Republican cloth coat, and I always tell her that she would look good in anything."

He would not quit, he said, because he was not a quitter. And Pat was not a quitter either—"after all, her name was Patricia Ryan and she was born on St. Patrick's Day—and you know the Irish never quit."

But the choice was not his, he said. He would do nothing to harm the candidacy of Dwight Eisenhower. Let the Republican National Committee decide and let the listeners wire and write the Committee, telling it whether they think he should quit or remain. He would abide by their decision. Pat sat like a waxen figure throughout the thirty-minute speech.

The results were spectacular. Nixon had run overtime

and had forgotten to announce the address of the Republican National Committee. But cards, letters, and telegrams went to GOP headquarters all over the country, more than 300,000 to the Washington office alone. Western Union offices were swamped. Nobody could count the number of telephone calls which lit up switchboards at radio and television stations and any place that sounded like a Republican headquarters. There were almost no dissenters.

But still Eisenhower hesitated. He sent Nixon a telegram asking him to come to Wheeling, West Virginia, his next campaign stop, for a face-to-face discussion. But the wire did not reach Nixon; it had been lost in the flood of other messages sent to him after the telecast. And he and Pat had heard a news bulletin that Ike was not yet convinced. "It is obvious," the General had told a crowd in Cleveland after the speech, "that I have to have something more than a single presentation, necessarily limited to thirty minutes, the time allowed Senator Nixon."

Pat exploded when she heard the news. "What more does that man want!" she demanded. Nixon admitted he, too, "blew his stack." He ordered a telegram of resignation to be sent to Eisenhower but Murray Chotiner dissuaded him from sending it. The day after the speech, Arthur Summerfield, the Republican Party chairman, telephoned and asked if Nixon would fly to Wheeling. Chotiner said he would come but only if Eisenhower would tell the country that Nixon was completely exonerated. Summerfield assured Chotiner that would indeed happen.

And it did. In Wheeling, when Pat and Dick stepped out of the plane, Eisenhower ran up the steps to greet them. Nixon was astonished. "What are you doing here, General?" he asked. "You didn't have to come out here to meet us."

"Why not?" Eisenhower beamed at them. He put his arm around Nixon and said: "You're my boy."

Pat smiled at him, but it was a long time, her close friends told me, before she forgave him.

INCURABLY DOMESTIC

All through Nixon's first term as Vice President, the family lived in their small Spring Valley home. Sightseeing buses put busy Tilden Street on their scheduled tours and paused in front of the house as the guides explained that the nation's second family lived there. Once Julie, in a Brownie uniform, emerged with Pat; they stood there gaping at a loaded bus whose occupants gaped back.

Pat hired a full-time Swedish housekeeper and had a man come in half a day a week to clean the floors and windows. These people were always hidden from public view because Pat, who was developing an increasingly acute sense of what worked politically, believed she could help win more votes for Dick by projecting the image of the determined housewife. There were never any pictures of the housekeeper or of any other help—only of Pat pressing Dick's suits and running a vacuum cleaner.

But Pat Nixon was doing much of the work anyway; she had done it too long and couldn't change her habits. She needed the help because, with the demands on her time, she was unable to do it all. She would rush home from official receptions, change, and go directly to the local supermarket. And most of the time, she'd prepare the meals.

Eventually, though, the family outgrew the small house. There was no room to entertain official guests, who had to be taken to restaurants, and no study where Nixon could work. The children's possessions, too, were spilling all over the place: their dolls, many from foreign lands brought home by their parents; Tricia's multiplying herd of miniature horses, her giant sea turtle skull, and other aquatic and biological specimens; Julie's parakeets and goldfish, her sets of tiny furniture, tea services, and dishes which seemed to increase by the week.

After Nixon was renominated in 1956 and re-elected with Eisenhower, they found a larger and more secluded residence at 4308 Forest Lane in Wesley Heights, an upper-middle-class section of Washington. A fieldstone English Tudor house once owned by Homer S. Cummings of Connecticut (former chairman of the Democratic National Committee and President Franklin D. Roosevelt's Attorney General), it was on a dead-end street and had a large backyard surrounded by dense woods. It also had more room than either Pat or Dick had had in their lives. There were eleven rooms, including a bedroom with private bath for each of the girls, a special one for their possessions, an all-electric kitchen, a large master bedchamber with bath and dressing area, a dining room and a living room, and a hideaway study for Nixon midway between the first and second floors.

"We're moving up," Nixon told Pat the day they bought it. And they were: they had sold the Spring Valley home for $41,000, the same amount they had paid for it, and purchased the new one for $75,000. Pat not only supervised the moving but tried to do some of it herself, and sprained her back in the process. "I thought I was Tarzan or something," she said ruefully. "I picked up a piece of furniture and, spang, something gave way." They hired a live-in couple, Susie and James Johnson; Susie helped with the cleaning, James did everything else inside and out. Again, as in the case of their former Swedish housekeeper, Susie and James were never photographed with them.

Pat was still on top of everything. She planned the menus, drew up the food shopping lists, and then drove to the supermarket in the family's 1955 Oldsmobile. She cooked double or triple the amounts they needed and froze the rest. Although she had had years of hard experience in money management, she found they were unable to save on Nixon's $30,000 salary, double his income as a senator, plus his $10,000 allowance for expenses. To her irritation, she found doctors were charging them "twice as much as they did before." There was need, too, for many new clothes to attend official functions. "We were also buying gifts for visitors," she says, "and though we were told that no entertaining was necessary, we did it anyway." But she saw to it that they did not go into debt. She was firm about living within their means. "I shop very carefully," she said,"and I count the pennies."

She was constantly after the girls to turn off lights that were unneeded, would shut off the heat in winter in rooms not in use, and, having read somewhere that leaking faucets add up to extra dollars paid to the water company, would examine the faucets regularly; if they did leak, she knew how to install new washers.

Nonetheless, Pat need not have counted the pennies quite so carefully. Their frugal years were now behind them, and the family lived well. They joined the Columbia Country Club in Bethesda, Maryland, and went there for Sunday dinner as often as they could. Pat's wardrobe was enlarged considerably and her Wesley Heights home contained expensive gifts from countries the Vice President had visited. Flanking the fireplace in the living room were a pair of butterfly-shaped floor lamps from an ancient Korean temple. A jewel chest decorated with twisted threads of delicate gold with a base of pure ivory stood on an Oriental table; it was described as "priceless" in one account. There were mahogany chests atop which were lamps with brass bases and a golden four-sided globe which contained, on each of its faces, a barometer, clock, thermometer, and hygrometer (a humidity-measuring instrument). On the shelves, mantel, and walls were delicate figurines from Siam, an Oriental brass plate, lamp brackets of sculptured dancers, and landscape scenes from Japan.

It is hard to believe that the much-publicized pressing of the vice presidential suits by the nation's Second Lady was not part of the "act." But it was, of course, one of her links to the hard but happy past life that she was reluctant to snap. Even Nixon now saw its absurdity and urged her to stop. They could afford the best tailors in town, he told her. "He scolds me," she admitted, "but I've always done it, and I like to." She also repaired and altered Julie's and Tricia's clothing as well as her own.

Approaching her middle forties, Pat continued to look extraordinarily youthful. There was no gray in her beige-blond hair, no wrinkles, no extra poundage—and her energy was awesome. She would rise at six-thirty and prepare breakfast for the family in her sunny-yellow kitchen, with her hand-sewn curtains on the windows and yellow daisies she had grown in the backyard on the table. Nixon would be picked up by his official limousine at eight and the girls would be off to the Horace Mann Public School.*

Already becoming apparent were the differing personalities of the Nixon daughters that would come to the attention of the world when Watergate exploded. Tricia was reserved, quiet, "introverted"—Pat's own word for her, as she added "like I am." At home, Tricia was called "the Thinker" and Julie "the Speaker." Julie would be precisely that while Tricia remained in the background all during the Watergate scandal.

Pat knew that she was fighting a losing battle to create a normal home environment for them, and this saddened her. Nixon would try to be home for dinner once or twice a week, but often he would not see his daughters except at breakfast. On the night of a Brownie father-daughter dinner, the biggest event of her year, he telephoned Julie that he couldn't make it. Julie cried. He would usually come home about midnight or shortly before, and then he and Pat would take an increasingly plump Checkers for a walk. The girls had acquired four cats by now as well.

The Nixons usually retired shortly after midnight, but on September 24, 1955, a Saturday evening, they came home after 5 A.M. from the wedding of Drusilla Nelson, one of Richard's former secretaries, and Henry Dworshak, Jr., son of the Republican senator from Idaho, Henry C. Dworshak. They were still living on Tilden Street at the time. Pat had gone upstairs to get ready for bed when the telephone rang. James C. Hagerty, President Eisenhower's press secretary, was on the line.

---

*Later they transferred to the Sidwell Friends School, a Quaker institution.

"The President," Hagerty told Nixon, "has just had a coronary." "Oh my God!" Nixon said. Eisenhower had been stricken in Denver and Hagerty had been called.

Within fifteen minutes, the small house was surrounded by news reporters and photographers. The telephone rang so constantly that Pat called Dorothea Cox, one of her husband's office assistants, to rush over and help take calls. Tricia and Julie peered down wonderingly and Pat prepared a morning snack. Tricia, who overheard them talking, raced down the stairs crying, "The President isn't going to die, is he?" she asked. "No," Nixon replied. "He's going to be all right." Within minutes, Bill Rogers, then assistant attorney general, elbowed his way through the throng at the door. Pat peered outside and saw that the crowd had now been augmented by television crews and spectators.

Two hours later, Nixon and Rogers left for the Rogers home and Pat was left alone to think, to wonder, and to pray.

During the ensuing weeks of Eisenhower's recuperation from his seizure, Pat had more company than she had bargained for: dozens of reporters, cameramen, and TV crew members camped in their small basement rumpus room. There was never any quiet while they were present; when the shifts changed in the middle of the night, the men going and coming woke up all the Nixons. Pat, outwardly unruffled, would keep bringing down pots of coffee.

By early October, the crisis had eased and the siege lifted.

Outwardly, she was still tightly controlled, poised, gracious, and, where the press was concerned, very, very cautious. "I never discuss politics" was still her standard remark at the start of news conferences, and she didn't. Nixon wanted it that way. He knew that some candidates' wives from time to time made "stupid" remarks that could prove harmful. "Pat's smart enough to say the right things and avoid the sticky question," he once said. She would go to great lengths to maintain the flawless image. During the 1956

Republican Convention in San Francisco, with Nixon a candidate for renomination, she wore high heels as she walked the daunting hills of that city. Most women would have switched to flats or low heels, but not Pat, who insisted she was "very comfortable."

But in private, she could stop performing and be a delightful companion. The smile unfroze and became genuine; she laughed, made jokes, and even teased her husband. Guests who attended their parties at Spring Valley and Wesley Heights were astonished at the contrast. Mazo, who visited their homes on a number of occasions with his wife, Rita, found her "a very *haimisheh* girl," a Yiddish word meaning "informal, warm and cozy."

Nixon was especially proud of his collection of miniature elephants in jade, ivory, bronze, porcelain, and rare woods which he had put in the bookcases in his study. "He was pontificating about them one evening," Mazo recalls, "telling us that 'this one came from Burma, that one from Indonesia,' when Pat walked in with a tray.

" 'Try some of these,' she told us. 'They're better than that baloney he's handing out.' "

Haimisheh also means unpretentious, and she was that, too. She would be seen rummaging through the racks of downtown Washington stores, hunting for bargains. Early one afternoon, Rita Mazo was waiting for an elevator at Woodward & Lothrop, a large department store, when the doors opened and Pat emerged from the throng of shoppers with Tricia and Julie. "Oh, Rita," Pat exclaimed. "I'm so glad to see you. We've done some shopping, been to the dentist, and now we're going to lunch. Come join us."

Rita replied: "I'm sorry, but I can't. I must get home to meet the children when they get home from school."

Rita Mazo: "This whole thing happened as crowds surged around us in a store. Here was the wife of the Vice President of the United States asking me to lunch, and here I was saying no to her. It just didn't occur to me that she *was* the wife of the second man in the country. She was just a mother taking her two children shopping and to the dentist and I was another mother on her way home to meet her children when they came from school."

She loved auctions. On infrequent free afternoons, she and a group of friends would drive into Virginia hunting for bargains in antiques. Rita Mazo tells a story about one of these expeditions:

"We packed picnic lunches, jammed ourselves into a car, and off we went. At one large auction, Pat and I somehow became separated from her friends while it was going on. After a while, the auctioneer brought out a Rosenthal china tureen. It looked magnificent. She adored it at once. It would make a perfect centerpiece for flowers, she said, and so she began bidding for it.

"From another side of the room came a second bid and Pat quickly offered a higher one. But the other bidder topped her again, and again she bid higher. And so it went until finally it was knocked down to Pat, who knew she was paying more than she should, but she wanted it so much.

"It turned out that the other bidder was one of her friends who had known Pat was looking for just such a tureen and was unaware that she was bidding against Pat Nixon. It's a good enough story, but it got even better when Pat took it home, unwrapped it, and discovered what it really was. She found it had only one handle, which she had not noticed from far away, and that it wasn't a tureen at all, but an elegant chamber pot!"

9

Nightmare in Caracas

The Horace Mann Public School, which Tricia and Julie attended, had no cafeteria and discouraged its pupils from bringing lunch. That was why the girls were home at noontime on Thursday, May 8, 1958, a warm, sunny day in Washington. Tricia, who was then eleven, flipped on the radio as they ate.

She and Julie heard a news bulletin that terrified them. Their father had barely escaped from an ugly, rock-throwing mob in Lima, Peru. Shouting "Death to Nixon" in Spanish, the crowd had followed his motorcade to the hotel where he was staying with Pat, and was milling around the entrance.

Tricia, in a panic, dialed her father's office and screamed into the mouthpiece: "What are they doing to my daddy and mommy in South America?" Loie Gaunt, one of his secretaries, listened aghast. Nobody knew about the events: It was the first information the Vice President's office had received that big trouble was happening in South America and that Pat and her husband were in grave personal danger.

Five days later, a mob in Caracas came close to murdering the Nixons. Pat, inside a locked limousine, was caught in the midst of a screaming, stone-throwing mass of people gone wild with rage against the United States. Had the attackers been able to open the car doors, she

117

would almost surely have been killed.

Pat, of course, had had no notion of what lay ahead when she told her two tearful daughters that their parents would be traveling once again. She had hugged them and assured them both that she and their father would be home before they even realized they had been away.

There had been many long trips for Pat, the first soon after Nixon assumed office early in 1953. President Eisenhower had asked him to visit the Far East on a non-specific mission to cement diplomatic ties, and had added: "Take Pat." That initial journey lasted ten weeks, during which they covered twenty-one countries and traveled more than 45,000 miles.

It was followed not long after by another tour, a one-month trip through the Caribbean and Central America during which they visited twelve nations and the Canal Zone. In 1956, Pat was gone for five days in February while they attended the inauguration of the Brazilian president; then in June there was a twelve-day trip to Asia, which included visits to Honolulu, Manila, Turkey, and a long trip home by way of Spain. The following year they went to Africa and Italy for three weeks. Then, in 1958, came the danger-fraught trip to South America. The year after, the Nixons visited the Soviet Union.

All these trips added up to a new record: as the wife of the Vice President, Pat Nixon had done more global traveling on official diplomatic missions than any Second Lady in history.

She was often highly praised for the pleasantness, poise, and good manners she brought to her role as an American ambassador of goodwill in foreign countries. Britain's Prime Minister Harold Macmillan once wrote to Richard Nixon after he and his wife visited London: "Your speeches have deeply impressed the public . . . your personality and that of your charming wife have 'got over' in a wonderful way."

In those years of widespread Cold War tension, Pat and her husband often found themselves threatened in

THE LONELY LADY OF SAN CLEMENTE

1914. The house in Artesia, California, now called Cerritos, where Pat grew up. Originally containing five rooms, it was improved over the years. In 1974, the home was refurbished and converted into a museum and youth center as part of Pat Nixon Park. In 1978, the interior was damaged by a homemade firebomb.

About 1928. The youthful Thelma Ryan, later Pat Nixon, at the beach in California during high school days. Thelma *(center)* is flanked by two childhood friends who lived next door to her in Artesia, where she grew up. Myrtle Raine (now Mrs. Cecil Franz) is at left and her sister Louise Raine Gwinn, now widowed, is at right.

1929. Her class picture from the yearbook of Excelsior Union High School in Norwalk, Calif. In her senior year she was class vice president and secretary of the school student body. *(UPI)*

1937. Pat Ryan at twenty-five. This is the photograph she gave to the placement office at the University of Southern California when she registered for a teaching job after graduation.

About 1950. A reunion of the "Committee of One Hundred," the group of Republican businessmen, bankers and party workers of the 12th Congressional District in California, which launched a drive in 1945 to find a candidate to oppose Representative Jerry Voorhis. The committee, headed by Roy O. Day, the district's GOP chairman, chose Richard Nixon. The reunion took place in a restaurant in Pomona, California, a few years later. Nixon and Pat are in the center; Roy O. Day is second from left, seated.

1950. The Nixon family relax at their Whittier home after Richard's nomination for the Vice Presidency. Pat is holding Julie, two; Tricia, four, is on Nixon's lap. (UPI)

1952. Pat Nixon accepts a bouquet in front of the Southern Pacific Railroad Station in Pomona, California, at a ceremony launching Nixon's transcontinental tour as Vice Presidential candidate. The man at Pat's right is George Murphy, then still a movie actor and later a senator from California. The two girls are Linda and Diana Day, daughters of Roy O. Day.

1952. At the El Capitan Theatre in Los Angeles after Nixon delivered his famous "Checkers" speech. (UPI)

1957. The Nixon family at the inaugural ball in Washington on January 20 after his re-election as Vice President. Julie was eight years old, Tricia ten. *(UPI)*

1958. President Eisenhower greets the Nixons in Washington on their return May 15 from their eighteen-day South American journey; Julie and Tricia are also on hand for the welcome home. *(UPI)*

1959. Pat swings mightily, but the champagne bottle she slams against the bow of a Boeing 707 to inaugurate jet service between Washington and Los Angeles wouldn't break. After her seventh futile attempt, American Airlines president C.R. Smith *(right)* finally broke it for her. *(UPI)*

1959. Pat Nixon, visiting Russia in July with her husband, is flanked by wives of high Soviet officials at Usovo, Premier Nikita Khrushchev's summer home. At left is Mrs. Anastas Mikoyan; to Pat's right are Mrs. Khrushchev and Mrs. Frol Kozlov. *(UPI)*

1959. Pat Nixon struggles to hold back tears as she listens to her husband tell Republican campaign workers at the Hotel Ambassador in Los Angeles that the Presidential race against John Kennedy appears to be lost. Moments later, when Nixon finished speaking, the tears came. (UPI)

1959. Pat, Tricia and Julie in the backyard of their home at 4308 Forest Lane, Wesley Heights, during Nixon's Vice Presidency. Julie's the one in the air on the trampoline. Pat is cuddling one of the girls' pet cats. (Queensborough Public Library—New York Herald-Tribune morgue)

1964. It was a year when she was "out of the rat race," a private citizen's wife for a while. At Pat's right is Hannah Nixon, Richard's mother. Julie and Tricia *(at left)* share an open sightseeing car on a visit to the New York World's Fair on a bright June day. *(UPI)*

1965. Pat fixes Tricia's hair at the Hotel Astor in New York, where the elder Nixon daughter was introduced to society at the International Debutante Ball on January 2. *(UPI)*

1968. On the eve of Richard Nixon's nomination for the Presidency, Pat, Julie, Tricia and David Eisenhower chat at the convention hall in Miami. *(UPI)*

1968. Pat and her daughters—Julie is in the center—smilingly watch the traditional hoopla after Nixon's name was placed in nomination at the Miami convention by Spiro T. Agnew, then Governor of Maryland. *(UPI)*

1969. In a rare quiet moment, the First Lady sits in the large, graceful Yellow Oval Room in the family quarters on the second floor of the White House. *(UPI)*

1971. After Tricia Nixon, then twenty-five, married Edward F. Cox, twenty-four, in the Rose Garden outside the White House, the bride danced with her father and the groom with his new mother-in-law at a reception in the elegant East Room. *(UPI)*

1971. The First Lady and President Nixon, walking back down the aisle after the wedding ceremony. *(UPI)*

1971. Pat is greeted by throngs in Tijuana, Mexico. She had stepped across the border after officiating at ceremonies just to the north, deeding 372 acres of Federal land to California for a park. *(UPI)*

1972. Pat Nixon in Moscow's Red Square with Mrs. Andrei Gromyko, wife of the Soviet foreign minister. At left is the famous GUM department store, which the women had just visited. *(UPI)*

1972. Pat and the President walk along the top of the Great Wall of China on February 24. Secretary of State William P. Rogers is at the right. Pat was the first First Lady ever to visit China. *(UPI)*

1972. A handshake for the Chinese salesman who helped her shop for jade during a visit to Peking. *(UPI)*

1972. Pat Nixon in an exuberant mood on her 32nd wedding anniversary, June 21. She appeared at a "Salute to Education" gala in Washington, then returned to the White House for a celebration with the President. *(UPI)*

1974. In March, as the Watergate investigations were building toward a climax, Pat went on a six-day goodwill trip to South America. En route home, her staff and accompanying journalists surprised her with a party, cake and all. Pat was sixty-two. *(UPI)*

1974. It looks like a happy family photograph, but it is not. After the President made his decision to resign, White House official photographer Ollie Atkins was summoned to the family quarters on August 8. He reported later it was obvious that all three women had been crying. Pat and Nixon are flanked by Edward and Tricia Cox at the left, and Julie and David Eisenhower on the right. *(UPI)*

1974. Anguish is etched on Pat Nixon's face as she leaves the White House for the last time as First Lady on August 9. She is accompanied by Betty Ford, her successor. *(UPI)*

1974. Pat and her daughters arrive at Memorial Hospital Medical Center in Long Beach, California, where the former President was listed in critical condition after undergoing surgery for phlebitis. *(UPI)*

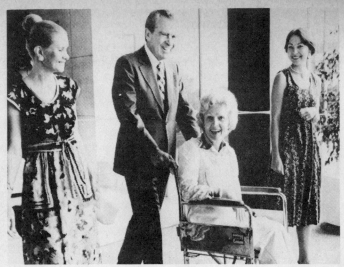

1976. Pat is checked out of the hospital sixteen days after she had suffered a stroke. "I feel fine," she said as she left in a wheelchair, and added jokingly: "But I'm a little frightened about the driver." Nixon smilingly pushed the chair to a waiting car. Tricia is at left, Julie at right. *(UPI)*

1977. At *La Casa Pacifica*, their San Clemente estate, Pat and Richard Nixon celebrate the former President's sixty-fourth birthday on January 9. *(UPI)*

foreign lands by angry Communist-agitated anti-American demonstrators. On her first overseas mission with her husband, in Pegu, Burma, on Thanksgiving Day in 1953, the Nixons, on their way to a Buddhist temple, were confronted outside the local city hall by a mob of abusive, sign-carrying hecklers. Government officials had tried to persuade them to ride to the temple in a limousine, but Nixon had insisted on going by foot. "I also insisted that Mrs. Nixon and I walk first and alone—not surrounded by Burmese officials and guards," he wrote later, in his book *Six Crises.* "This is just what we did. When the first demonstrator accosted us, I asked him to point out the leader of the group. I walked up to the leader, asked what his grievances were—and by this direct action put him completely on the defensive and, at the same time, swung the crowd to my side. We then went on our way with a now overwhelmingly friendly crowd following along behind."

But the anti-Nixon demonstration in Caracas, Venezuela, on May 13, 1958, turned into the most terrifying experience of Pat's lifetime.

The Vice President had agreed, only after much persuasion from President Eisenhower himself, to undertake that journey to several South American countries, mainly to attend the inauguration of a new president in Argentina. Nobody in the United States government had expected him to encounter any trouble on the trip. Nixon himself had told journalists in Washington that very little, if any, important news would be likely to develop on the journey and advised them not to bother covering it if they could possibly avoid it.

Many members of the press corps took his advice and stayed home. The trip to Argentina, which Nixon tried to limit to one week away from Washington, turned out to be a two-and-a-half-week tour of eight South American countries, plus a stop in Trinidad.

The first week of the tour was pleasant and uneventful, although at Uruguay, the Nixons' first stop in

South America, there had been a few Communist demonstrators carrying signs that said, FUERA NIXON ("Go Home, Nixon"). In Argentina, along with the various ceremonies of President Arturo Frondizi's inauguration, Pat accompanied her husband to discussion meetings at universities and labor union halls, and enjoyed a huge *asado,* a beef barbecue dinner, with the hide still on the side of beef as it was cooked on an outdoor grill. She learned that the trick was to eat the beef like a slice of melon, leaving the hairy skin.

The favorable impression made by the Nixons in Uruguay and Argentina produced strong Communist-inspired demonstrations on the later stops on their itinerary in Peru, Colombia, Bolivia, and Venezuela. Violent rallies were stopped by the police of Colombia. A planned protest march by miners in Bolivia was canceled when the government blew up a railroad track connecting the mining area of the country with the capital city of La Paz. When the Nixons visited the president of Bolivia, Hernán Siles Zuazo, they were startled when he pointed to pictures on the wall of his office of two previous presidents and said that one of them had committed suicide and the other had been hung by a mob on a lamppost on the street outside.

When the Nixons flew from La Paz to Lima, the capital city of Peru, they were given a formal reception by government officials at the airport. But they felt an atmosphere of strain as they drove into the city. The streets were strangely deserted. The few people who did recognize the Vice President of the United States either coldly ignored him or gave him the Latin American boo or raspberry—a high-pitched whistle. Not expecting trouble in Lima, the Nixons were astonished to learn that the city had been flooded with leaflets calling for the ouster of the Vice President. "Students, Workers, Employees—Join Us," they read. "Out Nixon—Death to Yankee Imperialism." The leaflets urged the citizens to join in a big demonstration against Nixon when he appeared the next day as a speaker at San Marco University. It was signed by "The Communist Committee, Lima District."

The Nixons attended a three-hour luncheon given in their honor by President Manuel Prado, and then went to a formal dinner that evening at the American Embassy. Before the embassy dinner, the American Ambassador in Peru, Theodore Achilles, and Roy R. Rubottom, Jr., the Assistant Secretary of State for Latin American Affairs, who was traveling with the Nixons, asked to have a private meeting with the Vice President. They warned him that the Communists were planning a violent and perhaps dangerous demonstration at San Marco University the next day and urged him to consider canceling that appearance. The local chief of police had urged one of Nixon's staff members to call it off.

Nixon asked an aide to telephone the rector of the university and ask his opinion about canceling the appointment. The rector said that he was afraid of a violent disturbance but he was also afraid to cancel the university's invitation to Nixon. Such a move might be interpreted, he said, as a public admission that he could not keep peace on the campus and might turn the wrath of the Communists against him. Then Nixon asked for an opinion from the chief of police, who said that privately he hoped that Nixon would cancel the visit, but he, too, would not make a public announcement of the Nixons' withdrawal for fear of turning the Communists' anger against himself and the police force. The decision to go or cancel was put to Nixon.

He decided to face the Communists but advised Pat to remain in their hotel room. She waited and worried the next morning while he went to lay a wreath at the tomb of General José de San Martín, the statesman and soldier who is honored as a liberator of Argentina, Chile, and Peru from Spanish domination. All night long crowds had been pressing close to their hotel; she could hear clearly their "Fuera Nixon" repeated through the night.

The crowd followed when he emerged from the hotel and walked across the square to the liberator's tomb. While standing at attention after the wreath-laying, he decided to go on to the university, where a much larger, far more dangerous mob, later estimated at about 3,000, was waiting.

Just before the gates of the university, Nixon left his car and, with Colonel Vernon Walters, his interpreter, and agent John Sherwood of the Secret Service, walked toward the whistling, shouting crowd. Surprised by this move, the crowd quieted down and moved back from the approaching Vice President, who reached out and shook a few hands. Nixon said a few words to the people about why their leaders were trying to deny him the right of free speech. He accused the Communists of being afraid to listen to him because they were afraid to hear the truth. Nixon, of course, spoke in English with Walters shouting a Spanish interpretation.

"For a few moments, I thought I might get the situation under control," Nixon wrote in Six Crises. "Those in front of me continued to give way and I walked directly into the mob. Some of the younger students started to quiet down. But the older ones in the rear, the ringleaders, saw what was happening. They tried to whip up a frenzy again, egging the younger students on, just as if they were driving them with whips. They shouted insults at those who shook hands with me. . . . Just as it seemed that the balance might be tipping in our favor, I felt something glance off my shoulder. Sherwood put his hand to his mouth. Walters whispered in my ear, 'Mr. Vice President, they are throwing stones.' I leaned toward Sherwood: 'OK, all right, let's get out of here. But move back slowly, keep facing them.' "

As the men backed toward the waiting car, more rocks flew around them. In the car, Nixon stood up and shouted at the crowd, with Walters translating in rapid Spanish, "You are cowards! You are afraid of the truth! You are the worst kind of cowards!" The rocks continued to fly. Nixon asked to have the car head for Catholic University, where his arrival was a big surprise, although the rector had known that he might pay that institution a visit. There he spoke for a few minutes, and answered questions, and was warmly received by the students, although a few Communist hecklers tried to interrupt him. Sherwood, the Secret Service agent, who had had one of his front teeth knocked out by a rock at San Marcos, whispered to Nixon, "We'd better get out of here. The gang from San Marcos is on its way."

The motorcade began its return trip to the hotel just ahead of a shouting, stone-throwing mob racing from San Marcos. The rest of the crowd was milling in front of the hotel.

Pat Nixon, peering out anxiously through the draperies of her window, saw that many were armed with clubs and rocks. She watched as Nixon's car approached the entrance. The door opened and, flanked by the interpreter, a Secret Serviceman, and an embassy aide, he forced his way through the mob to safety.

The Nixons' visits to Ecuador and Colombia during that weekend were comparatively quiet. Then the party moved on to its final stop of the tour, Venezuela, where the hatred spilled over even more venomously. Caracas, the Venezuelan capital city, had the strongest Communist organization in South America and the group's aim was to kill the Nixons. The Secret Service, which relayed the death plot to Nixon from Washington, beefed up the guard around him and Pat: in Venezuela, they would be protected by a dozen Secret Servicemen instead of the usual three or four.

The Communist newspaper in Caracas published a front-page photograph of Nixon, labeled "Tricky Dick," with the picture altered to make the Vice President look like a snarling beast. The city was covered with FUERA NIXON signs with the "F" painted out and replaced by an "M," changing the FUERA to MUERA, making it DEATH TO NIXON. The weak junta government made public appeals pleading for the people in the city to treat Nixon courteously.

When the Nixons' plane taxied to the terminal at the airport in Caracas on the morning of May 13, a big and noisy crowd of people, most of them young, was waiting to greet them. Colonel Walters, hearing the shouts of abuse and reading the Spanish slogans on the placards, whispered to the Nixons, "They aren't friendly."

Pat and Richard Nixon stood at attention during the playing of the United States and Venezuelan national anthems, but the noise of the mob almost drowned out the band's music and the firing of the traditional 19-gun vice presidential salute.

The Vice President and his wife made their way toward the terminal building where they met Foreign Minister Oscar Garcia Velutini and his wife, who were to escort them to the city. Noting the hostile and roaring crowd, Nixon decided to dispense with any speeches at the airport and to head as quickly as possible toward their cars, which were waiting in a parking space beyond the terminal building. As the party reached the door of the terminal, under a large balcony jammed with shouting people, the band started to play again the Venezuelan national anthem.

Again the Nixons stood at attention, but the music could not be heard above the roaring of the mob. On the balcony the crowd leaned over the rail and began spitting upon the North Americans; to the astounded Vice President it seemed as though rain was falling from a clear sky. Pat's red suit, newly bought for the journey, quickly became splattered with the ugly spittle, some of it loose and brown-stained from the mouths of tobacco chewers.

While the band was still playing the anthem, a teenaged girl standing near Mrs. Nixon was spitting at her and shouting insults. Pat reached for the girl's hand and shook it. The girl's eyes filled with tears and she turned away, obviously embarrassed. While the Nixons and members of their party tried to reach their waiting limousines, a little girl was escorted forward to present a bouquet of flowers to Pat, the first gesture of welcome that she had seen since landing at the airport. Pat bent down and kissed the child. "Thanks!" she said to her quietly. A teenaged boy grasped Pat, turned her around, and asked her why Nixon had tortured black children at Little Rock.

"He was one of those very mean young boys," Pat later told Earl Mazo. "I pretended that I didn't understand him. I just said, 'How are you? So nice to be here,' and a few things like that which I thought he and the others might understand. . . . They must have been told that we were horrible people."

American Secret Service agents and a few Venezuelan plainclothes policemen helped the Nixon party squeeze through the roaring crowd to their limousines. There seemed to be no uniformed policemen in sight. Soldiers in the guard of honor stood rigidly at attention, doing nothing to quiet the crowd. A Marine Corps sergeant from the United States Embassy and Sam Moskowitz, the embassy's second secretary, were pushed and mauled while they tried to attach American flags to the Nixon cars. Foreign Minister Velutini and Nixon were shoved while they climbed into the back seat of one of the lead cars, in which Colonel Walters and Secret Service Agent Sherwood were to ride on the jump seats in front of them. Another agent, Wade Rodham, sat on the front seat beside the Venezuelan chauffeur from the embassy. Mrs. Nixon and Mrs. Velutini took seats in the second official car with Major James D. Hughes, the Vice President's military aide, and two Secret Service agents. Mrs. Nixon had to wipe a large quantity of spit off her seat in the car while her Venezuelan hostess tried to apologize. A large truck filled with reporters and photographers led the procession into the city from the airport, and, behind the two cars carrying the Vice President and Mrs. Nixon, there were seven other limousines with other Secret Service agents, military aides, and members of the Nixon party.

As the procession drove along the highway leading from the airport to Caracas, the Foreign Minister's wife again apologized to Mrs. Nixon for the behavior of the crowd. To change the subject, Pat mentioned that she had talked that morning, while flying to Caracas, with her two daughters in Washington over a short-wave portable radio operated by the pilot, Colonel Thomas E. Collins, Jr. The Vice President's party planned to make its first stop in Caracas at the National Pantheon, the tomb at the end of a narrow cobbled street where Simón Bolívar, South America's greatest hero, and other national leaders are buried. The Nixons were scheduled to place a wreath at the tomb, but Major Hughes and Dale Grubb, one of the Secret Service agents in Pat's car, decided it would be wiser for Mrs. Nixon to remain in the limousine during that service.

During the twelve-mile drive from the airport to Caracas, carloads of demonstrators drove beside the Nixon limousines, shouting, spitting, and throwing cans and bottles. Coming into the city proper along the Avenida Sucre, a six-lane divided highway, the Nixons noticed few people on the streets and stores closed. A Secret Service agent and an administrative assistant from Nixon's staff, who had gone ahead to the site of Bolívar's tomb to arrange for the ceremony there, had seen mobs of club-armed men and youths waiting for Nixon's arrival at the Pantheon and had tried to warn the vice presidential party by radio to stay away from the tomb. But the warnings never reached the Nixon party. Soon the motorcade came to a halt behind a traffic jam. The limousines were quickly surrounded by a mob that ripped off United States and Venezuelan flags and battered fenders and doors. Agents rushed from the Secret Service cars to push the rioters away from the Vice President's limousine.

The procession managed to push ahead slowly for a few blocks. Then it was halted again near the Pantheon Plaza. More crowds of men and some women poured out of a side alley waving clubs, pieces of iron pipe, and banners and placards. Startled reporters watching from the truck in front of the Nixon limousines figured that at least five hundred of them attacked the Vice President's car, while other mobs pounded and shook the other limousines.

Rocks smashed against the limousine windows, splintering the shatterproof glass and sending bits of it into the faces of some of the passengers. Walters was spitting blood and the Venezuelan Foreign Minister was moaning about a wound in his eye. A glass splinter nicked Nixon and another fragment struck Sherwood.

"Several times I glanced back at the car behind us," Nixon said later. "Pat appeared to be talking to the Foreign Minister's wife as calmly as if the trouble was no worse than an afternoon traffic jam on the Hollywood Freeway.''

A big rock bounded off the window beside Pat Nixon's seat. A huge man, armed with a great club, struck her car repeatedly. She was wondering if the windows in the limousines would stand up under the pounding that they were getting, or if the doors would be ripped open, or the whole automobile turned over on its side. ''I had visions of all those things,'' she said later. ''We got a few good knocks on our car, but that didn't frighten me. I kept watching what was going on ahead of me. I couldn't believe that none of the police were doing anything. I tried to calm the Foreign Minister's wife. She felt horrible that this was happening in her country.''

Without pulling a gun, the Secret Service agents around the vice presidential limousine kept the mob of attackers away from the door handles simply by shoving them off balance with expertly timed thrusts of their shoulders, feet, or open hands. Sometimes an agent would knock down a dozen Venezuelans with a quick jab of his elbow. The attack on the limousines and deft defense of the door handles went on for twelve minutes without a let-up. Then the men in the mob began to rock Nixon's car, trying to turn it over. The Vice President noticed that, curiously, all of the police around him had disappeared, except for a few who were making no attempt to stop the violence.

Finally, after twelve minutes that seemed like twelve hours, the driver of the press truck in front of the Vice President's limousine managed to work his way across the dividing line between the two one-directional lanes of the highway. The Vice President's car and Mrs. Nixon's hurried after it.

Fortunately, Nixon and his Secret Service guard, John Sherwood, quickly decided against going on to the planned wreath-laying ceremony at the Pantheon Plaza or to the government guest house where the group was supposed to be billeted. They stopped on a side street, checked the damage to their cars, and headed for the United States Embassy. If the Nixons had gone to the

Pantheon, where a mob of several thousand Communist sympathizers was waiting, both Vice President and Mrs. Nixon and several other people in their party probably would have been killed. A subsequent investigation showed that the agitators were planning to bomb the Nixons with explosives hidden in a home near the plaza.

The Vice President found his wife calm and unruffled after the strain of the ordeal, "probably the coolest person in the whole party," as he said later.

"I felt a great sense of relief when it was over, naturally," Pat said afterward. "On an occasion like that, it isn't your own personal fear that you think of particularly. You just feel sick that anything like this could happen to mar what was meant to be a goodwill trip."

At the American Embassy Residence, where gin and tonics were waiting, Nixon slumped in a chair exhausted, called off or rearranged the rest of the day's appointments, and then went to sleep for forty minutes, his first daytime nap in twelve years.

In the meantime, Washington was throbbing with anxious excitement. A breakdown in communications had interrupted a brief report on the mob violence before further news of Nixon's safe escape reached the White House and the Pentagon. President Eisenhower ordered airborne Army and Marine combat troops to Caribbean bases to back up demands that Venezuela guarantee the Nixons' safety.

In a telephone conversation with the President, Nixon straightened out the confusion and assured Eisenhower that military intervention would not be necessary. Before hanging up, Eisenhower said, "Give my love to Pat," The Nixons flew to Puerto Rico to spend a night with Governor and Mrs. Luis Muñoz Marín. "You are safe here," Mrs. Muñoz Marín said when she kissed Mrs. Nixon. "You are home now."

Earl Mazo, who saw it all, was a combat correspondent for *The Stars and Stripes* during World War II when I was managing editor of the Paris edition of the soldiers' newspaper. In his Washington home, Earl recalled for me those terrible hours when Pat had escaped death at the hands of the murderous mob. He was utterly frank.

"If I were in an infantry platoon somewhere," he told me, "I wouldn't mind being led by those two people. If I myself had been in that predicament, I would have been frantic. . . .

"That lady showed no fear. She didn't panic, not even remotely. She was utterly calm. She was even calming the reporters, all of whom were scared silly.

"In Puerto Rico, we were still shaken, but not Pat. We were all staying at the same hotel and, believe this, that evening she was coming out of an elevator when Bob Hartmann [Robert T. Hartmann, Washington bureau chief of the Los Angeles *Times*] and I were waiting to go upstairs to file our stories. The hotel's nightclub was just off the lobby.

" 'I hear music,' she said gaily to us. 'Why don't we go dancing?' Dancing! After an experience like that! Bob and I begged off."

Later, Pat organized and was president of a "Rock and Roll Club," named after the rocks thrown at them and the rolling of their cars by the crazed mobs. The Rock and Roll members met for some years afterward on the anniversary of the incident in May at the Nixon home and recalled their grisly experience.

When Pat and Richard returned to Washington, aboard a DC-6B, the personal plane of Neil H. McElroy, the Secretary of Defense, they received a welcome unprecedented in the history of the vice presidency. The State Department had brought out its red carpet and rolled it out in front of the ramp. When Pat and the Vice President emerged, President Eisenhower practically skipped over for a greeting but he was beaten to them by Tricia and Julie, who rushed up the ramp. Pat swept them into her arms. They clambered all over their parents as a beaming Eisenhower stretched out his hand. By now, Pat was suffering from aftershock, and was looking pale and drawn.

The national greeting was extraordinary. Both the

Republican and Democratic leaders of Congress, several Cabinet members, fully half the Senate and busloads of representatives, along with many Latin American diplomats, were there. Two high school bands, with their pretty drum majorettes, played welcoming marches. More than 15,000 persons roared a hello and another 85,000 lined the route from the airport to the White House.

After the welcoming speeches, Eisenhower insisted that the Nixon family ride with him in the presidential limousine to the White House for a visit with Mamie. Pat sat with her husband and the President in the rear seat, Tricia and Julie in the jump seats.

That night, Nixon went to a reception by the Women's National Press Club, then to the White House for a stag dinner where he discussed the Latin American situation with leaders of the financial and business communities and a number of top government leaders. Pat stayed home with Tricia and Julie.

10

"Out of the Rat Race"

PAT VS. JACKIE

It seems paradoxical that a woman who hated politics because it robbed her of much of the precious privacy she craved would fight so hard to win a campaign that would give her none at all. Yet such was the total commitment of Pat Nixon that, when Richard Nixon decided to run for President in 1960, she became the most active and visible wife of a presidential candidate in American political history.

She ran harder than ever before, fully earning the dedication in his book *Six Crises,* with its unfortunate phrasing: "To Pat, she also ran." She traveled with and without him, her daily schedule crowded with the customary news conferences, chats with women's groups, receptions, visits to hospitals and homes. She did it all with her usual calm, clear-eyed aplomb, and nobody, of course, knew about the quarrels there had been in Wesley Heights over the candidacy.

She didn't want him to run, but he did. And, as always, he prevailed.

Although they were offering the country their customary antiseptic image of the couple who had made the American Dream come true, there had been trouble in their paradise even before the discord about the 1960

131

race. Pat, as already noted, had a temper. Some of their quarrels were minor, others more serious.

When he was unable to handle them, Nixon would telephone his mother in Whittier and ask her to talk to Pat. Hannah had her ways and, with her sympathy and understanding, would smooth things over. On at least one occasion, a quarrel was so serious that Pat wouldn't talk to her husband for days and intervention by telephone did no good. Hannah, though into her seventies, got on an airplane, flew to Washington, and moved into the house to act as peacemaker. Her way was to ignore her son and concentrate on Pat and her grievances. She listened well and, before long, Pat's anger ebbed and she unfroze. Hannah remained a few days to make certain all was well, then returned to Whittier.

Her opposite number as a candidate's wife, thirty-year-old Jacqueline Kennedy, probably did not suspect that Pat was as reluctant a campaigner as she was. Never a gung-ho Kennedy like the other women in the family, Jackie had had a taste of the political whirl and hadn't liked it much. Bobby's wife, Ethel, and her husband's sisters—Eunice Shriver, the then Patricia Lawford, and Jean Smith—had plunged enthusiastically into John Kennedy's House and Senate campaigns. And Rose Kennedy was, well, Rose—politics was bred into her genes. But Jackie was bored by the game.

The contrast between the two wives was sharp. Jackie gave an interview while lounging in purple Pucci slacks on the carpet of her Georgetown home. Pat gave interviews with her hands folded in her lap, wearing one of the five new dresses she had bought in one fast hour's shopping, guided only by whether they were conservative enough and how well they would pack. Pat talked about homemaking as a practicing housewife with full credentials. Jackie couldn't make a bed (and didn't) or cook or handle bills. Pat ironed and mended her own things. Jackie insisted on having her personal maid iron her stockings and change the sheets after she had taken an afternoon nap. Pat watched her words with infinite care and talked in clichés that caused even some GOP leaders to grind their teeth: "Dick's candidacy is an American Dream come true"; "I am proud to have a chance to serve my country." Jackie was hip, elegant, and made wisecracks. When *Women's Wear Daily* wrote that Jackie spent $30,000 a year just for Parisian clothes, she quipped: "I couldn't spend that much unless I wore sable underwear."

The biggest difference was in their campaigning. Pat never stopped; Jackie helped only minimally. She opened the New Hampshire primary campaign with Jack in February, then in March and April went to snowy Wisconsin. The construction gangs at factory gates flocked around her more than around him and she drew more crowds on sidewalks than he did. Once in a Kenosha supermarket she asked the manager if she could use the loudspeaking equipment over which the daily specials were announced, and then she delivered a breathy plea for votes. But it was also in Kenosha that she pulled a gaffe that made John Kennedy wince. She appeared on a stage one evening and tried to "warm up" the crowd until the candidate arrived. Suggesting that they all join in a song, she came out brightly with her choice for a starter: "Southie Is My Home Town." The Kenoshans looked at each other in wonderment. The song, written by a song and dance man named Benny Drohan, is strictly Boston Irish and about as familiar outside the city as "Turkey in the Straw" would be in Outer Mongolia.

After the nomination, she made some appearances at Kennedy's side, held several press teas at their home at 3307 N Street in Georgetown, was coaxed into some interviews and delivered short talks at neighborhood rallies. In ethnic areas she was able to speak a few sentences in faultless Spanish, Italian, and French—thanks to Miss Porter's School, Vassar, and her long vacations on the continent—which never failed to please the crowds.

Her pregnancy—she gave birth to John, Jr., on November 25—was responsible in some measure, but not entirely. Even before the doctor had advised her to avoid exertion because of her history of obstetrical difficulties, she had made it plain that campaigning was not her cup of tea. She had never cared for political types,* preferring the arty set. She was more at home with talk of high fashion, modern art, the latest plays, and the Beautiful People gossip than analyses of which way the vote would go in the 14th ward. Before Los Angeles was selected as the site for the 1960 Democratic Convention, a leading Democrat turned to her at a dinner party and asked if she had some thoughts about a suitable city. With a straight face she replied: "Acapulco."

Meanwhile, the Democratic leadership was noting that Pat didn't miss a single day on the campaign trail. Keenly aware of the importance of the women's vote, they worried that the country's housewives might be wondering about Jackie's infrequent appearances. Kennedy alone, they felt, was effective but he needed help. Looking backward at the Camelot years, it may be hard to realize that Kennedy, campaigning in 1960, had not yet become the glamorous figure he was to become afterward. His romantic appeal at the time was more to the youthful set, young girls who would jump up and down when they watched him in parades and sit with their thighs pressed closed together as they stared at him at rallies. Many of them were too young to vote anyway, since the federal voting age had not yet been lowered to eighteen. It may be even harder to believe that Richard Nixon, slender, still darkly handsome at forty-seven, and obviously hard working and serious minded, had a greater appeal for women voters than the millionaire newcomer with the Boston accent.

While Jackie's pregnancy had been announced before the convention, campaign leaders urged Kennedy to remind his audiences in case they had forgotten. In late summer, his speeches contained references to the fact

---

*Not long after Kennedy was nominated, she was playing golf at Hyannis Port when she met an old friend. "Oh God," she said. "Why didn't you tell me you were here? When I think of those awful politicians!" The "awful politicians" were virtually camped in her home at the Kennedy compound, planning the campaign.

that Jackie was "at home, having a boy." (Astounded reporters asked how he knew the sex of the baby in advance. He replied: "She told me. You would have to ask her.")

Mud was thrown at the families of the candidates as well as the candidates themselves. Old Joe Kennedy was attacked as a "whisky baron" in dry areas; Kennedy was reported to be an "unreliable sick man." Bruce Felknor, of the Fair Campaign Practices Committee, said that by election day "both members of each ticket were depicted to Jews as anti-Semites and to anti-Semites as Jew lovers." Pat's "perfect-wife image" was cruelly caricatured, but Jackie got even worse treatment. One of the rumors that found their way into the gossip columns was that the story of her pregnancy was a hoax, deliberately devised to keep her out of the campaign because American housewives resented her glamorous image. (Kennedy heard the rumors. After he won, he invited a few friends for supper, among them Tony Bradlee, then the wife of journalist Benjamin Bradlee. Tony, like Jackie, was pregnant. Kennedy grinned at the women. "Okay, girls," he said, "you can take out the pillows now. We won.")

Considering Jackie's enormous popularity during and after her tenure as First Lady, it may sound almost unbelievable that she came out second best to Pat during the 1960 campaign. For just as John Kennedy was not yet highly charged with glamor, neither was Jackie. It was not until Kennedy's election—by the narrow margin of barely more than 100,000 votes, one of the closest in history—that Jackie reached superstardom.

Pat took the loss harder than most suspected. As she stood by Nixon's side on election night, the strain showed in her face and there were tears in her eyes. The hurt was deep and it emerged in private.

Around eleven that night, she had come down from her fifth-floor suite at the Ambassador Hotel in Los Angeles to his rooms on the floor below and urged him not to concede until all hope was gone. The news was not good, he told her and Tricia, who began to cry. He said he had to go to the ballroom, which was jammed with campaign supporters, and make some kind of statement.

Pat agreed he should. But she also said: "I simply cannot bring myself to stand there with you while you concede the election to Kennedy." Address his backers, yes; but he must not go down and make even a conditional concession.

He composed his remarks and, just after midnight Pacific time, he and Pat descended to the ballroom. She stood beside him in a print dress with green flowered motif as he spoke. Her face was contorted and she was grinding her teeth.

It was minutes before the screaming stopped and he could speak. He talked about his appreciation for their help. Then the tears came to Pat's eyes when he said, as he had told her, "While there are still some results to come in, if the present trend continues, Senator Kennedy will be the next President of the United States." At this point, Pat looked stricken, her face sadder than anyone had seen before.

Standing close was Marion Nichols, her friend and fellow teacher at Whittier High. Marion, now retired and living in Capistrano Beach, caught Pat's eye and waved. Marion watched her friend closely.

"Then I saw the tears coming. She broke. He was talking about the probability that the election was lost. I've always seen her stolid, very much in control, but this time the tears began rolling down the sides of her cheeks. She never used a handkerchief to dry them because that would have been a dead giveaway. She held her head up and, when he was finished, she left with her head up."

Afterward, away from the people and the cameras, she sobbed.

For months thereafter, few people saw her. Rumors spread that she had been so hurt by the narrow loss after she and Richard had worked so hard that she didn't want to face the world. She denied strongly that she was secluding herself, asserting that she was busy with home and children and had little time for much else.

Pat was certain in her heart that her husband had

been cheated of the election. Even ten years later, when Nixon was halfway through his second term, she was still bitter at the Kennedys, convinced that old Joe Kennedy's millions had bought the election for his son. Nixon himself believed that there had been voting frauds in Illinois and Texas but soon found that a recount in Chicago's Cook County would take some eighteen months and that there was no legal way for him to obtain a recount in Texas.

On Inauguration Day, she pointedly snubbed Jackie.

Kennedy, accepting his party's nomination, had made an unusual, sharp personal attack on Nixon that surprised politicians and angered Pat. "We know that our opponents will invoke the name of Abraham Lincoln on behalf of their candidate," he had said, "despite the fact that his political career has often seemed to show charity for none and malice for all." And he added: "Mr. Nixon may feel it is his turn now, after the New Deal and the Fair Deal—but before he deals, someone is going to cut the cards."

During the campaign, Kennedy had continued to flick at Nixon with rapier thrusts of wit; he also made remarks about him in private that quickly came back to the Nixons.*

The snub came inside the White House that cold Friday morning, January 20, 1961, the day after one of the worst snowstorms in Washington's history. The Nixons had arrived about ten-thirty and were ushered into the Red Room, where some two dozen dignitaries were gathering before moving out to the inaugural stand on the steps of the Capitol's East Portico. Mamie Eisenhower was there; the new Vice President, Lyndon Johnson, and Lady Bird Johnson soon arrived.

A few minutes after eleven, Kennedy and the next First Lady drove up and were greeted by Eisenhower, who had been standing inside the doors at the North

---

*At one point he told Ben Bradlee, then the chief correspondent of *Newsweek*'s Washington bureau: "Anyone who can't beat Nixon doesn't deserve to be President." After the election, Kennedy paid a courtesy visit to Nixon at Key Biscayne. Nixon did most of the talking. On his way back to Palm Beach, Kennedy told Dave Powers and Kenny O'Donnell, two of his aides: "It was just as well for all of us that he didn't quite make it."

Portico. Ike escorted them into the Red Room, where coffee and little cakes were being passed around.

Jackie, in a beige cloth coat with a narrow sable collar and beige felt pillbox hat, found a seat on a sofa next to Pat Nixon. Pat acknowledged Jackie's presence, then turned away and spoke to another woman on the couch until it was time to leave. John Eisenhower, Ike's son and his aide for top-level security matters, saw Jackie sitting alone and went over to chat.

The day belonged to the Kennedys, who made the most of it. They swarmed all over the inaugural stand. Even Joe Kennedy, who had remained discreetly behind the scenes during the campaign, was there telling everyone: "This is what I've been looking forward to for a long time." Nixon hid his disappointment well as he sat smiling only a few feet from the new President in the front row. Pat was behind him, for the most part ignored. After the ceremony, the Nixons slipped away to Wesley Heights as new snow began to fall.

OUT AGAIN, IN AGAIN

Now they had to think of the future. They had no savings and just enough cash for day-to-day expenses. Offers had started to come in from law firms, businesses, universities, and foundations. One company sweetened its bid for Nixon to become its head with $500,000 in the company's stock, which was considered to be gilt-edged. But Nixon soon made up his mind that he wanted to resume the practice of law and that he would do it in California. Pat agreed happily.

Nixon telephoned an old friend, Earl C. Adams, senior partner of the prestigious law firm of Adams, Duque and Hazeltine in Los Angeles and a member of the original group which had chosen Nixon to oppose Voorhis fifteen years before. Adams flew to Washington and, over lunch, urged Nixon to remain in Washington or go to New York rather than sequester himself on the West Coast. Nixon, however, insisted he would go either to San Francisco or Los Angeles. He had a few discussions with New York law firms but soon gave up and decided to join Adams's firm in Los Angeles. His salary was to be $60,000 annually, to which would be added a quarter of all the fees from business he brought to the firm; thus, his total income was expected to reach about $100,000.

In March, Nixon flew west to start his new job while Pat remained behind until Tricia and Julie, then fifteen and thirteen, could finish out their school year at Sidwell Friends. Pat began the job of packing, which was harder now than ever before. There had never been so many belongings, including livestock. In addition to the famous Checkers, then a venerable nine years old, there were Puff and Nicky, the cats, and the goldfish and the birds. In June, Nixon returned and helped with the packing. After the last of forty-nine barrels had been stuffed into the huge transcontinental moving van, he said wryly: "Now I've got something in common with President Kennedy—a sore back."

The Nixons sold their Wesley Heights dwelling for $101,000—$25,000 more than they had paid, though they had spent about that much for improvements. Nixon had purchased a large house in a new development called Trousdale Estates, near the exclusive Bel-Air section of Los Angeles, for about $100,000. Until construction was completed, he rented an attractive two-story house at 901 Bundy Drive in Brentwood from Walter Lang, a motion picture producer. It was here that the family went upon arrival. The Brentwood house had a large swimming pool, a bath house, and a little guest house. Fred MacMurray and his wife, June Haver, lived nearby; other neighbors were Joe E. Brown, Cesar Romero, and Cecil Kellaway.

By the end of the year, the Nixons were in their new home at 410 Martin Lane—long, low, and ranch-style, with seven baths and four bedrooms. There were three fireplaces, a living room 30 feet long, a spacious library, and, of course, a swimming pool. Here, too, the neighbors were mostly movie folk. Groucho Marx lived nearby and made it clear that he wouldn't be dropping by to say hello. "I don't know my neighbors," Groucho said, "and I don't expect to associate with them unless there's a bomb and we all meet in the same hole in the ground. That's called the fusion ticket—or is it fission?"

But also by the end of the year the Nixons were in something else much more familiar than a big house with a pool.

It was another campaign.

Pat had had a few happy months. She visited with her old friends from California, went shopping, spent time with Tricia and Julie, swam a lot, gardened. Life was peaceful for the first time in fifteen years.

Ever since Nixon's defeat in 1960, there had been reports that he would try to unseat the Democratic incumbent governor of California, Edmund (Pat) Brown, in 1962. In February 1961, Whittaker Chambers wrote to him, "strongly" urging him to run. Before Nixon moved his family out of Washington, he had had a brief conversation with conservative writer Ralph de Toledano. "Do you think I should run for governor?" he asked de Toledano, who countered with: "Can you win?" Replied Nixon: "They tell me I can."

The pressure to run was growing, but Nixon, too, was enjoying his new life, especially the money flowing in from law fees. He had also received a handsome advance for the book he had begun to write, *Six Crises*.

When early polls showed Nixon ahead of Brown 53 to 37 percent, national leaders urged him to go in. Eisenhower said it was his "duty"; Senators Barry Goldwater, Hugh Scott, and Thomas Kuchel added their voices. So did Murray Chotiner and Leonard W. Hall, the Republican National Chairman. They told him that unless he made the race, he would lose his standing as a national political leader. Everyone, it seems, said "go"—except Pat Nixon.

On September 26, 1961, Nixon called his family together, asked them, and got a firm "no" from his wife. Julie wasn't anxious either. "Why you?" she wanted to know. "Can't someone else carry the ball for a while?"

Recalling that night, Pat said: "As nearly as I can define my attitude, it was, Let's not. Let's stay home. Let's be a private family. Let's take a vacation trip when we want to. Let's not be leaders but instead make our contribution in other ways."

The family kept talking it out. Then, as Pat tells it, Tricia suddenly rose and embraced her father, crying: "Daddy, come on—let's show 'em!"

The next morning, Pat said, she told the aging Checkers: "Well, Checkers, here we go again. I am once more a candidate's wife—and proud to be, too."

After losing the gubernatorial race, having taken only 47.4 percent of the vote, Nixon made his astonishing speech to a hundred newspeople who had gathered in the ballroom of the Beverly Hilton Hotel to hear Herbert G. Klein, his press secretary, officially concede the election.

Nixon was not supposed to be there, but at ten-fifteen he left his suite to go down to the press conference. Pat, unable to face another agonizing concession, was secluded at home with Julie and Tricia. Five minutes later, Nixon stepped before the microphone and stunned the nation with an assault on the press coupled with generous doses of self-pity. At the start of his rambling seventeen-minute talk, he said he had "no complaints about the press coverage" but at the end he unleashed his true feelings:

"I think that it's time that our great newspapers have at least the same objectivity, the same fullness of coverage, that television has. And I can only say thank God for television and radio for keeping the newspapers a little more honest. . . .

"I leave you gentlemen now and you will now write it. You will interpret it. That's your right. But as I leave you I want you to know—just think how much you're going to be missing."

Now the bitterness that had been gnawing at him for years burst out in a remark that would become a national joke:

"You won't have Nixon to kick around any more

because, gentlemen, this is my last press conference. . . .''

He turned and strode from the room, telling the astounded Herb Klein: "I know you don't agree. I gave it to them right in the ass. It had to be said, goddammit. It had to be said.''

Time magazine titled its story about the speech "Career's End." President Kennedy thought that the speech showed that Nixon was "mentally unsound." He told Ben Bradlee: "Nobody could talk like that and be normal.''

Nixon's misery was absorbed by Pat, as it always had been. He was devastated, and so, therefore, was she. It took them both a long time to recover from this one.

By the following summer, they had made a decision: they were going to sell their California home and move to New York, as private citizens.

Pat told a friend: "We're out of the rat race.''

AND ONCE AGAIN

On June 1, 1963, the Nixons moved into a twelve-room apartment at 810 Fifth Avenue, overlooking Central Park, from where Richard commuted to work by limousine to the law firm of Mudge, Stern, Baldwin & Todd at 20 Broad Street. Not long after, the company's name was changed to Nixon, Mudge, Rose, Guthrie & Alexander; and not long after that, the name of John N. Mitchell was added when the firm merged with another company.

The living was gracious on Fifth Avenue, and the neighbors even more distinguished than they had been in California. Nelson Rockefeller, then Governor of New York, was one; William Randolph Hearst, Jr., son of the publisher, another. Their cooperative, which had cost $135,000, with an annual cost of $10,000 for maintenance, had two fireplaces. Pat made no effort to furnish it in any special period but brought in her lifetime accumulation of comfortable sofas and chairs and rotated from storage accessories such as lamps, vases, and assorted bric-a-brac. Prominently displayed was an

Indonesian landscape painting, a gift from President Sukarno, a floral scroll brushed and signed by Madame Chiang Kai-shek, and a painting of the chapel at Gettysburg by Dwight D. Eisenhower. Another Eisenhower original, "Welcome to Gettysburg," which pictures trees from all fifty states lining the driveway to his home, was on loan from Ike and hung in the living room.

The long journey had ended at last for Pat. Her husband's political obituary had been written by every pundit and political leader and there seemed no possible chance of breathing life into it. No chance whatever.

She had what she wanted: stability, privacy, and comfort. Her husband was earning $250,000 a year and, though he traveled on business fairly often, spent a good deal of time at home too. They belonged to exclusive country clubs—Blind Brook and Baltusrol, in Westchester County and New Jersey respectively, both short drives away. The girls were attending the fashionable Chapin School on East End Avenue, and soon Tricia would be formally introduced to society at the International Debutante Ball.

On weekends, like many other New York couples, the Nixons would go out for dinner: to the House of Chan, a well-known Chinese restaurant on Seventh Avenue; to Chez Vito, where a strolling violinist played at the tables. Some afternoons Pat would walk, alone or with a friend, along Madison and Fifth avenues, stopping to examine the windows of the shops, browsing in the boutiques, buying things in the department stores.

It was family living and she loved it. At home, she would cook and bake for her husband and the girls: dinners of spaghettini and meatballs; Mexican hamburgers with chili, string beans with almonds cut into slivers, and a green salad tossed with her own dressing of oil and wine vinegar, and for dessert, a fruit pie; a "shrimp superb" dish, combining cooked shrimp with hard-cooked eggs and blue and cheddar cheese. And, of course, the soon-to-be-famous meat loaf. "He knew very well what a good cook he was getting before we were married," she said gaily during those years. "I started collecting recipes as a young girl and never stopped. One of the reasons he married me was because he was crazy about my strawberry shortcake!"

But Pat could not give up the habits of a lifetime and become a lady of total leisure. So several days each week, often three or four, she would go to Richard's office and, as he put it, "help out."

Mazo told me: "I've seen her there working her ass off. She'd come to the outer office early in the morning and sit at a desk near Rose Mary Woods [Nixon's long-time secretary] and work like the devil, pecking away at a typewriter. And I'd say, 'Hey, what are you doing here?' And she'd say jokingly, 'Can't afford another secretary.'"

If Nixon confounded the country by his comeback, he did no less to his family. None of the three women dreamed that he would ever want to re-enter politics. Julie said in 1967: "For a long time I thought Daddy would be happier out of it all. Now I can see that he wouldn't. This is Daddy's whole life."

Pat began to see it, too, several years after they went to New York. When Kennedy was assassinated in 1963, a few political columnists spoke of Nixon as a possible Republican candidate in 1964, but she had paid little attention. Then, as the convention drew near, she could see his absorption. He spoke at the GOP convention, introducing the nominee, Barry Goldwater, and was given a rousing ovation. Later, he campaigned vigorously for Goldwater.

He was even active in the off-year of 1965, traveling to thirty-five states on behalf of eighty-six nominees for local and national posts. Incredibly, his star was rising again. In 1966, he campaigned again and helped many Republican candidates win.

The handwriting was clearly on the wall and Pat was reading it. He had not left politics; he was not dead politically; he would rise from the ashes, and the old, familiar, rigorous routine would begin all over again.

On Wednesday, January 31, 1968, five years after they had moved to New York, Nixon wrote a letter addressed to the "Citizens of New Hampshire," where the country's first presidential primary is traditionally held. He wrote: "I have decided to enter the Republican Presidential primary in New Hampshire."

Once again Pat had tried to dissuade him and once again she had failed. At least this time, she thought, the children were grown and the campaign would not be so hard on them.

She sighed, shopped for campaigning clothes, and went into the cold of New Hampshire with him for the start of the most grueling ordeal of all. But this time they won.

11

First Lady

MOVING IN

In the East Wing of the White House, just inside the entrance, a door at the right opens into a 20-foot-square reception room decorated in gold brocade. I had gone to Washington in October of 1974, two months after Nixon's resignation, to interview members of Pat Nixon's staff, most of whom were still there serving the new First Lady, Betty Ford. From a white telephone in a corner of the reception room, I talked for a long while with Julie Nixon Eisenhower, who was then working in the capital as an editor for the *Saturday Evening Post*.

By then, Julie had been married almost six years to Dwight David Eisenhower II, Ike's only grandson. The wedding had taken place on December 22, 1968—twenty-nine days before her father took the oath of office as 37th President—in the Marble Collegiate Church, New York City. Dr. Norman Vincent Peale had conducted the ceremony in the 118-year-old church where Julie attended services during the time her family was living in the city. Julie and David had met when Julie was a student at Smith College in Northampton, Massachusetts, and David was attending Amherst near by. Mamie Eisenhower had brought them together, telling young David it would be nice if he would ''look

146

up" the younger Nixon daughter who was studying only a few miles away. He did, a romance blossomed and they became engaged on Thanksgiving Day, 1973.

For a long time Julie spoke in impassioned tones of her mother's contributions during her five and a half years as the President's wife. Far too little was known, she said, about her mother's positive accomplishments as First Lady.

Julie told me: "She did so much. She has been one of the most unique First Ladies in the history of the country, only not a lot of people realize it. She never tried to create an image for herself by doing it in Madison Avenue style, publicizing herself. She did so much quietly. Dr. Kissinger considers her a diplomat without peer. Since 1953 she traveled everywhere with my father as an ambassador for the United States and she never made a mistake."

Julie knew the statistics by heart: Besides crisscrossing the country more than a dozen times, she said, since 1953 her mother had traveled some 500,000 miles in trips to 74 foreign countries, plus Hong Kong. Two years before, she said, Mrs. Nixon had gone to Africa, China, and the Soviet Union; in 1974 she had flown with the President to Belgium, Russia, Latin America, and the Middle East. She had supervised the redecoration of fourteen of the thirty-six rooms in the main house, raising all the money herself from private sources because no government funds are available for this purpose.

Julie: "She began the practice of displaying national treasures, taken from the upstairs rooms, in the East Room, so that visitors to the White House from all over could see them. Among the items shown at various times were Thomas Jefferson's inkwell, Lincoln's handwritten Gettysburg Address, and James Madison's medicine chest.

"My mother would spend four hours each day on the mail because she believed that everyone who wrote to her should receive a personal reply. And she invited so many groups to the White House to give them recognition, not famous ones but little-known people and organizations, such as teachers with their children. These were not important enough to be publicized, so the reporters never mentioned them. But my mother continued to receive them all through the years.''

Nixon himself shrewdly observed: "Any lady who is First Lady likes being First Lady. I don't care what they say. They like it.'' If there were any happy times in Pat Nixon's public life, these were the years. A goal had been reached and there was for her fulfillment of a kind. For the fringe benefits were, to say the least, quite fabulous.

She was hostess to kings, princes, prime ministers, and the world's most talented and prestigious men and women. When she traveled to foreign countries, she was received with full honors. Gifts of jewels, furs, and priceless antiques poured into the White House, and were hers to wear and use as she pleased. She had cars, jet planes, and helicopters at her disposal. At the executive mansion alone, there were thirty-five servants to wait upon her. She had a vast wardrobe, necessary because she was constantly being photographed. She was the center of attention wherever she went.

Nixon was right. The life, Pat admitted, was "glorious."

The White House years began on the morning of January 20, 1969. She and her husband, the President-elect, and their daughters came to the White House to have coffee, sweet rolls, and toast with Lyndon and Lady Bird Johnson, and with the Spiro Agnews and the Hubert Humphreys, the incoming and outgoing vice presidential couples, before going to the Capitol for the inaugural ceremonies.

The Nixons and the Johnsons had been friends for twenty years in Washington, and Pat and Lady Bird had become more intimate during the previous two months when they met often to discuss the Nixons' move to the White House. So there was none of the rather stiff formality that usually prevails at pre-inaugural breakfast meetings. Pat and Lady Bird embraced each other warmly and kissed. Before Bruce, the senior doorman, could usher the Nixons into the reception hall, they were wildly greeted by their own two dogs, Pasha, a Yorkshire terrier, and Vicky, a poodle, who had already moved into the mansion the day before.

At the threshold of the White House, Lady Bird paused, smiled, and gestured for the Nixons to go in ahead of her. Pat shook her head politely and said, "No, until twelve o'clock, you are the First Lady." Lady Bird laughed and led the way to the Red Room, where the coffee was being served. Pat noted that President Johnson, who had delivered his own inaugural address in a business suit, was rather uncomfortably dressed in a cutaway coat and striped trousers in deference to her husband's preference for formal clothes at the ceremony.

After the inauguration and Richard Nixon's address pledging an end to the Vietnam War, and after sitting through the parade in dreary, freezing cold weather, the Nixons and their close friends and relatives hurried back to a reception at the White House before getting dressed for that night's several inaugural balls.

Protocol decreed that none of the Nixons' personal belongings, furniture, or clothing could be moved into the White house until after the inauguration at noon. So while the new President was delivering his address at the Capitol, trucks from New York were delivering trunks and boxes full of the Nixons' belongings at the south entrance of the executive mansion. Under the direction of Manolo and Fina Sanchez, the new First Family's luggage was unpacked and arranged in the upstairs living quarters by the White House staff. The Nixons brought very little with them except personal effects, but as one of the staff members said at the time, "All you need to move into the White House is your clothes and a toothbrush."

The Nixons had put their Fifth Avenue cooperative apartment up for sale at a reported $425,000, which included $60,000 worth of bulletproof glass installed in its windows by the Secret Service after the election in November. Some of the apartment's furniture had been shipped to Julie and David Eisenhower's apartment in

Northampton, Massachusetts. The rest was sent to Key Biscayne, Florida, where the new President had recently bought two beachfront houses. The Johnsons' personal furniture and Mrs. Johnson's valuable collection of china had been shipped to the LBJ Ranch in Texas a few weeks earlier, but there was more than enough furniture and porcelain in the White House's basement to replace those furnishings and dishes in the upstairs living quarters.

Tricia and Julie and David moved into the two bedrooms formerly occupied by Luci and Lynda Bird Johnson.

The President and Pat had adjoining bedrooms across the hall, beside the large, graceful Yellow Oval Room with its Truman Balcony—the parlor and living room in the second-floor apartment—which had been called the Trophy Room during the Eisenhower administration. Roosevelt and Truman had used it as a study. Like Jacqueline Kennedy and Lady Bird Johnson, Pat quickly decided that the room was her favorite in the White House.

Mamie Eisenhower, Julie's grandmother-in-law, had attended the inauguration and the reception at the White House after it, but she declined to stay for the Nixon family's dinner that evening in the upstairs family dining room. She wanted to get back to Walter Reed Hospital where Ike was then confined, suffering his last illness.

While Pat was deciding what to order for dinner—her family's first dinner alone in the White House—David Eisenhower opted for steaks. Pat telephoned the chef, Henry Haller, who had supervised the kitchen for the Johnsons, and ordered four steaks to be served in the upstairs dining room for the President, Julie, Tricia, and David. "I'd just like a bowl of cottage cheese in my bedroom," she said.

J. B. West, then ending his long years of service as the White House's Chief Usher, or staff manager, later recalled the frantic scene that took place in the kitchen in his memoirs, *Upstairs at the White House:* "Steaks we had—juicy, fresh prime filets . . . waiting in the

White House kitchen for a family who, we'd heard, loved steak. But cottage cheese? . . . So the head butler, in a White House limousine, sped around the city of Washington until he found a delicatessen open with a good supply of cottage cheese. The kitchen never ran out, after that.''

After the dinner, the Nixon family left the White House to spend the evening appearing at the six inaugural balls in the city. Pat wore a glittering, jewel-studded mimosa silk yellow gown, designed by Karen Stark of Harvey Berin, with a bell-shaped skirt and a small stand-up collar. With the gown, she wore a long-sleeved jacket and narrow cummerbund. The jacket, collar, and cummerbund were embroidered with Byzantine scrolls of gold and silver bullion and ornamented with Austrian crystal jewels. The exquisitely intricate embroidery had taken 260 hours of labor to put together.

The gowns of pink and white worn at the inaugural balls by Tricia and Julie, respectively, were designed and made by Priscilla Kidder, known professionally as Priscilla of Boston, who had designed the bridal gown and the gowns of the bridesmaids and the bride's mother for Julie's wedding to David Eisenhower a month earlier.

''Mrs Nixon asked me to make a dress for her to wear to Julie's wedding,'' Priscilla said at the time, ''because she couldn't shop for one in New York. She was mobbed by crowds of people in every store she went into, so she gave up and called me. We had known each other for a long time because years before she had asked me to make a formal gown for Tricia. She couldn't find a dress anywhere in New York to fit Tricia because Tricia is so tiny, a little bit of a thing, only size three, believe it or not.''

The Nixons did not try to dance at any of the six crowded balls that night. When they were leaving the last one, the new President said with a broad grin: ''They gave me the key to the White House. I have to go there now and see if it fits.''

The next morning Pat slept until eight-thirty, had

coffee in her room, and did some unpacking. At ten-thirty she went downstairs to attend the first of a round of social events in the White House that were not to let up for the next five and a half years—a coffee and pink lemonade reception for 1,300 women campaign workers. That afternoon, after more unpacking, she answered some personal mail, met with delegations who sought her endorsement of disease-fighting fund drives, and saw to the hanging of new pictures in the West Wing.

Pat made some changes in the upstairs living quarters. She asked to have the big canopied bed removed from the President's room and replaced with a simple double bed from the White House storeroom, a bed that Harry Truman had slept in. At her husband's urgent request, Pat saw to it that the extra-powerful, skin-searing shower head, installed by Lyndon Johnson in the presidential bathroom, was removed and replaced by one with a softer spray. Johnson's shower had almost ripped Nixon apart the first and only time he tried using it.

SOMETHING NEW

Pat also acted quickly to remove reminders that the Kennedy family had lived in the White House.

On the mantel in the First Lady's room was a plaque inscribed in Jackie Kennedy's handwriting; it had been placed there at her request when she left the house after her husband's death. It said: "In this room lived John Fitzgerald Kennedy with his wife Jacqueline during the two years, ten months and two days he was President of the United States, January 20, 1961–November 22, 1963." Jacqueline had it placed directly below another plaque reading: "In this room Abraham Lincoln slept during his occupancy of the White House March 4, 1861–April 13, 1865."

Pat Nixon asked the chief usher to have Mrs. Kennedy's plaque removed and put in the White House basement, where it still remains. She also replaced the mantelpiece itself with a historic one designed by Benjamin Latrobe.

Mrs. Nixon also wanted other tokens of the Kennedy occupancy banished. After the assassination, Jackie had gone to considerable trouble and expense to select a suitable painting which would be donated to the White House and hung there in the late President's memory. James W. Fosburgh, a noted art collector, had chosen a selection of twenty, including a Corot, a Whistler, a Cézanne, and a Monet, culled from galleries and dealers in New York. The priceless array was stacked in the hallway on the second floor and around the yellow Oval Room as the Kennedy family spent hours studying them. Finally, they decided on Claude Monet's *Matinée Sur la Seine—Beau Temps*, a seascape depicting morning on the Seine in beautiful weather. It was hung in the Green Room. Below was placed a plaque reading: "In Memory of President John F. Kennedy, by His Family."

Pat Nixon ordered the painting rehung in a far less prominent spot in the Vermeil Room on the ground floor. Not long after, a beautifully landscaped area which Lady Bird Johnson had named the "Jacqueline Kennedy Garden" was quietly changed to the "First Lady's Garden."

She arranged for separate quarters for herself and the new President, explaining that she would occupy the First Lady's room. "Nobody could sleep with Dick," she said. "He wakes up during the night, switches on the light, speaks into his tape recorder or takes notes—it's impossible."

Pat also ordered that in the future all state dinners would be formal white-tie and tails affairs—no more black tie informality, as the Kennedy and Johnson dinners had relaxed into after the white-tie Eisenhower regime. She said that she wanted no beauty parlor in the executive mansion, and asked to have the black leather chairs in the President's Oval Office reupholstered in cheerful cherry red.

On their second evening in the White House, the

Nixons, accompanied by West, were taken on a long tour of the rooms in the mansion by its young and historically knowledgeable curator, James Ketchum. The President looked at the long formal table in the State Dining Room with its mirrored plateau centerpiece and asked if any Presidents and their families ever had dinner there when no invited guests were present. West told him that Herbert Hoover had dinner in the big downstairs dining room every night, even when he was alone.

"That figures," Nixon replied.

At the end of the tour, Nixon told West that he was planning to have religious services every Sunday morning in the large East Room of the White House, something that no other President had ever done. Then the Nixon family went to the mansion's moving picture theater and watched the three-hour religious film *The Shoes of the Fisherman*, even though the President had already seen it once before.

The Nixons' close friend the Reverend Billy Graham preached the first sermon at the Sunday services in the East Room before a congregation of two hundred invited guests, seated on small bentwood chairs that had been bought by Bess Truman and later banished to the basement by Mamie Eisenhower, who denounced them as fit only for "a children's party." West produced an altar that had been used at the Lynda Johnson–Charles Robb wedding, but the President pointed out that the services would be interdenominational. "I don't want an altar," he said, "just a podium." The East Room was rigged with wiring for an electric organ and a raised platform for the choir singers.

Less than a month after the Nixons moved into the White House, Pat astonished the lady members of the press corps by inviting all of them to a sit-down luncheon at the big table in the State Dining Room. They drew numbers for seats at the table, and Pat drew a number, too. The women reporters could hardly remember the last press conference given by a First Lady in the White House, back in Eleanor Roosevelt's time. In 1947, after several months of trying, the women of the press finally succeeded in getting Bess Truman, probably the most reticent First Lady of the century, to answer a number of questions which they submitted in writing. Her penciled replies, read to the correspondents by two White House secretaries, have never been surpassed for non-communication. Twenty-five of the forty questions were answered with "no," "no comment," and "yes."*

Five years later, after the White House had gone through a major reconstruction, Mrs. Truman agreed to show a group of women correspondents through the renovated mansion. One of them asked her if she would like to spend another term there.

"That is a question to which you are not going to get a yes or no out of me," Mrs. Truman said.

"But could you stand it if you had to?"

"Well, I stood it for seven years."

End of interview.

Mamie Eisenhower, a cheerful, sociable, and outspoken woman, never gave interviews to reporters. Jackie Kennedy ignored the press completely. When a reporter tried to approach her at an airport or at a White House function, Jackie would silently ignore the questions or would turn her back and walk away. She once referred to the ladies of the White House press corps as "harpies."

Lady Bird Johnson sometimes carried on a pleasant

---

*A few of the questions and answers:

Q: If you had a son, would you try to bring him up to be President of the United States?

A: No.

Q: Would you want Margaret ever to be the First Lady?

A: No.

Q: Has living in the White House changed any of your views on politics and people?

A: No comment.

Q: How does supervising the White House compare with supervising your own home in Independence, Missouri?

A: With a housekeeper, there is not the personal responsibility.

Q: Will you go to the Democratic National Convention in 1948?

A: Expect to—wouldn't miss a Democratic convention if I could help it.

Q: What experience since you have been in the White House do you consider the most worthwhile?

A: No comment.

casual conversation with a correspondent on a plane trip. But her relations with the press were firmly handled by her capable public relations secretary, Liz Carpenter, who did most of her talking, much of it concerned with Mrs. Johnson's crusade for conservation and restoration of America's scenic beauty.

A press conference, then, by a First Lady—and this First Lady, at that, who had never spoken her mind on anything even remotely resembling a controversial question—was eagerly awaited.

She still said nothing of substance, but some of her more discerning listeners at that first press conference luncheon remarked on the differences between Pat and her predecessors. Here, they thought, was a different kind of First Lady.

Eleanor Roosevelt and Jacqueline Kennedy were both from wealthy Eastern backgrounds, and Lady Bird Johnson was uppercrust Texas. Mamie Eisenhower, from a wealthy Denver family, was Army High Society, used to being waited on all of her life. ("When I go out," Mamie ordered her White House staff, "I am to be escorted to the diplomatic entrance by an usher. And when I return, I am to be met at the door and escorted upstairs.") Bess Truman and Pat Nixon were both from middle-class America, and they both believed in the virtues of family, country, loyalty, and discipline, but Mrs. Truman never had to work for a living.

"She's dedicated to America in a way that might seem corny to the average person," one of Pat's friends said after she became the First Lady. "Mixing in high society in Washington and New York did not impress her at all." On the morning after Inauguration Day, Pat shouted happily to the crowd of campaign workers in the East Room: "You'll all be invited back! We're going to have our friends here instead of all the big shots!" Impressed by her lack of affectation, most of the women at the press luncheon found themselves, to their surprise, liking Pat Nixon for the first time very much.

At that first meeting with the ladies of the press, Mrs.

Nixon talked about the various things that she was planning to do as First Lady. She said that she did not intend to confine herself to one special project. One program that she planned to give her active support to, Pat said, would be a drive to enlist women in various kinds of volunteer work—in hospitals and in schools as teachers' aides and in providing home care for elderly and mentally retarded people. Although she did not mention it at that early date, probably her biggest contribution in the years to come was to refurbish the interior decoration of the whole executive mansion, which had declined since Mrs. Kennedy's brief term as First Lady, and to assemble in the mansion the finest collection of great American works of art ever seen in the White House.

To the astonishment of her critics, Pat Nixon also became a warmly welcomed and highly praised traveling ambassador of goodwill in such sensitive foreign nations as Russia, China, and the African and South American republics. "I have known the wives of several American presidents," said Mrs. Andrei Gromyko, wife of the Soviet foreign minister, "but Mrs. Nixon is the nicest."

But such acclaim and prestige were at least three years in the uncertain future when Pat Nixon was getting accustomed to her new duties and problems as First Lady in the winter of 1969. She quickly worked out a daily schedule that began at 7 A.M. During the morning she looked over and answered some of her mail, signing each letter of reply herself, a task that took four hours a day. She once explained why she gave the answering of mail such a high priority. "When a letter from the White House arrives in a small town," she said, "it's shown to all the neighbors, and often published in the local paper. It's very important to the people who receive it."

While she worked on her mail and looked at the day's newspapers, Pat talked with Lucy Winchester, her social secretary, about plans for a dinner in honor of a visiting prime minister and with chef Henry Haller about the menu for the dinner. There were other discussions during the morning with Mary Kaltman, the chief housekeeper, about shopping lists, and with the White House florist about flower arrangements.

After a lunch, usually with Tricia—often consisting of a sandwich, small salad and milk—the First Lady spent her afternoon as a hostess at a ceremonial function, perhaps a reception for a group of Mexican folk dancers, a tea for Urban Service Corps volunteer workers, or (as happened more than once) a reception for as many as 4,000 or more Republican women, coming and going in four or five shifts.

If there was no formal social event planned for the evening, Mrs. Nixon would have dinner with the President and any members of their family who happened to be in Washington, in their second-floor private dining room. The White House was staffed by three chefs—Haller and his assistant, Hans Raffert, and Heinz Bender, the pastry cook.

At dinner, there was rarely a first course, but occasionally clams or baked grapefruit were served. Their favorite main courses were swiss steak, broiled steak (usually a sirloin), broiled or baked fish, broiled, barbecued, or baked chicken (a real favorite), chicken pot pie, and, of course, the famous Nixon meat loaf, served once a month.*

After dinner, the President usually went back to work at his small hideaway office across the street in the Executive Office Building or in the Lincoln Sitting Room in the White House. Pat would go back to work on her mail, spend some time with Tricia, or read until

---

*The dish was so highly publicized during the Nixon administration that the White House printed the recipe and sent it to all who asked. Hundreds of thousands did. The recipe: One and one-half pounds of lean ground beef, three tablespoons of bread crumbs, two tablespoons of whipping cream, two tablespoons of tomato sauce, one egg, one tablespoon of chopped parsley, two teaspoons of salt, a quarter teaspoon of ground black pepper and a teaspoon of seasoning salt. Mix all ingredients well with the meat and form a loaf. Place the loaf in a pan and spread some additional tomato sauce thinly over the loaf. Bake for 50 minutes, with the oven set at 375 degrees for the first half-hour and then turned down to 350. Serves six.

she went to bed, usually between twelve and one o'clock.

During her first three years in the White House Mrs. Nixon entertained more than 109,000 guests at formal state dinners, receptions, luncheons, and teas, making herself the busiest hostess in the history of the executive mansion.

One week alone, her guests included Indira Gandhi, President Tito of Yugoslavia, and Prime Minister William McMahon of Australia. For her first formal White House dinner, eleven days after the Nixon inauguration, she invited the entire Washington diplomatic corps. There were three reception lines. The President and the First Lady, wearing the same gown that she had worn at the inaugural balls, first received guests in the Green Room. They then moved on to the Blue Room to meet Vice President and Mrs. Agnew and to the Red Room, where they were greeted by the new Secretary of State and Mrs. Rogers. The procession went from the Red Room to the State Dining Room, where a buffet dinner was served with champagne.

One of the most spectacular social events staged in the White House by Mrs. Nixon during her first year as First Lady was a seventieth birthday party for Duke Ellington, the famous jazz pianist, composer, and band leader, who received that evening from President Nixon the Presidential Medal of Freedom, the highest civilian award given by the government. About eighty guests, including many big names in the jazz world, attended the dinner and another hundred people came in later to attend the concert and dancing that followed. Among the musicians who performed that night were Dave Brubeck, Paul Desmond, Earl "Fatha" Hines, J. J. Johnson, Billy Taylor, Urbie Green, and Gerry Mulligan. The jam session went on long after one o'clock in the morning.

Andrew Wyeth, the realist painter from Chadds Ford, Pennsylvania, who remained a staunch Nixon supporter throughout and long after the Watergate ordeal, was honored at a special dinner when his works were exhibited at the White House. Most of the big names in the art world attended the dinner, including the film tycoon Joseph Levine, who loaned five of his twenty-one Wyeth paintings to the exhibit. Wyeth was asked to select the musician to entertain at the after-dinner concert, and he picked his close friend Rudolf Serkin, who brought his own piano to the White House, playing two Chopin selections and Beethoven's Pathetique Sonata. Serkin stayed on for the dancing, with music by a Marine Corps jazz combine, until after midnight.

Violinist Isaac Stern and composer-pianist-conductor Leonard Bernstein performed at Mrs. Nixon's reception for Israel's Prime Minister Golda Meir, and pianist Eugene List was the guest star at a concert following a dinner for Emperor Haile Selassie of Ethiopia. Henry Mancini, the composer of "Moon River" and other hit songs, conducted a performance of his compositions after a dinner honoring the Apollo 10 astronauts.

Mrs. Nixon arranged a series of entertainments called simply "Evenings at the White House" featuring such stars as Red Skelton, Bob Hope, the cast of the Broadway musical hit *1776*, and the famous British actor Nicol Williamson, who asked for the American jazz band of Yank Lawson and Bob Haggart to appear with him before an audience of 275 guests, including many big industrial and business names. Williamson varied his program by switching from *Hamlet* to jazz music, then to Samuel Beckett, excerpts from Arthur Miller's *Death of a Salesman*, Robert Benchley's "The Treasurer's Report," and T. S. Eliot's "The Love Song of J. Alfred Prufrock." After his performance, Williamson quickly changed into a velvet dinner jacket and black tie and joined the Nixons in the receiving line to shake hands with the guests. Then Williamson and the jazz band moved into the State Dining Room, where they staged another impromptu show after the buffet supper, featuring such numbers as "The Dark Town Strutters Ball" and "When the Saints Go Marching In."

Mrs. Nixon established another precedent as a White House hostess on her first Thanksgiving Day in the executive mansion when she invited 225 elderly people from District of Columbia nursing homes and homes for the aged to dinner, which was served in the State Dining Room and the East Room. Julie Eisenhower recited the blessing before dinner in the State Dining Room:

> "Thank you for the food we eat;
> Thank you for the air so sweet;
> Thank you for the birds that sing;
> Thank you, God, for everything."

In the East Room, Tricia Nixon sat at the head table beside Mamie Eisenhower and Mamie's granddaughter, Susan, who gave as the blessing the Saint Agnes Prayer, which, she explained, was her grandparents' favorite. President Nixon, after welcoming the elderly guests, slipped upstairs and ate a lunch of cottage cheese salad alone. He returned later and stood beside his wife, shaking hands with each of the guests as they left the White House. He told them that they had been invited to dinner "as part of our family—the American family."

After her first year as a hostess in the White House, and as a world-traveling First Lady, Pat Nixon seemed to be gaining a self-assurance and poise in public that continued to surprise the women of the press who were covering her activities. One of them noted that Pat was certainly not the stiff and rather wooden figure that she had appeared to be before moving into the White House.

"She is warm and kind and she goes that extra mile to shake a hand and greet a stranger," Helen Thomas, the veteran United Press International White House reporter said at that time. "She is concerned about people's feelings. Mrs. Nixon is a very strong woman, and sometimes a very stubborn woman. As a hostess, she has kept her promise of not entertaining just the big shots. She never forgets her days of poverty when she was growing up. . . . She obviously is not much involved in the intellectual ferment of her time, but she reads the papers, and she is bright."

In the often embarrassing give-and-take of press conference questioning—there were many after that first one—Pat was looser than before, keeping her cool, volunteering quips she'd never dared voice in years gone by, but parrying the hard questions with her usual skill. Talking about a recent trip around the world, she remarked, "I was pleased to learn that the prestige of the United States abroad is at an all-time high."

"Who told you that?" Helen Thomas asked.

"Well," Pat came back quickly, "judging from what people said abroad, and by the size of the crowds that came out to meet us."

At the same meeting, she was presented with a gold medal commemorating the Nixon inauguration by an official who remarked that the inaugural committee had earned $470,000 selling such medals. "Boy, I think I'll go into that business," Pat said. After the conference, a reporter said to her, "Do you like to talk to the press?"

"Well, you know, I really do," she said. "I admire the press. It isn't easy to go out day after day and get news. You deserve a medal, and I'm going to give it to you."

"You mean," the reporter asked, "that you're not going to call us 'harpies' after you leave the White House?"

Catching the reference to Jackie Kennedy's remark, Pat Nixon smiled and said, "Certainly not."

Her new brightness irritated at least one veteran and much revered Washingtonian, Alice Roosevelt Longworth. Mrs. Longworth, daughter of President Theodore Roosevelt, is a great wit and raconteur, and a totally uninhibited personality. (When Lyndon Johnson was photographed exhibiting the scar of his gall bladder surgery, she observed that the country should be grateful that LBJ did not have an operation on his prostate gland.) Mrs. Longworth liked Pat and said so. But she also said: "I wish she wouldn't call people 'kiddo.' She called me 'kiddo' just the other day, and frankly I can't stand it.'' Mrs. Longworth was then nearing her ninetieth birthday.

Now that she was First Lady, Pat's pants-pressing routine finally ended and she also stopped making her own clothes. She went *haute couture*, embracing Geoffrey Beene, Mollie Parnis, Adele Simpson, and Count Sarni. She dabbed on Norell perfume and had her hair done by Rita de Santis at Elizabeth Arden in Washington. Her shoes were coordinated by Beth Levine. And she took Tricia in hand and convinced her to lengthen her thigh-high skirts to top of the knee.

She would wear slacks but never inside the White House, only at Camp David or aboard the presidential yacht, *Sequoia*. The executive mansion, she felt, was a showplace that called for dignity in dress. She didn't like her staff to wear pants or very short skirts either, and would let them know, though never by direct order. To a girl in a mini, she would say: "My, what pretty dimpled knees you've got!" The young lady got the point.

Her sense of dignity was affronted when Joan Kennedy, the blond wife of Senator Edward Kennedy, showed up at the White House in a silver-sequined cocktail dress that revealed six inches of her thighs.* The occasion was the First Lady's annual reception for members of Congress, always a formal affair. The President was in black tie and Pat wore a floor-length gown and long white gloves. When Joan in her mini reached the head of the reception line, Pat could not help but stare at her exposed limbs, though she said nothing. Later, however, Pat and the President discussed the incident upstairs and wondered what had prompted Joan to appear in the outfit, which caused a furore when the story hit the papers. The following year, just prior to the reception, Pat wondered aloud to the President about what Joan was likely to wear this time.

*One woman guest at the reception asked Senator Hugh Scott of Pennsylvania if he thought Joan was an exhibitionist. "I don't know," Senator Scott answered, "but she sure exhibits well."

* * *

For Pat Nixon, probably the most memorable of the many social events during her years in the White House was the wedding of Tricia and Edward Finch Cox, son of a wealthy New York family, which took place in the Rose Garden on June 12, 1971.

That afternoon was cloudy and drizzling. At four o'clock, the appointed time for the outdoor ceremony, the weather was still so wet that the President tried to persuade Tricia to move the wedding inside to the East Room, but she refused to be married indoors.

Fortunately, twenty minutes later, the rain stopped and the four hundred guests hurried to the garden to watch the ceremony, which was performed under a 12-foot high, open-sided domed pavilion by the White House chaplain, the Methodist Rev. Dr. Edward Gardiner Latch. The bride—who wore an embroidered white organdy dress with a sleeveless fitted bodice and a pearled Juliet cap and carried a bouquet of sweetheart roses, babies' breath, and lilies of the valley—was led to the altar on her father's left arm. Then he stepped back to join a radiant Pat as the couple knelt on a wrought iron prie-dieu. Julie Eisenhower, whose husband, David, was on sea duty, was matron of honor, and Mary Ann Cox, the groom's sister, was one of the attendants. At 4:35, Cox slipped the ring of thirty full-cut chip diamonds in a platinum setting on Tricia's finger; the minister recited the Lord's Prayer, pronounced them man and wife, and offered a prayer and a benediction. Then she and the groom rose and went directly to their parents before walking back down the aisle, which was bordered with snapdragons, lilies, and white chrysanthemums. Tricia kissed Pat and her father, then crossed the aisle to kiss the groom's parents. Then, at 4:48, the rain started falling again and everybody hurried back indoors for the reception. There, a friend in the receiving line, shaking the President's hand, said that he was sorry about the rain. "Oh, no," Nixon said quickly. "Soft rain caresses a marriage."

Among the guests at the reception, much to the surprise of everyone there, was one of President Nixon's severe critics, consumer advocate Ralph Nader. Ed Cox had worked on Nader's staff during a summer vacation while he was studying at Princeton. Other guests included Billy Graham, Red Skelton, Chief Justice Warren Burger (but none of the other Supreme Court justices), Ethel Waters, J. Edgar Hoover, Mrs. Bob Hope, Art Linkletter, the author Victor Lasky, and Martha Mitchell, in a dazzling orange and white ankle-length gown.

The President, who admitted he had tried all night to figure out a way to avoid it, finally got out on the floor with the bride, muttering, "My parents were Quakers. They didn't believe in this sort of thing." He made it through "Thank Heaven for Little Girls" without stepping on her foot once. Two-stepping in a little circle, he looked embarrassed, like someone who had had just one quick lesson the night before and hadn't learned any too well. Still, he got a round of applause and, somewhat encouraged, proceeded to dance with Julie, Lynda Robb, and Pat.

When the bridegroom's father, Howard Cox, led Mamie Eisenhower out on the floor to dance, the crowd cheered. Champagne flowed, all of it from California and New York State. Luci Nugent startled and embarrassed J. Edgar Hoover by giving him a big kiss. Finally, the bride, still wearing her wedding gown, and the bridegroom ran off to a waiting limousine while the band played "Toot, Toot, Tootsie, Goodbye." The President started to tease newspeople about where they were going for their honeymoon. "Well," he volunteered, "they're not going out of the United States. We've taken care of that." Pat, looking surprised, stopped him. "Now wait a minute," she said. He didn't exactly spill the beans but hinted broadly that it could be the estate of his wealthy patron, Robert Abplanalp, in the Bahamas.

Conspicuously absent from the guest list were members of Congress, including Speaker Carl Albert and a Michigan representative named Gerald R. Ford. However, three previous White House brides were there—Luci Johnson Nugent, Lynda Johnson Robb, and Alice Roosevelt Longworth.

Mrs. Longworth was cornered by reporters and asked if the occasion brought back memories of her own wedding. As a twenty-two-year-old girl, she had been married in the East Room in 1906 to Representative Nicholas Longworth, later Speaker of the House, before a thousand guests.

"No," she replied, "it doesn't bring back one goddamned memory."

12

A New White House

FIXING UP

Many of the guests at the Nixon-Cox wedding who had not visited the White House in recent months noticed the extensive redecorating and refurnishing of the executive mansion that was then beginning under Mrs. Nixon's direction.

The Nixons had never been invited to the White House during the Kennedy administration, but Pat had read in the newspapers about the complete renovation of the mansion by Stéphane Boudin, an interior decorator from Paris who worked under the personal direction of Mrs. Kennedy. Jackie had the Blue Room repainted in white, and she prominently displayed her favorite paintings by Cézanne. To finance the work, which could not be paid for by government appropriations, Jackie established a Fine Arts Committee, headed by Henry Francis du Pont, an authority on American antiques who soon began to complain that the Gallic influence was too pronounced. But Jackie seemed to have no trouble persuading wealthy patrons and patriotic organizations to contribute money and works of art. She wangled prized antiques out of private homes and raised funds for redecorating by selling White House guide books to sightseers at the mansion.

167

When Pat Nixon moved in five years after President Kennedy's death, she was astonished to find the mansion looking run-down and seedy. The heavy traffic of more than a million and a half sightseers and fifty thousand invited guests every year for almost ten years had taken its toll, and the Lyndon Johnsons had done little or no work to keep up the appearance of the downstairs public rooms. The wall fabrics in the Red, Green, and Blue rooms were worn threadbare. The upholstery on the furniture was ragged. Only four of the fourteen chairs in the Blue Room seemed presentable.

Busy with many other new problems during her first year in the White House, Mrs. Nixon was unable to make plans for, or to figure out how to finance, the urgently needed redecorating of the mansion. Like Jackie Kennedy before her, Pat learned that the supposedly plentiful supply of nice furnishings in the White House's storage rooms available as replacements simply did not exist.

For help, Mrs. Nixon turned to Clement E. Conger, an expert on antiques from an old Alexandria, Virginia, family which traces its ancestry back to William Ramsay, the lord mayor of that town under British rule in 1724. The Nixons met Conger at the State Department, where he was the curator of antique furnishings, and they had little trouble persuading him to take on the same duties in the White House, replacing Johnson's curator, James Ketchum, who had also worked with Mrs. Kennedy.

"I made a date to meet Mrs. Nixon at the White House one Sunday afternoon in January at two-thirty," Conger told me in his White House basement office, "and we spent three hours looking at every room in the house. She told me exactly how she wanted to change every room, and all of it was in her head. She didn't carry a notebook. And every change that she suggested was the right one. She has a marvelous eye for line, color, and design."

Later, Mrs. Nixon and Conger met with an architect and designer, Edward B. Jones of Albany, Georgia, who had designed period rooms at the Metropolitan

Museum in New York and had supervised historic restorations all over the country.

Clem Conger described to me in fascinating detail how they worked:

"The three of us planned, room by room, how the restoration of the White House would be done. We decided that we wanted to restore as many rooms as possible back to what they had been in the early nineteenth century, the golden era of the White House—the era of the Adamses, Jefferson, Madison, and Monroe—when the house probably looked its best, before designing started to go downhill during the Machine Age. We met in the mornings, afternoons, and at night to determine how certain colors looked in certain rooms at different times of the day and at night, because, you must remember, the White House is used as a museum in the morning and as a place for meetings and entertainment during the rest of the day and at night.

"Now reds, blues, and greens for the three principal drawing rooms literally change color in front of your eyes due to the differences in light. So we tried the things by the morning sunlight, the afternoon sunlight streaming into the rooms, with, of course, electric lights on too in the rooms, and in the night under completely artificial light. The reds can change colors—go very dark at night.

"The previous red in the Red Room had a blue tone to it which made it very dark at night and somewhat controversial in the minds of some people. We selected a red which would stand up all day long. We called it Dolly Madison Red because it was taken from the red in the back of the chair in the portrait of Dolly Madison now in the Red Room, which had been there in Dolly Madison's day and in that same room. So we knew that was an accurate red for the room and it was Mrs. Nixon, personally, who called it Dolly Madison Red. In the Blue Room, where we had French wallpaper, which was quite a departure from recent history but more correct to what it might have been in the first quarter of the nineteenth century, the blue paper has a very light, general background but there are blue classical designs on the border of the paper near the chair rail and up by the corners of the ceiling.

"And all the upholsteries in the room and the draperies, the blue and gold, had to match the blue in the wallpaper and they, too, had to stand the test of time. Blue changes perhaps more with the light than almost any other color and the blue, which was very light and pretty in the morning and afternoon, could go almost black at night.

"So, again, every one of these things was studied many, many times and Mrs. Nixon was in on every step of this operation."

Valuable art objects and paintings that decorated the White House a century or more ago are now scattered all over the country in museums and private homes. Some past Presidents, like Chester A. Arthur, sold them off when they moved out of the executive mansion; not until the early 1920s was there a federal law declaring that the contents of the White House were government property.

Conger happened to discover the prized Gilbert Stuart painting of Dolly Madison one day when he was poking through the storage basement of the Pennsylvania Academy of Fine Arts in Philadelphia. When he asked to have the portrait loaned to the White House, the museum officials turned down his request, explaining that it was against their policy to lend artworks to any institution outside Philadelphia.

Mrs. Nixon then wrote to the Academy, making a formal request for a loan of the painting and it was soon shipped to the White House. Apparently it had disappeared from the Red Room during the burning of the mansion by the British in 1814, toward the close of the War of 1812. Mrs. Madison, who was First Lady at that time, was too busy during the fire saving Stuart's famous full-length portrait of George Washington to be bothered about her own picture.

While she was planning the restoration of the White House to its early-nineteenth-century elegance, Mrs.

Nixon had to raise the funds to pay for the redecoration and the acquisition of much of the artwork that she wanted to bring to the mansion. Congress had stopped paying for White House decoration and luxuries after Andrew Jackson caused an uproar by spending $4,308 of the taxpayers' money on a silver service for his dining room. Along with contributions from private donors and foundations, the First Lady's sources for such financial support were the sales of White House guide books and royalties from the sales of the Franklin Mint's commemorative Presidential and First Lady silver medals.

Conger also contributed, and still contributes, fees that he receives for illustrated lectures about the White House art treasures. The three White House guide books on sale in the mansion during sightseeing hours—*The White House—An Historic Guide, The Living White House* (an illustrated history of First Families), and *The Presidents of the United States*—bring about $100,000 a year to the decorating and art acquisition fund. As Conger points out, such a sum even in Jackie Kennedy's time could buy quite a few important decorative items, but today it scarcely covers the cost of a few choice antique pieces.

In the fall of 1970, Pat Nixon spent a considerable sum of donated funds designing, with engineers and electricians, a system for lighting up the whole exterior of the White House at night for the first time in history. It was all her idea. If the Lincoln Memorial and the Washington Monument could be lit up from dusk to dawn, she asked, why not the White House?

Telling the President nothing about her plan, she worked on it for six months and then arranged to have him see the spectacularly lighted mansion for the first time one evening when they were flying home together in a helicopter from a working vacation trip. Along with the fifty-six floodlights hidden in shrubbery, terraces, and porticos, and illuminating the whole outside of the building, other lights on the roof shone on the American flag flying above the White House. The President was so delighted that he asked the helicopter pilot to circle around the shining mansion four times before making a landing.

As funds became available, Pat decided to renovate only one or two rooms in the White House at a time so that the work would not disrupt her busy social schedule.

One of the first rooms completed was the impressive new and enlarged Map Room on the ground floor, so called because President Roosevelt hung military maps there during World War II. She turned it from a warren of small offices into a handsome new reception area and had it furnished in American Chippendale, including several rare pieces. She was delighted when the only known American Chippendale library table was purchased for $25,000 and donated to the White House by the late Mrs. Charles S. Payson, John Hay Whitney's sister and the owner of the New York Mets and co-owner of the Greentree racing stable. The large table still stands there. The Map Room also exhibited a 1775 antique map of the Maryland, Virginia, and District of Columbia area, drawn by Thomas Jefferson's father. The newly created room was first used for a meeting by President Nixon and Lyndon Johnson on May 27, 1970, before they went to a luncheon tribute to Speaker of the House John McCormack.

A few months later the China Room, with its display of china pieces used by past First Families, was opened to the public after its renovation. On the wall was one of the most popular paintings in the mansion, a portrait of Mrs. Calvin Coolidge in a red dress that matched the red velvet lining in the surrounding showcases of chinaware. There were several new acquisitions in the room: an 1850 hand-woven English carpet and an 1800 English Regency chandelier, as well as new additions to the White House china collection—a French porcelain cup and saucer owned by Presidents James Monroe and James Madison, two compotes from the White House service of Franklin Pierce, and other dishes from the dining rooms of Madison, Monroe, Jackson, and Polk.

The next two downstairs rooms refurbished by Mrs.

Nixon were the Diplomatic Reception Room, with a pair of rare Sheraton 1795 mahogany cane settees and an English Regency chandelier of 1810, and the Vermeil Room, with new draperies, an 1860 Hereke rug from Turkey, a rare American drum table, and andirons made in Philadelphia between 1750 and 1770. The Red Room, redone in American Empire style instead of Jackie Kennedy's pale cerise and gold, was unveiled on November 8, 1971, with five important new pieces of furniture, including an invaluable secretary-bookcase made by the great New York cabinet designer Charles Honoré Lannuier between 1810 and 1815, and a pair of rosewood card tables made in Boston around 1815.

Perhaps the biggest hit in Mrs. Nixon's newly decorated White House was the Green Room, with its collection of Duncan Phyfe 1800–1815 American Sheraton furniture, including two rare and unusual work tables and an armchair inscribed by Phyfe's upholsterer. Berry B. Tracy, curator of the American Wing at the Metropolitan Museum of Art in New York, called the Green Room the finest example of a federal period furnished room in America.

The Blue Room was repainted back from Jackie Kennedy's white to its traditional blue by Mrs. Nixon and refurnished in James Madison's French Empire style with wallpaper modeled after 1800-style French Directoire wallpaper and a mantel of early-nineteenth-century carrara marble. An outstanding piece of furniture in the Blue Room was a *bergère*, an armchair made to order for President Madison in France in 1817 and used by him in the same room during his presidency. Two of the greatest American portrait paintings were hanging in the Blue Room when its renovation was complete in the spring of 1971—Rembrandt Peale's life portrait of Thomas Jefferson and Gilbert Stuart's portrait of James Madison.

Mrs. Nixon searched far and wide for an outstanding portrait of John Adams, the first President who lived in the White House. She found one, painted from a life study by Trumbull, in Harvard University's Fogg Museum, and arranged to have it loaned to the White

House. The hanging of the Adams portrait in the executive mansion gave the First Lady one of her proudest moments. She also acquired several highly valuable American landscape and cityscape paintings, such as Ferdinand Richardt's "Philadelphia in 1858"; Jaspar Cropsey's "Under the Palisades in October," a handsome 1895 picture of the rocky cliffs along the Hudson River; Richardt's 1858 "View on the Mississippi 57 Miles below Saint Anthony's Falls, Minneapolis"; George Inness's 1869 "The Rainbow in the Berkshire Hills"; and George Henry Durrie's 1858 "Farmyard in Winter."

Critics and art dealers were astonished by the high and discerning quality of Mrs. Nixon's tastes and wondered how such a quiet-mannered and not particularly stylish woman from a country background could have selected the faultless collection. "The sheer quality of the acquisitions and the volume of them has never been equaled," Clement Conger said at that time. "When the Nixons moved into the White House, about one-third of the furnishings were authentic originals. Two-thirds were reproductions, most of them cheap reproductions. Mrs. Nixon has turned that around. Now 65 or 70 percent of the furniture and furnishings are original American antiques. We have built up a much greater and much more valuable national collection of White House furnishings than Mrs. Kennedy ever did, but she deservedly gets credit for starting it."

The amount of interior redecorating and acquisitions of furnishings during Mrs. Nixon's five and a half years in the White House is astonishing. While she was First Lady, the mansion acquired 65 highly valuable paintings, 156 pieces of original-designed furniture, 19 chandeliers, and 22 rugs. Fourteen rooms were redecorated and largely refurnished, including not only the downstairs state rooms but also the President's Oval Office, the Cabinet Room, the Roosevelt Room in the West Wing, and the Yellow Oval Room and the President's bedroom on the second floor of the mansion.

The upstairs living quarters of the First Family were

opened to groups of visitors more often than in previous administrations. And Mrs. Nixon made a special effort to make the morning tours of the downstairs rooms and halls more interesting for sightseers. To relieve the boredom of people waiting in line along the South Lawn fence before entering the White House, she installed loudspeakers that gave them recorded talks on what they were about to see in "the only place in the world where an elected head of state opens his official home to visitors."

Along the first-floor hallways, she arranged displays of state gifts to the President from foreign governments. In the East Room, during the morning visiting hours, she placed exhibits of special historical items that had been kept upstairs during previous administrations. She also ordered the White House guards to keep their gun belts and pistol holsters carefully hidden from view under their blazer jackets. One day she happened to hear a guard giving a short and inadequate answer to a visitor's question about a painting in the Green Room. She then arranged to send a group of the guards to Winterthur, the du Pont residential museum in Delaware, to learn "how things are done in a real museum."

JACKIE'S VISIT

During the winter of 1971, when her renovation of the White House was still mostly in the planning stage, Mrs. Nixon made arrangements for a public unveiling of Aaron Shikler's portraits of President John F. Kennedy and Jacqueline Kennedy Onassis, which were to be added to the collection of paintings of past Presidents and First Ladies in the executive mansion. Pat decided to invite Mrs. Onassis and her two children, Caroline and John, for a private look at the paintings on the day before the public unveiling ceremony. Jackie had never returned to the White House, not even for a brief visit, since she and her children moved out two weeks after her husband's death. Mrs. Johnson had invited her to attend the dedication of the Jacqueline Kennedy Garden on the White House grounds a few months later, but Jackie had politely declined.

Somewhat to Pat Nixon's surprise, Jackie Onassis warmly accepted—on one firm condition. There was to be absolutely no publicity or advance notice to the press before she and her children came to Washington. Mrs. Nixon, no publicity lover herself, immediately agreed.

An Air Force jet picked up Jackie and her children in New York and flew them to the capital, where a presidential limousine drove them to a back door of the White House late in the afternoon of February 3. Helen Smith, Mrs. Nixon's press secretary, had been told nothing about Mrs. Onassis's visit. She received a phone call about it from Helen Thomas, the alert UPI correspondent, who seldom missed anything newsworthy that was happening at the White House. After checking the tip with Mrs. Nixon, who was somewhat annoyed, Mrs. Smith called Mrs. Thomas back, promising to give her the details later if Mrs. Thomas agreed to hold the story until after Jackie and her children had left and returned to New York.

Mrs. Onassis and the Kennedy children looked at the Shikler portraits in the lower round hall of the mansion and then had a roast tenderloin of beef dinner with the President and Mrs. Nixon and Tricia and Julie in the upstairs family dining room. After dinner, Caroline and John were escorted by the Nixon daughters on a tour of the living quarters and a visit to the Oval Office, where John remembered hiding under his father's desk when he was a two-year-old youngster.

Mrs. Nixon took Jackie for a tour of the downstairs state rooms, describing her plans for redecorating, which Jackie warmly approved. "I think it looks lovely," Mrs. Onassis said later about the Nixon White House. "I never intended Boudin's work to remain in the White House forever. Every family that lives there should put its own imprint there." Later, Jackie wrote a thank-you note to Pat Nixon, calling the evening "a moving experience."

"After Jackie left, about nine-thirty that night, Mrs.

Nixon called me and gave me the details about the dinner and what they did later," Helen Smith told me. "I gave it to Helen Thomas and gave her an hour to break the story before I gave it to the other reporters, who hadn't known a thing about Jackie's visit."

13

. . . And a New First Lady

Early in 1972, the year of President Nixon's landslide reelection, when his popularity was at its all-time high, newspapers all over the United States were running headlined feature articles about the emergence of "a new Pat Nixon."

"Until recently Richard Nixon was the star, Pat Nixon the star's wife," Marlene Cimons wrote in the Los Angeles *Times*. "But something has happened. Pat Nixon has clearly begun to emerge in her own right. The Pat Nixon who would never discuss controversial issues has had something to say about abortion and women's rights. She has lobbied for a woman on the Supreme Court. The Pat Nixon who said she would never wear pants in public—her husband disapproved of them—is casually modelling pants in the current issue of a national magazine. In a recent television interview, she wore a pants suit. Clearly there has been a major change in the First Lady."

Speaking out in favor of women's rights and abortion, or wearing pants, hardly seem startling today, but for Pat Nixon in 1972 these were bold departures indeed, even if her comments on those then controversial issues were actually rather mild. President Nixon had said earlier that abortion was "an unacceptable method of population control." Now, the "new" Pat Nixon said, "I think abortion should be a personal decision." A few years earlier she had belittled the women's liberation movement, defending the glories of motherhood and claiming that woman's place was in the home. Now, as First Lady, she said, "I would campaign for women candidates, even if they were not Republicans. I've always believed in supporting the person, not the party." Even if they were not Republicans? Supporting the person, not the party? This was a new Pat Nixon indeed.

Helen Smith said at that time, "I think she's gained much more self-confidence than she's ever had."

The warmth, vivacity, and good humor she had bottled up all during Nixon's political climb began to emerge publicly in the late 1960s. And the country got a good look at all these qualities on national television at the Republican Convention in Miami in 1972. Nobody had expected to see the controlled, almost glacial Pat Nixon do a little frug in the hall to the thumping of a rock band, to laugh aloud, toss quips, and look very much like she was having a grand old time. Which she was. Earlier, she had waded into a throng of three thousand at the airport, shaking hands, hugging and kissing people, calling them "kiddo." She acted at ease and, for the first time in all those long years when fear of damaging Nixon had haunted her, she *was* at ease.

In October, 1972, she broke even newer ground: she undertook her first solo campaign tour, a 5,500-mile swing through seven Midwestern and Western states. "I'm taking the White House to the people," she announced, and headed for Chicago. There, on a hot Indian summer's day, she walked through the noon throngs on Michigan Boulevard, shaking hands, chatting amiably with all comers, jiggling a little to a rock version of "Hail to the Chief" blared from a Nixon campaign headquarters. Upstairs, in the seventh-floor offices, she was in a wonderfully happy mood. She sat next to a volunteer who was calling prospective voters, listened a while, then took the phone, identified herself to the astonished woman on the line, and asked for her support. When a test pilot at a National

Aeronautics and Space Administration research center in California took her for a spin in a flight simulator, she yelled after a few minutes: "Hey, I'm getting seasick!" But she was dauntless where it counted. In Billings, Montana, she spoke into a howling forty-mile wind at the airport, when even the Indians, accustomed to the cold, were chilled to the bone. In Riverside, California, an orange sun beat down on her head as, with the mercury soaring to 102, she dedicated a new wing of a community center. In Yellowstone's National Park, she sat for an hour at a ceremony honoring the park's second century as sleet and rain stung her face and numbed her gloveless hands. Her spirits never dimmed.

She had gained enough confidence to speak her mind about amnesty for Vietnam War draft dodgers and deserters. "I think that those who ran should not be accepted back at the moment," she said in 1972. "I do feel that if they decided to serve, maybe in a volunteer capacity or something like that, and earn their way back into the country, that would be another thing."

She agreed with her daughter Julie, who had raised something of a ruckus when she announced that she would be willing to die for South Vietnam. "I would be willing to die to save freedom for 17 million people who are now having aggression against them with the idea of taking away their freedom and their country," she said.

In Riverside, California, she dedicated a cornerstone to the memory of Hannah Nixon and stated: "Under the Nixon administration, the senior citizen is not forgotten. Instead, he is the remembered one. So far, there have been improvements in every segment. Under the Older Americans Act, federal funding has increased eightfold."

None of these utterances was especially bold and, as she made them, there were clear traces of the old timidity in her demeanor: she chose her words with great care and seemed anxious to cut her questioners' time short. But her behavior did represent a breakthrough at last. The Pat Nixon who still kept insisting that "I never talk politics," was doing precisely that.

Mrs. Nixon's first public appearance tours as a First Lady, planned to encourage various volunteer work projects, had taken her to the West Coast and later on an extensive 4,130-mile journey throughout the country to college campuses—not a comfortable place for a President's wife to be during those days of bitter student protests against the Vietnam War. Though obviously uneasy, she handled herself in delicate situations with tact. At one stop in Cincinnati, she talked with students who had just wildly applauded an anti-war speech by William Kunstler, the fiery attorney for the Chicago Seven protesters. Reporters noted that the students praised Mrs. Nixon almost as warmly as they had praised Kunstler. One of them, with a bushy beard and a peace button, gave her a big kiss. "She reminds me of my mother," he said. Mrs. Nixon laughed and said, "His beard tickled." Another student said after talking with her: "She wanted to listen. I felt like this is a woman who really cares about what we are doing. I was surprised. I didn't expect her to be like that."

During her first year as First Lady, Pat accompanied her husband on a tour around the world, visiting wounded and ill American soldiers in hospitals in Vietnam, waving to crowds in humid heat in Indonesia, surviving a monsoon in Thailand, and calmly keeping her cool while visiting hospitals, schools, and orphanages in 100-degree weather in India and Pakistan. But her first really exciting and rewarding goodwill mission on her own was a quickly arranged flight to Peru after that country had been hit by a catastrophic earthquake in the spring of 1970.

Mrs. Nixon took with her two planeloads of supplies and medical equipment and $30,000 in hurriedly collected private donations, including "a little check from Dick," and promises of continuing American aid until "everything is rosy once again." Peru, of course, was one of the South American countries where Pat and

Vice President Nixon had been booed and spat upon by hostile crowds in 1958, but on this mission of mercy to the disaster scene in the Huaylas Valley, she was cheered everywhere.

She stopped often to hug small children and to listen to tragic stories. To one homeless woman, she said emotionally, "You are going to have good times again." Diplomatic relations between the United States and Peru had been strained recently, and most Peruvians felt that the Americans had been slow in coming to their aid after the earthquake. Pat Nixon's warm visit seemed to relax that tension. One high-ranking Peruvian official said at the time, "Her coming here meant more than anything else President Nixon could have done. It meant more than if he had sent the entire American Air Force."

La Prensa, the Lima newspaper, warmly praised Mrs. Nixon in an editorial:

> Leaving the relaxation of a weekend with her husband and children, Mrs. Nixon undertook a long and tiring journey Sunday, continuing the following day to the official requiem mass at the Cathedral of Lima in honor of the earthquake victims, and afterwards traveling to the Callejon to see the destruction at the scene of the indescribable catastrophe. Certainly an act like Mrs. Nixon's is not common in an age in which the rules of international protocol are limited to formal and conventional response such as a telegram, as befits the high station of a First Lady of a nation. In her human warmth and identification with the suffering of the Peruvian people, she has gone beyond the norms of international courtesy and has endured fatigue in an example of solidarity and self-denial.

Pat Nixon's eight-day, 10,000-mile trip to Liberia, Ghana, and the Ivory Coast early in January of 1972 was the first visit of an American First Lady to those West African countries, but the widely traveled Mrs. Nixon had been there before, in 1957 on a state visit with her husband, then Vice President, celebrating the new independence of Ghana. William R. Tolbert, the new president of Liberia whose inauguration she attended, was a Baptist minister and an old friend of Billy Graham, who was traveling in Mrs. Nixon's party along with Bernard Lasker, a former chairman of the New York Stock Exchange's board of governors, and Mrs. John H. Johnson, wife of the Chicago publisher of *Ebony* magazine. Liberia, of course, has close ties with the United States because that republic was established in 1822 by freed black slaves from America.

When Mrs. Nixon arrived at the airport in Liberia, she was given a 19-gun salute. Marching in time to the blaring music of a military band, she reviewed the ranks of honor guards. Then she rode beside President Tolbert in an open car along the forty-mile road to the capital city of Monrovia, cheered by crowds of people in every village. She saw a big change in Liberia since her last visit fifteen years earlier. Then the road from the airport was a narrow dirt trail; now it was a paved highway and Monrovia was dotted with highrise buildings. In the 100-degree heat at the outdoor inaugural ceremonies, Pat seemed cool and comfortable in her red, white, and blue gown as she listened to the new president praising her presence as "testimony of the strength, solidarity, and permanence of this special relationship between our countries."

The next day she watched native dancers performing and enjoyed a ceremony in which she was dressed in a bright blue lappa African suit by two women, who also crowned her with a tall blue head tie. At the inaugural, she was the guest of honor and was awarded Liberia's highest decoration, the Grand Cordon in the Venerable Order of the Knighthood of Pioneers of African Redemption.

Mrs. Nixon's next stop was Ghana, where she was greeted by an elderly tribal chief, Nana Osae Djan II, who had welcomed her on her previous visit to that nation fifteen years earlier. Pat and the chief sat together at his home in Aburi while princesses in his tribe presented her with a garland of kente cloth and a basket of fruit. One of the Ghanaian chiefs delivered a speech declaring that Mrs. Nixon was cementing a friendship between the United States and his country that "not even a lion could destroy."

Later she was entertained in Accra at his hilltop mansion by the president of Ghana, Edward Akufo-Addo, and interviewed by the press. Pat said that her husband's chances of being re-elected seemed "very good." One reporter asked if she would do any political campaigning for him. "I thought that's what I've been doing," Pat said, getting a big laugh. There were more ceremonies at the Ivory Coast's capital city, Abidjan, where she was greeted by a crowd of a quarter of a million people. She visited a school for homemaking and was the guest of honor at a lavish banquet in President Félix Houphouët-Boigny's palace, where the French-speaking mobs outside shouted, *"Vive Madame Neexon!"*

Pat Nixon's goodwill trip to Africa was highly praised in newspaper editorials all over the United States, in major cities and in Middle America. "Mrs. Nixon's week-long tour of West African nations was a triumph from beginning to end," the *Seattle Post-Intelligencer* said. "The great crowds which turned out to see her were obviously delighted by the gracious visitor from America who joined in their dances, donned their costumes, and knelt to examine the artwork of their children." And in Sioux Falls, South Dakota, the *Argus-Leader* declared: "Other First Ladies of the land have performed in undertakings of this kind but none has done as well as Mrs. Nixon. She isn't too sleek or too chic. She is demure, but not so much so that her personality is erased. She is well-dressed, but not overdressed. She has an inviting smile and heart-warming humility. She deserves a top honor as the nation's best First Lady in a long period of years."

A month later Pat Nixon scored her most impressive diplomatic triumph when she accompanied her husband on a visit to China—the first American First Lady ever to tour that country.

It was reported before that trip that the Chinese government had not been too eager to entertain a

President's wife. She was given long and detailed briefings on China and its government leaders by Henry Kissinger and his staff, learned some Chinese phrases, and "read everything I could get my hands on" about China. Pat took her hairdresser, Rita de Santis, from the Elizabeth Arden Salon in Washington, along with her and Miss de Santis also acted as Pat's secretary and wardrobe mistress. Of course somebody asked Mrs. Nixon if she could use chopsticks. "I'll do all right with them," she said. Both of the Nixons, Chinese food fans, had been using chopsticks for years.

As usually happened on such official visits to foreign countries, Pat saw many more Chinese people and much more of the sights than her husband was able to see between his long talks with the Red government leaders. She visited stores, schools, hospitals, museums, and communes. Reporters noted that she seemed to make a very favorable impression on Premier Chou En-lai and his wife, Teng Ying-chao. "She gave Chou a little girl curtsy when they met," one correspondent noted, "and from then on, he was ready to eat off Pat's chopsticks. The ailing Madame Chou, who normally does not make it past the salad course and seldom shows much affection, stayed up late one night to laugh and gesticulate with Pat and even hugged her when she left." Mrs. Nixon later told reporters that Chou "was a real charmer." She said the President had given the Prime Minister a gift of two oxen, and Chou in return had presented the Nixons with two giant pandas, which they planned to turn over to an American zoo.

After the Nixons' return from China, *Women's Wear Daily* published an assortment of comments from well-known people on Mrs. Nixon's performance as a good-will ambassador under a two-page headline, "Pat Nixon—Her Charms." Marion Javits, wife of New York's liberal Republican senator, was quoted as saying, "Pat Nixon has a new grown capacity and assurance. Just the way she stands next to the President is much more individual. Something very special has happened to her as an individual." Happy Rockefeller said, "She did a magnificent job. She's made a great contribution for all of us,'' and Alice Roosevelt Longworth declared, ''I don't think anyone could have done it better.'' Mel Elfin, chief of *Newsweek*'s Washington bureau, said, ''She was Pat Nixon, which means she was not Simone de Beauvoir, or not, on the other hand, Martha Raye. And maybe that's what they wanted in China. Ultimately, maybe it's better for us to have someone like that rather than a Jacqueline Kennedy.''

Late in May during that presidential election year of 1972, Pat Nixon made headlines seeing sights in Moscow while her husband carried on summit talks with Soviet leaders. Accompanied by Mrs. Leonid I. Brezhnev, Mrs. Andrei A. Gromyko, and Mrs. Anatoly F. Dobrynin, wife of the Russian ambassador in Washington, Mrs. Nixon visited a secondary school and rode in a glittering subway train, one of Moscow's prides. Later she toured Moscow University, shopped in the world-famous GUM department store, visited the Bolshoi ballet school, and watched a circus performance.

Pat's sightseeing tour was a strange experience for the three wives of the Soviet officials who were with her; nobody in Moscow could remember Mrs. Brezhnev, Mrs. Gromyko, or Mrs. Dobrynin making appearances in public before. The ladies were surrounded on a visit to a first-grade reading class by a crowd of news reporters, photographers, and two television crews that far outnumbered the children in the classroom. One of the TV crews was making film to be used in President Nixon's re-election campaign. Pat complained on the subway tour later that she was so surrounded by newspeople that she was unable to talk with any of the passengers on the train. While the school children stared wide-eyed at the television cameras and the throngs of reporters, their teacher kept reassuring them, ''Don't be afraid. It's nothing terrible. It's nothing terrible.''

Pat exclaimed over drawings done by the children and hugged and kissed one little girl who recited a poem. She and Mrs. Brezhnev, who stuck with her bravely throughout the whole day, picked their way through a maze of microphones, tape recorders, and cameras to visit a physics class, a music recital, a home economics class, and a basketball practice. Mrs. Nixon presented the basketball squad with American basketballs. The squad members scrimmaged before her so nervously that they missed their first fourteen shots at the basket.

When a reporter asked Mrs. Nixon how women's fashions in Moscow compared with those that she had seen on her previous visit in 1959, she made the mistake of saying, "They're much the same." But she quickly added, "I mean they're very fashionable, as they were then." Her own brightly patterned and belted dresses sharply contrasted with the quiet colors worn by the Russian women. At the Moscow Circus performance, Pat managed to keep her poise when she was introduced to an acrobatic bear, who extended a paw for her handshake.

After their stay in Moscow, the Nixons visited Iran and Poland. In Warsaw, as in Moscow, Pat was annoyed to find herself continually surrounded by a cordon of police during outdoor public appearances. One day in a park, after attending a Chopin concert, she asked the policemen if she could shake hands with some of the people crowded around her. Her request was ignored. Pat then pushed one policeman aside and elbowed her way past two others, grasping, hugging, and kissing small children and a few women while the crowd roared its approval. "Hi, honey!" Pat called to the youngsters.

Pat Nixon made her last trip as a diplomat in March, 1974, while the White House was undergoing the trauma of Watergate. She traveled to South America, attending the inaugurations of new presidents in Venezuela and Brazil. Her visit to Caracas marked her first appearance in that capital city since she and her husband, as the Vice President, had been stoned and spat on by angry mobs there in 1958. She was greeted warmly this time, not only by the Venezuelan people, but by delegates from seventy-nine other nations attending the inaugural events, many of them friends from the seventy-five other foreign countries that she had visited in her travels since her husband first became Vice President in 1953. Along with her official duties at the inaugural festivities in Venezuela and Brazil, she visited art museums, schools, day care centers for children, and watched folk dancing exhibitions and seemed to enjoy herself immensely at every stop.

This 9,195-mile journey—her third solo excursion as First Lady—brought Pat Nixon's foreign travels since she had moved into the White House up to more than 108,000 miles, including 27,860 by herself and 80,610 with the President.

Her journeys around the world and the nation, together with her exposure to the game of politics for so long, developed in Pat Nixon some shrewd judgments. As one close friend put it: "She didn't like it, never would, but she had gotten the feel, the instinct if you will, that all political people need to possess if they want to survive."

The irony is twofold: she was not asked to contribute her judgments, nor did she volunteer them because she acted on the principle that Richard Nixon knew best. And, when she did finally take her husband aside and offer him some wise counsel, her advice went unheeded and the house came crashing down around his head.

14

Watergate

"DESTROY THE TAPES"

Until July of 1973, nobody knew but the President, a handful of his chief aides, and four or five men in the Secret Service who handled the equipment. Pat was just as amazed as anyone else when Alexander P. Butterfield dropped his bombshell soon after the Senate Watergate Committee reconvened for its afternoon session on Monday, July 16, in the ornate Caucus Room of the Senate Office Building.

Butterfield was then head of the Federal Aviation Administration, but for several years he had served as assistant chief of the White House staff under Bob Haldeman, with an office right next to the President's. In February, 1971, he had been given instructions which he carried out in his customary brisk, efficient manner. He began the job of supervising the placement of listening devices, which included microphones secreted in lighting fixtures and desks, so that everything spoken in the President's offices would be recorded on a series of Sony 800B tape recorders which were placed inside closets. To guard the secret, the installation was done in the White House and at the EOB after the staff had gone for the day.

Afterward, Rose Mary Woods, Nixon's fiercely loyal

secretary who had worked for him since 1951, telephoned Butterfield and told him: "You dirty bastard. You have contributed to the downfall of the greatest President this country ever had. You are on the other side."

At the time, Pat Nixon foresaw no such cataclysm. But she did tell her friends—emphatically—that whatever information was on the tapes had never been intended for public disclosure. "If they had been *my* tapes," she told Helene Drown in the upstairs quarters of the White House, "I would have burned or destroyed them because they were like a private diary, not public property."

As the controversy over the tapes mounted in intensity, Pat did something virtually unprecedented for her—she offered the President some political advice. She urged him to get rid of the reels.

She had no inside information about their contents. She had no reason to suspect that her husband had incriminated himself in any way and that the tapes would reveal damaging evidence. She was to learn what was on the tapes only as the conversations were disclosed piecemeal, first voluntarily by the President in an abridged version, finally in their entirety under direct order of the United States Supreme Court.

In her lovely apartment on Eaton Place in London, diagonally across the street from the mansion where the immensely popular *Upstairs, Downstairs* television series was filmed, Helen McCain Smith, Pat's former press secretary, recalled for me in detail what actually happened upstairs in the White House during those months when the nation went through one of its worst traumas.

Mrs. Smith, an attractive brunette, took over as Pat Nixon's press secretary in 1969 and was a confidante of the family. Her reliability and credibility are unassailable. Helen Thomas said of her: "People trust Helen, which is more than you can say for other press secretaries around here."

When I interviewed her, she had gone back to England to serve as an information officer at the

American Embassy in Grosvenor Square in London. My wife and I had spent a delightful evening with Mrs. Smith and her mother at dinner near Eaton Place, then returned to their apartment to talk about the Nixons and especially the woman to whom she has remained devoted.

"Mrs. Nixon believed that the whole idea of the tapes was ridiculous," she said. "They simply never should have been done, and as time passed and the crisis grew, she became more and more certain of this. Over and over, she would say as the arguments grew shriller: 'How foolish to have made them.' She had shrewd political sense and lots of savvy.

"Very early, before they had become the subject of litigation, she urged him to destroy them.

"But he did not listen to her."

Nixon has explained that he refused to destroy the tapes because he never believed their contents would ever become public knowledge, and that, had he done so, it would have been "an open admission of guilt." Political observers believe, however, that he could have weathered the storm of disapproval that would have followed. And Nixon himself admitted to David Frost during their television interviews in September of 1977 that had he known then what he knows now, he "sure as the dickens would have destroyed them."

Mrs. Smith disclosed that in the years preceding the Watergate crisis, a silent but bitter feud was raging between the East and West Wings. The East Wing was the so-called women's department where the First Lady's staff was stationed, and the West Wing contained the offices of the President's aides.

It was a White House battle of the sexes, with H. R. Haldeman heading the male side and Pat Nixon's entire crops of assistants opposing him. The feud was never brought to public attention, and the President himself apparently did not know it existed.

Haldeman, Mrs. Smith told me, and some of his aides believed that Pat was a political liability to Nixon and that her public visibility should be sharply downplayed.

"And so over in the West Wing," she said, "they

were always pushing, pushing, pushing the President to keep her away from the public, to dump her, advising him not to take her on trips because he would do better on his own.

"I couldn't believe that Haldeman could be that stupid. He simply did not realize her potential and her very significant assets. Our feeling in the East Wing was that Pat and Dick had always been a team all through their political lives, a successful team. She had won great affection wherever she went.

"Haldeman had the last word in presidential planning. It was he who passed upon the itinerary and the personnel who would be along. Many times we would receive staff memos from Haldeman informing us that the President was about to go somewhere, and we would see that the First Lady was not included.

"It's important to understand that, while the memos came down from the President's office, the staff system—not unique in this administration by the way—was such that the President himself would not see the memos. And so he never knew what was being planned.

"Perhaps there were times when Haldeman would simply forget to include her but at other times I feel it was quite deliberate.

When the memos arrived without Pat's name on the list of travelers, the East Wingers would be outraged. "It was an uphill battle all the way to get her added," says Mrs. Smith.

Early in Nixon's presidency, Haldeman and Ehrlichman did not want an independent East Wing. Mrs. Nixon's first press spokesman was Gerry Van der Heuvel, a former newspaper columnist, who remained for a year before she was transferred to the press office in the Rome Embassy. Mrs. Van der Heuvel makes it clear why she was moved out. "I was replaced," she says, "because Ehrlichman and Haldeman wanted one of their own people in the job."

Her successor was Connie Stuart, whose husband, Charles, had worked for Ehrlichman as an advance man during the 1968 campaign. Mrs. Stuart, a tall redhead, had little press experience when she came to the job, having worked in the public relations department of the phone company in New York. She remained until 1971, when Helen Smith took over.

Pat Nixon's staff believed that the opposition to the First Lady was compounded of one part ignorance of her true value, one part jealousy, and one part male chauvinism. ("You wouldn't believe the sexist attitude some of those guys had," one former staff member says. "And Haldeman was the worst of the lot.")

Pat Nixon was aware of the West Wingers' antagonism. Although her staff tried to shield her as much as possible, jokes about her reached her ears. (Just one: "When she goes on trips she takes along her hairdresser—and her embalmer.") But she was not about to be put down by Haldeman or anyone else. When she wanted to go on a trip or felt she could be helpful, she would go to the President and tell him bluntly: "Dick, I want to go too." And she did.

The First Lady had no love for Haldeman, never sharing her husband's early high regard for him. She looked upon him as an opportunist and was concerned over his growing influence upon the President. She also clashed with Haldeman on a number of occasions and won.

When Haldeman commissioned the construction of a new Air Force One, the presidential plane, she examined the plans and discovered that little provision had been made for the privacy of the First Lady. Quietly, she ordered him to change them to include a private compartment just behind the President's. It was done.

Another time, the West Wingers ordered the construction, at considerable cost, of tiered seats for the 87-foot-long East Room, the largest and most famous in the mansion, which is used for public receptions. Pat was not consulted but she had the last word. She considered the seats unattractive and more appropriate for basketball at a high school gym than the White House, so she rarely allowed them to be used.

Once Haldeman gave approval to Johnny Cash, the famed Country and Western singer, to record a concert he gave at the White House and to market the recording. The disc was to be titled *Johnny Cash at the White House.* When Pat got wind of it, she put her foot down. It won't be permitted, she said, and it wasn't.

Pat Nixon had her first encounter with the Watergate problem in the fall of 1972, during the presidential campaign.

The great events had been set in motion on June 17 of that year by a bungled burglary that received scant attention: five men were seized on the sixth floor of one of the Watergate office buildings in Washington, apparently attempting to burglarize the Democratic National headquarters. Investigations were started, and the first faint rumbles began to be heard in Washington. There were reports that some persons important in the administration might be involved in the curious affair.

Pat was asked in Chicago: "Are you concerned that the investigation of the Watergate bugging incident will hurt your husband in the election?" Instantly, her face froze into the familiar mask. "No, I don't," she replied. Then, showing that she was studying the barometers carefully, she added: "The polls haven't indicated that. They know he has no part in it."

"When you and your husband discuss the election and the campaign," she was asked, "does the Watergate situation concern him?" She replied: "We don't discuss it."

Nor did they. As later events revealed, Nixon was carefully watching developments but was not talking them over with his wife and family.

A newsman insisted: "Does what you read in the papers concern you?" She answered firmly: "No, I think it has been blown all out of proportion." Someone threw her a hard one about Martha Mitchell, the late wife of then Attorney General John N. Mitchell, who had charged that security guards had overpowered her in a California hotel to prevent her from speaking out about Watergate, ripped her phone from the wall, beaten her, and held her down while a tranquilizer was injected into her buttocks. Pat said she didn't know what had happened in that room. Then someone asked her how she managed to stay so young and vibrant and she was on safer ground.

As Watergate began to escalate during the following year, her schedule remained as full as ever. The official White House calendar for October of 1973, probably the most turbulent month in the recent history of the presidency, listed sixteen events for her and she went through each with an easy grace.

Yet that was the month the beleaguered President was clinging to Watergate-related tapes and other communications that had been subpoenaed by the U. S. Court of Appeals, and then, in an electrifying switch, announced he would release them. It was the month of the "Saturday Night Massacre,"* the month when hundreds of thousands of letters, telephone calls, and wires flooded legislators' offices demanding her husband's ouster, when resolutions calling for his impeachment went one after the other into the hopper of the House, when the Senate Judiciary Committee announced it would hold public hearings on the "massacre," and when the House Judiciary Committee began scouring the nation's law schools for the most able person to head up its impeachment staff.

It was a disastrous time. Yet, the Sunday after that fateful Saturday night, Pat astounded visitors who arrived for the fall garden tour of the White House grounds. Many did not expect her to attend at all, and few would have expected her to appear smiling and gracious as she welcomed them, shook hands, made pleasant small talk, and presented awards in the Rose Garden to Washington school children who had done

*On Saturday, October 20, Nixon ordered his Attorney General, Elliot Richardson, to dismiss Archibald Cox from his post as special Watergate prosecutor. Cox had been calling for tapes that Nixon was refusing to turn over, citing executive privilege. Richardson refused and was fired. The President thereupon named William Ruckelshaus, the Deputy Attorney General, to Richardson's post and ordered the dismissal. Ruckelshaus would not accept the job, and he too was fired. Solicitor General Robert Bork was thereupon designated by the President as acting Attorney General and directed to relieve Cox of his job. Bork agreed and sent Cox a brief note. Later that night, press secretary Ron Ziegler announced the dismissals and said that, as of 8 P.M., "the office of the Watergate Special Prosecution Force has been abolished."

the most to beautify the capital. On Tuesday, October 23, when it was announced that the number of impeachment resolutions had risen to 24, she was again the smiling hostess at a reception for members of the American Association of Medical Assistants on the State floor of the White House.

There was worse to come. The next day, George Meany, president of the powerful AFL-CIO, issued a devastating statement that "the events of the last several days prove the dangerous emotional instability of the President." Pat, immaculately dressed and coiffed, went to the Map Room on the ground floor where whe knelt to hug tiny Michael Newsome, that year's muscular dystrophy poster child. She whispered to him and played with him as the photographer took their pictures.

And so it went for the rest of that tumultuous month, and the long months that followed.

She gave no sign at any of these events that she was bored, distracted, or troubled, through everyone who came close, even heads of state, was scrutinizing her face and watching her actions for evidence. The prime minister of a small African republic was heard to remark at a diplomatic reception: "How amazing. I could see his [Nixon's] hands were shaking and he looks gray. But she has such control."

The fact is that she did not hate their critics, as Nixon hated them; she was resigned. "They're out to get us, Clem," she told White House curator Conger one day after a particularly virulent press barrage. "They want us out of here. But it's all politics and it will go away." Conger saw no bitterness in her statement. Only once did she utter a remark that sounded bitter but was actually said in sadness. "It's right out of the *Merchant of Venice*," she told Helene Drown after an official function during which she was besieged by newspeople. "They're after their last pound of flesh."

Once, late in January, 1974, a swarm of reporters gathered around her while she greeted wives of members of the National Religious Broadcasters in the State Dining Room of the White House. They peppered her with questions about Nixon—was he sleeping badly, does he rise in the middle of the night to play the piano? Pat was angered at the tone of the questions. Clenching a fist and thrusting her arm upward, she told them: "The President is in great health and I love him dearly and I have great faith."

Then, as the women went through the receiving line, she gained control and, responding to their expressions of confidence, she told them to pray for the press. When the newsmen got wind of this, they asked her: "Does the press need prayers?"

"Who doesn't?" she answered. "We all do."

One newsman called out: "Is the press the cause of the President's problems?"

She headed for the White House elevator to the family quarters. Over her shoulder, she called back: "What problems?"

"The truth sustains me," she said when she was asked how she bore up so well in the crisis months.

She laughed merrily when somebody sent her a popular poster showing a kitten suspended from a curtain rod, with a caption reading: "Hang in there, baby." She took it to the President's bedroom, where it hung for a few days.

And it was she who, through the awful months, bucked up the sagging morale of her staff instead of the other way around. Young Terry Ivey, a pretty blond assistant press secretary, told me: "Whenever we spoke to her on the telephone on official business or went to see her, she was telling *us* to cheer up. "Keep your chin up,' she'd tell me many times. When I had to call her about a story in a newspaper that wasn't too complimentary, she gave it a light twist and, somehow, it made us all feel just a little bit better. Again and again, she'd tell me, 'We'll have better days.' She was truly fantastic."

Pat was "ebullient and confident," a close friend reported. And Julie said: "I don't know how she does it. She's an inspiration to the rest of us."

She could joke, too, about the worsening situation. Once, at a reception, she picked up a copy of a

Pennsylvania newspaper and glanced down at the headlines. "Well," she said, "I don't see Watergate on the front page. Something's wrong here!"

She wasn't missing a thing. Inside the White House, Pat followed all the Watergate developments with great care. When the President, after months of legal maneuvering, finally released edited transcripts of his taped conversations with John Dean, Haldeman, Ehrlichman, and others about the Watergate scandal, she read every word in the 1,254 pages. It took her close to twelve hours to get through them.

And yet, for all this, the first fissures were beginning to appear in the granite as the vise tightened. Outwardly, she was still bucking them all up, including the President himself, but the strains were starting to show.

Except for the functions in and out of the White House, she stopped going out alone or with friends. She would no longer browse and shop in the Washington stores, go "antiquing" with friends in Virginia, or lunch in public places. She went out to lunch only once in 1974, when Eleanor Howard, wife of Scripps-Howard executive Jack R. Howard, and a few other friends invited her to Sans Souci, one of the capital's best-known dining spots. Mrs. Howard told me she was astonished when Pat accepted. "We chatted about unimportant things," Mrs. Howard said. "Never once did she refer to the scandal and I, of course, never brought it up." Pat's lunch caused headlines. Observers felt she chose the Sans Souci, where leading Washington figures and newspeople lunch, to refute charges that she was becoming reclusive. "What in the world do they expect me to do," she complained to her friend Helene Drown, "go streaking along the Tidal Basin?"

But she never went out in public again, except for solitary midnight walks, when she would wrap a scarf around her head and stride down deserted Pennsylvania Avenue or in Rock Creek Park, followed, of course, by Secret Servicemen. Occasionally, Julie would join her on these walks.

WATERGATE

199

Sometimes, she and the President would visit Julie and David in Bethesda, once bringing along the dinner. It was Mexican food, Nixon's favorite, and they brought so much Julie froze half for another day.

Why was Pat so reclusive during these months? "She didn't want to face the press and all those torrents of questions," says Mrs. Smith. "It was one crisis after another. Everywhere she'd go, the press would follow. There would be long-range cameras picturing her every move and microphones stuck into her face. It was a difficult time for her."

When she had to face them and they asked their questions, she would turn cold and angry. She returned from Brasilia in mid-March after representing Nixon at the inaugurations of the Brazilian and Venezuelan presidents. It was her birthday and the newswomen who accompanied her decorated the plane with crepe-paper streamers and passed around champagne. One reporter wrote a little song in her honor. Pat, though running a slight fever, got into the spirit of things, sang along with the women, joked with them. She was having a good time until somebody asked a question about Watergate. Her face froze instantly. She gave her usual response, and the gay mood ended as though a light bulb had been switched off.

She was worried, too, about the tensions that she saw developing between her daughters and their husbands because of the growing scandal. Rumors began floating around the capital that the marriages of both couples were undergoing strains. Neighbors in Bethesda, where the young Eisenhowers lived, noticed that Julie and David no longer joined them in lawn volley ball games and shunned invitations to informal gatherings in the evening. David gave thought to transferring from the George Washington University Law School in the capital to the University of Chicago. His own emotions, he admitted, fluctuated between despondency and euphoria. He abandoned the idea of leaving town because it would have been interpreted as "running away."

Julie had turned to religion for inner peace. She sought spiritual counsel from Billy Graham, and early in 1974, she joined some other wives of senators and representatives at weekly Bible classes.

"It was difficult at home for both young couples," Mrs. Smith says. David, a law student, and Ed Cox, who was already a practicing lawyer, knew considerably more about the legal aspects of the situation than Julie and Tricia. The young wives, defensive about their father, argued emotionally, tending to ignore the realities; their young husbands, more logical, urged them to face and understand the facts, which were becoming increasingly ominous.

A rift developed between Julie and David. "It was bound to be," Mrs. Smith says. "They were both so very young and the conflicts, given their respective points of view, were inevitable." There were many arguments, too, between Ed and Tricia, though not so serious.

For her part, Pat Nixon was upset because David was talking too much to too many people.

Helen Smith: "She felt he was being too outspoken, giving too many interviews. Because David was readily accessible at the school, the press would catch him and ask their questions; and David would reply frankly. Too frankly, Mrs. Nixon thought. Many times, she felt he was speaking out of turn. She loved David and she loved Ed, and she preferred that neither one of them speak out at that delicate time because it was a difficult period for the family, and she didn't want them to get hurt and didn't want them involved in the whole controversy."

Weaker marriages might have dissolved. It is a tribute to the basic solidity of their unions that Watergate did not tear the young couples apart.

JULIE FOR THE DEFENSE

However, it was ultimately Julie—and not Pat—who did get involved, and very deeply, in defending the President.

In private, Pat Nixon was stone and iron, bucking him up in his depressed moods, telling him again and again that all would be well, and near the end urging him to reject capitulation. But she was never able to come to his support publicly.

As speculation grew that the cover-up of the Watergate burglary might reach as high as the Oval Office, television viewers and newspaper readers wondered why they were seeing and hearing Julie Eisenhower in spirited support of the President, and not his most logical first defender, his wife. Journalist Nora Ephron wrote at the time: "In the months since the Watergate hearings began, she [Julie] has become her father's . . . First Lady in practice if not in fact."

Julie's public defense of him began the day after he announced in a nationally televised speech on April 30, 1973, that his two "dedicated" aides, Haldeman and Ehrlichman—"two of the finest public servants it has been my privilege to know"—had resigned. She had gone down to Disney World near Orlando, Florida, the first member of the Nixon family to visit the park. After taking a boat trip through "jungle" waters where lifelike elephants and other denizens of the dense forests lived, she answered newspersons' questions, which were hardly directed at her reactions to the make-believe land she had just traversed, but dealt exclusively with her father's speech on the Watergate problem.

"I think that the GOP and the rest of the nation," she said, "will realize that this was just seven men who made a mistake, and others made a mistake by trying to cover it up. That speech last night was very heartfelt."

At the time, not much attention was paid to her remarks, but before the whole episode came to its disastrous end, Julie had given 138 interviews in all parts of the country. She appeared on television talk shows and held so many press conferences one would have thought she was campaigning for office.

She was not only accessible to the media but asked for some speaking engagements and TV appearances herself, knowing in advance that questions would be asked about Watergate. Moreover, as a member of the First

Family, she was highly visible. Her schedule of quasi-official functions, though not as heavy as her mother's, was heavy enough: often the White House scheduled as many as a half-dozen events for her each month.* She conducted garden tours for handicapped children, attended galas and jamborees, dedicated parks, education centers, and hospitals. At each of these, the event was overshadowed by the answers she gave to newspeople about Watergate and her father. Always she was charming, poised, attractive, and agile-minded. They loved her everywhere.

Julie even took her father's case to England. In the summer of 1973, she and David went to London where she appeared on BBC television and fielded question asked by British viewers. She was, as always, lucid in her replies, detailed and remarkably composed. And, as always, she never for a moment doubted her father's innocence. She counterattacked too, as she would continue to do for the next twelve months. One viewer asked if, looking back, she would have wished that Nixon had kept his promise to retire from politics in 1962 after his defeat for the California governorship. She answered: "I can't wish that when I've seen my father end the war in Vietnam."

In many of her appearances and special interviews, Julie took pains to stress that she was acting on her own, that the President had "never asked me to go out and take questions on Watergate."

But he never asked her to stop either, as authors Madeleine Edmondson and Alden Duer Cohen pointed out in *The Women of Watergate*. And *Time* magazine said in June, 1973: "She talks over with her father how to handle the thorniest questions."

Indeed, it does seem unlikely that the President was not giving her advice and support.

Item: On July 4, 1973, she had lunch with two wire service reporters at the San Clemente Inn, a mile from the estate, and made a sensational announcement

---

*In addition to her White House duties, Julie at the time had a $15,000-a-year job with the *Saturday Evening Post*, where she originated and edited articles, and was working on two books.

through them. The President, she disclosed, had considered resigning over Watergate but the family had talked him out of the idea.

Julie revealed that the President had summoned the family together at Camp David on May 4 and asked them all if they thought he should quit. "We said no," Julie said—and her statement made world headlines—"because resigning would be an admission of wrongdoing, and we also felt that he was the man for the job, and that he had started things and needed to finish them."

Item: On May 7, 1974, she stood with her husband David under a grape arbor in the East Garden and relayed to a throng of newspeople the President's determination to fight impeachment. There had been another family conference, this time aboard the presidential yacht, *Sequoia*, on the mounting moves to oust Nixon from office. He had made a decision, Julie announced. He was going to "take this constitutionally down to the wire." And she herself was out there answering questions because the media, she said, had been insistently asking how the family was reacting to the impeachment demands. "The media," she stated, "must be reassured from members of the family that my father is not going to resign." For forty minutes, as long as a presidential press conference, she stood there parrying questions as Nixon himself was inside the White House and Pat remained secluded.

The question is relevant: Was it Julie's idea to announce Nixon's intention to fight to the end, or did she believe her father was implicitly encouraging her to do so?

Was Nixon, in short, all along using the charm, youthful prettiness, and endearing devotion of his daughter to put his case before the American people and help still the rising clamor for his expulsion from office?

Possibly, there may have been more to Julie's headline-making role during the crises than she has suggested. I asked Helen Smith if she could shed some additional light.

Her statements to me, in a taped interview, were

revealing. The reader is reminded that Mrs. Smith is intensely loyal to the Nixon family and at the same time enjoys a lifelong reputation for thorough credibility.

"Television is the media of today," Mrs. Smith told me. "While Mrs. Nixon was very good one-to-one, she never, never, never was at home on television or speaking publicly. She felt that meeting people and being available and talking was her strength. Julie, being more the younger generation, was more accustomed to television and to public speaking, and this is why."

Q. "Was this a conscious decision on the part of the family?"

A. "Yes, it was. Julie was the one. Julie liked it."

Q. "A decision of the family?"

A. "Yes, I think it was, although mind you, I don't think either the President or Mrs. Nixon wanted Julie to take the brunt of it the way she did. But when it came to one person being the obvious one to do it [defend the President], it fell on Julie."

Q. "Did it fall automatically or did the family get together . . . ?"

A. "I think they obviously talked this over."

Q. "They talked it over?"

A. "Very definitely, yes. Tricia didn't want to do it. It was not Tricia's style and Julie had been doing a great deal of it anyway, and Julie was a very good public speaker, and Julie and David were more politically minded anyway. And somehow it became Julie's role. Julie herself wanted to do it."

To make the point absolutely certain, I asked the key question one more time:

"Was it a family decision?"

"It was a Nixon family decision," replied Mrs. Smith.

THE "DRINKING PROBLEM"

The statement about Pat Nixon that most arouses the fury of her close friends is the one buried in a paragraph of *The Final Days*, the best-selling book by Bob Woodward and Carl Bernstein. The "Woodstein team," as the young investigative reporters were known to capital journalists, played a major role in exposing the events surrounding the Watergate burglary and the subsequent cover-up. *The Final Days* is a graphic account of the events from the spring of 1973 to the President's resignation the following year.

These three sentences in the book made worldwide headlines: "She [Pat Nixon] was becoming more and more reclusive, and drinking heavily. On several occasions members of the household staff came upon her in the pantry of the second-floor kitchen, where the liquor was kept, in the early afternoon. Awkwardly, she had tried to hide her tumbler of bourbon on the rocks." The authors give no documentation but state in a foreword that each fact in their book was confirmed by at least two sources. Woodward and Bernstein place the drinking episodes in April, 1974, following Pat Nixon's return from her South American journey.

Nixon himself was enraged. Though not mentioning the authors by name, he told David Frost: "All I say is Mrs. Nixon read it and her stroke came three days later. I didn't want her to read it because I knew the kind of trash it was and the kind of trash they are. . . . This doesn't indicate that that caused the stroke, because the doctors don't know what caused the stroke, but it sure didn't help." He added: "I will never forgive them. Never." Pat watched him on a TV set in her bedroom as he said it.

How true was the allegation that Pat had taken to heavy drinking in the last hard months? Did she drink at all, and if so, when and how much? Here are the facts—documented:

To begin with, Pat was certainly no teetotaler. During the vice presidency years, when she would go antiquing in Virginia with friends, the lunch they packed would include Bloody Marys in a flask, Rita Mazo told me. Pat drank her share.

At the end of a grueling campaigning day, she would, on occasion, relax with a drink, though never in the presence of Haldeman, who disapproved of liquor and cigarettes. Author Theodore H. White tells an amusing story about that: Pat and her husband were staying at the estate of a governor in the East during a rigorous campaign schedule. Haldeman and other staff members were present too. During the evening, Pat took the wife of the governor aside and asked her if they could adjourn to another room. They did and Pat requested a dry martini, then another. "You know," she confided to the governor's wife, "I don't dare ask for a drink when Bob Haldeman is around."

Helen Smith adds: "You'd rarely see her take a drink at a party but upstairs, after she had shaken a few thousand hands, she would put her feet up and say, 'Wow!', and she would then have a highball.

"I remember the time we were in Florida during the 1972 campaign," Mrs. Smith says. "We were flying from one stop to another. A young woman reporter from the Los Angeles Times was with us. It was the first time she had flown with the First Lady. She saw her drinking something and asked me what it was. I told her it was a highball but said, 'For goodness' sake, don't say anything about her having one because it will simply stop her from being able to relax in front of the press.'

"Her editor, unfortunately, insisted that it go into her story and from then on, Mrs. Nixon never did it on the plane, even by herself. She had tremendous control. She never even smoked in public, ever, yet when she went upstairs after a long reception she would have a cigarette."

She had no taste for the liquor served to her in China, Julie says. During her visit she was faced with the problem of handling the frequent toasts made with the superpotent 120-proof brew. Julie says her mother did a masterful faking job, lifting the glass to her lips but never swallowing any.

But had she become a heavy drinker in those last hard months? I spoke to four women who were with Pat Nixon during much, if not most, of those days in the White House. Here are their reports:

Terry Ivey, her assistant press secretary, who is now

out of government and embarked on a wholly new career:

"I saw her sipping a drink at public functions where liquor was served—what's wrong with that?—but I never saw her high, at the parties or after. I never smelled liquor on her breath and I was close to her, literally. Lucy Winchester was even closer and she never did either."

Mrs. Winchester, an attractive, youthful divorcée, was for six years social secretary for the White House. It was her job to arrange for the state dinners, receptions, and other social functions; in that capacity, she worked closely with the First Lady. Nixon once said of her: "She runs the White House—and I mean the whole White House." After the Nixons left, Mrs. Winchester stayed on with the Fords for a short while, then left Washington for her native Kentucky, where she raises crops and livestock on a large farm in Woodford County, near Lexington. "I'm back to farming, where I came from," she told me. About Pat Nixon she said:

"The statement that she had been drinking heavily is a lie.

"I was with her from the time she arose in the morning, and often before. There was no sign whatever that she had been drinking. She was bright, cheerful, and ready to start the day.

"The assertion makes no sense. She was always punctual for her engagements and she remained at each event scheduled from the start to the end. If she had been drinking, she could not have done it. The statement is too ludicrous to be taken with any degree of seriousness."

Helene Drown: "I've traveled with her on campaign trips and when I would be so tired I couldn't hold my head up, she would still be fresh and strong and looking great. I would look like hell, and she would look as though she hadn't done a thing, even though the days had been terribly grueling. She never needed anything to buck her up. I've never even seen her take an aspirin.

"I was at the White House for ten days with Pat Nixon and left on Friday, August 2. [The President made his televised resignation speech the following Thursday night.] I was with Pat day and night and I know what is truth and what is fiction. The story that she sneaked down to get liquor is totally untrue.

"If Mrs. Nixon had been a lush, how could she possibly have appeared at all those White House receptions and other affairs and been able to maintain her poise and equilibrium hour after hour after hour? If she were drunk or drinking heavily, how in hell could she have managed to have gotten herself together to leave the White House as quickly as she did, giving orders on packing, supervising all the details. Remember, it was a sudden, mass exodus from the White House. [Nixon decided to resign on Wednesday, August 7. By eleven that Friday morning he and Pat had left the mansion.] All those clothes, all that packing, all those cartons—how could she have done it?"

Helen Smith: "I would see her in the morning, about eight-thirty or nine, looking immaculate. If someone is drinking heavily, he or she cannot do this. You're going to see signs. You're going to see baggy and bleary eyes, shaky hands, or slurred talk. There was never anything of the kind.

"Because of the crisis, she was not eating well and I was concerned about this and its possible effect on her health.

"But Pat Nixon never needed an alcohol crutch."

THEY DIDN'T KNOW

Up to ten days before Nixon resigned, Pat was convinced he would ride out the storm.

All through June and July, she was meeting with Lucy Winchester and Helen Smith, setting up the fall calendar of social events. She was planning a White House Christmas—the parties that would be held, who would be asked, what would be served. She was even blocking out a program of events for the following spring.

And more: She had been actively involved in plans to

choose a new set of china for the executive mansion, service for 250 persons which would bear the presidential seal and be called "Nixon china."

It was no small matter. Many Presidents have had their own chinaware named for them and used at official functions. Samples of these historic sets are on permanent display in the China Room on the ground floor next door to the Diplomatic Reception Room. The collection, in glassed cabinets on velvet-lined cases, includes the priceless French Sèvres china brought to the White House by Abigail Adams, the mansion's first mistress, and the lovely Castleton service with its wide gold bands ordered by the Eisenhowers. The Trumans had a gold-bordered Lenox service; the Theodore Roosevelt set was English Wedgwood; Ulysses S. Grant's was Haviland with a small seal in the border.*

Presidential china, preserved for history in the mansion, was a distinction that Pat very much wanted for her husband. But there was the question of money. Since Congress does not appropriate funds for White House acquisitions, the cash for these expensive sets has to be raised privately.

Clem Conger, the White House curator, told me that Mrs. Nixon had met with representatives of the Lenox China Company of Trenton, New Jersey, and a committee on selections. "They got so far along," Mr. Conger said, "as to narrow it down to something like theWoodrow Wilson service, a very beautiful white one banded in gold and with the presidential seal in the cobalt blue of the plates. The Lenox Company was to take 30 days to come up with a design for Mrs. Nixon's approval."

Pat Nixon saw no reason to halt the negotiations until

---

*When the Kennedys occupied the White House, Mrs. Kennedy felt the Eisenhower china was adequate but there was insufficient glassware. So she ordered six dozen each of water goblets, wine and champagne glasses from the Morgantown Glassware Guild, Inc., of West Virginia. They cost only six dollars a dozen, one of the few times Mrs. Kennedy made an inexpensive purchase anywhere. She ordered them because she had been strongly affected by the poverty she had seen in the region and felt the use of West Virginia glassware in the White House would act as a symbol of Kennedy's interest in the area's potential for economic growth.

the last week in July, 1974. Then, on July 27, 29, and 30, the House Judiciary Committee voted three Articles of Impeachment against her husband for "high crimes and misdemeanors." After the final historic roll call in Room 2141 of the vast Rayburn Office Building, she called Clem Conger. "She told me that she didn't think that it was an appropriate time to raise money for the china," Conger said, "and to let the matter rest." Conger said Pat's voice quivered when she spoke.

Almost to the end, then, Pat Nixon believed he would not quit. Again and again, she said to correspondents who covered her: "I know the truth and the truth sustains me."

The question must be asked: Would she have been sustained if she had really known the truth?

It is a harsh question, yet is it possible that Nixon lied to his wife and to his family, as well as to the country, about the full scope of his involvement in the cover-up of the Watergate affair?

Was he telling them one version too while he concealed another? While Julie was running around the country defending him and Pat was talking to her friends about the truth coming out, the clinching truth was on a reel of tape that answered the crucial question: How much did Nixon know and when did he know it? It proved he knew a lot and knew it early: and he had tried to cover up what he had known. In his memoirs, *The Ends of Power*, Haldeman states that Nixon "was involved in the cover-up from Day One."

The now-famous June 23, 1972, conversation he had had in the Oval Office with Haldeman was the "smoking gun" that finally doomed his presidency. Nixon fought hard to keep that and sixty-three other tapes from ever coming to light. He took the case to the United States Supreme Court, citing national security reasons, but on July 24, 1974, the court decided by an 8 to 0 vote that he must turn them all over to the Watergate Special Prosecutor.

The transcripts were finally made public on August 5. The June 23 tape consisted of three talks with

Haldeman, the first beginning at 10:04 A.M. and ending at 11:09, the next from 1:04 P.M. to 1:13, and the last from 2:20 to 2:45. They revealed that, only six days after the burglary and wiretapping of the Democratic National Committee in June of 1972, Nixon was aware that his former Attorney General, John N. Mitchell, who was then head of the Committee to Re-elect the President, had been involved. He knew, too, that E. Howard Hunt and G. Gordon Liddy, subsequently jailed for their parts in the crime, were also involved, and that the FBI was investigating the break-in and was "not under control."

The bureau was beginning to trace the source of money that had been paid to the Watergate burglars by the Nixon re-election committee. This was dangerous stuff. Haldeman told the President that both Mitchell and John Dean, then the White House counsel, were suggesting that the CIA tell the FBI to "stay the hell out of this."

Nixon thereupon authorized the cover-up saying "right, fine" to Haldeman's query: "And you seem to think the thing to do is get them [the FBI] to stop?" A few minutes later, Nixon once again said: "All right, fine. I understand it all. We wouldn't second guess Mitchell and the rest."

That was what the whole bizarre and anguishing Watergate ordeal was all about—a President conspiring to obstruct justice. Little wonder that General Alexander M. Haig, Jr., Nixon's chief of staff, who read the transcripts of the June 23 tape for the first time on August 1, rushed to confer with then Vice President Gerald Ford and alert him to be ready to take over the White House. The June 23 tape, Haig told Ford, would be "devastating, even catastrophic" for Nixon.

In October, two months after Nixon had left the White House, I asked Julie: "Did your father tell you about that tape?"

"No," she answered, "he had not."

She insisted that "he hadn't listened to them before." She added: "The pressures of the presidency are so heavy and he had been so occupied with trying to run the country that he had forgotten about them, and I believe him.''

On Friday, August 2, only three days before he was forced to admit publicly that he had tried to thwart the FBI probe of the Watergate crime, Nixon finally told his family—reluctantly, David Eisenhower remembers. "It was something he didn't want to talk about with his family," young Eisenhower said. "We sort of imposed ourselves on him to get to know the situation. He made the transcripts available to us.''

That night, Nixon's family gathered in the Lincoln Sitting Room on the second floor of the mansion, next to the Lincoln Bedroom. Here, in the intimate little chamber with its French provincial decor, green and yellow wall hangings, and striped curtains of red Paisley design, Pat, Julie and David, and Tricia and Ed Cox learned about the June 23 tape.

This small room, with its mementos of the Lincoln years, had been used often by Nixon as a hideaway office where he would work on speeches, read his official papers, or just sit, staring into the fire burning in the gray-marbled fireplace. King, his Irish setter, would follow him and curl up on the couch, watching as Nixon sat in a brown leather chair. There would usually be a large box of dog biscuits for him on the President's table.

Most recently, Nixon had come here to listen day after day, hour after hour, to the tapes which the Special Prosecutor and the courts were demanding.

It was shortly before 7 P.M. Nixon had ordered dinner on a tray and eaten little of it; the family had dined without him. He came to the room and took his place in the brown chair and stared into the fire, lit as he had requested, though the day was hot, muggy, Washington-mid-summery. As usual, the air-conditioning was on, turned high. The family entered, took chairs silently, and waited for him to speak. Pat, hands in her lap, was on the red and green couch with its curved dark wood ends. Cox, coming in on the air shuttle from New York, would arrive shortly.

The President did not come directly to the point. He talked at length about the situation, his enemies, the press, lashing out at "the people who won't rest until they get me." Then he said that there were some tapes that were damaging. General Haig and J. Fred Buzhardt, his special White House counsel in the Watergate matter, were pessimistic, he said. They gave him no chance to survive.

David asked for the transcripts and read them. By this time, Cox had come in, and he read them too. David at once saw the implications of the Nixon admissions. Cox said little. Julie felt neither shock nor surprise nor betrayal. "What sadness she felt," David said, "wasn't 'my world is exploding' or 'my forum has vanished,' but she was sad for her father, sad that the whole situation now was bringing down a presidency she thought was worth continuing, a man she loved."

Explaining the differences in their views, David says that he had been far more gloomy about the ultimate outcome than the family and others "who were involved in the everyday political atmosphere of Watergate." His own day-to-day exposure, he recalls, was with law students. Thus he could view and analyze the situation more objectively than Julie. "Her everyday experience was with supporters at rallies, political people. . . ."

However, he added that none of this meant that he and Julie were not united in support of the President. Did the ordeal have an impact upon their married life? David sighs as he answers: "It wasn't easy."

Nothing was decided that night. The family session ended at midnight. Pat had hardly said a word throughout the entire evening.

Julie and Tricia, opposing their husbands and the entire White House group advising the President, wanted him to fight it out from the dock at an impeachment trial. Nixon took them both into the solarium the next morning and told them there was no hope. Careful count had shown that even the small support he had in the Senate, which would try him, was eroding and conviction was inevitable.

But they pleaded with him, both tearfully, to

withhold his resignation. Apparently they convinced him that maybe—just maybe—a flicker of hope remained. He returned to his office and, a few hours later, he told Haig, his lawyer James St. Clair, and Raymond K. Price, Jr., one of his speech writers, that he had decided to go on national television. He would tell the country about the June 23 tapes and ask for their support. For a day, Nixon believed that he could re-play the Checkers speech and win again.

The decision made, he took the family, including Bebe Rebozo, to Camp David, where Price would follow and the speech would be written.

But the next day, on Sunday, the last ray was extinguished. Nixon changed his mind: there would be no last speech. He ordered the transcripts to be made public the next day, accompanied by a statement in which he admitted that the tapes were "at variance with certain of my previous statements."

Monday afternoon, the country heard. Shock waves rumbled all through official Washington; the nation itself was stunned. Now, even the most ardent Nixon supporter backed away from him and there was nothing left.

The President had decided to ride out the storm on a last voyage aboard the *Sequoia* with his family. Unknown to him, Julie arranged a send-off.

Terry Ivey: "The statement about the new tapes was released at four in the afternoon and, about five, I was getting ready to go home when Julie came down and invited some of us upstairs to say goodbye. We all trooped out and waited for them. The President came out with Mrs. Nixon, Julie, Tricia, David, Rose Mary Woods. We had all expected them to show some sign of being upset or unhappy. I couldn't believe it! Mrs. Nixon was like nothing had really happened. I mean, she was cheery, she was smiling, and even Nixon was joking, saying to David, 'Look at all the pretty girls. Have you ever seen so many pretty girls? Boy, if I was a young fellow like you . . .' Julie heard and she laughed.

"All of us were surprised at the contrast between what we had expected and what we saw."

Afterward, they were to realize that it was all a brave show. There was no one in the Nixon family who felt cheerful: their emotions ranged from despondency on the part of the President to sadness, but no higher up the mood scale. Helen Smith, who had returned to Washington from London, gets to the heart of the little charade: "The family," she says, "had closed ranks around the President. There was a determination not to allow their personal feelings to extend to the staff or to the outside world."

And what of Pat Nixon during those seven days between the time she learned of the June 23 tapes and the day she left the White House? She was deeply hurt, saddened, and worried. She stopped answering phone calls, even from friends she had known for years. Nor did she reply to memos from the East Wing, unusual for her. Her staff became alarmed.

It was a time of mourning for her, for a tragedy had occurred. There had been a real death in the family; and never, in all the crises of her hard life, had Pat Nixon needed sympathy or wanted others to share her grief. She would bear it alone, as she had borne all her other troubles.

On Wednesday, the President told her of his final decision to resign. Numbed as she was by the events, she knew that the job of moving from the executive mansion in just two days would be a gigantic one, and she was equal to it. The family's furniture, clothing, and personal belongings, accumulated over the years, had to be sorted; crates had to be ordered; packing had to be supervised. She got to work.

The anguish she felt finally emerged on August 9, that final day of the Nixon presidency.

She stood behind him in the magnificent East Room as he said goodbye to his staff, the East and West Wingers, the household workers, and all the others who had served his administration in the White House. It was nearly 10 A.M. and she was surprised to see that lights and television cameras had been set up. She hadn't wanted that because she knew that the mask was slipping.

The family formed a tight little semicircle in back of him as he spoke for almost twenty minutes. Pat, lovely in a pink skirt and open-necked sweater top, was to his left. It was a rambling speech, often maudlin, in which he talked about the courage of Teddy Roosevelt, the glories of the White House, his "old man," his mother. Many in the room were weeping.

Terry Ivey was there, in perfect control when she walked in. "I wasn't thinking of crying at all," she said. "But when I saw that look on Mrs. Nixon's face, I just burst out crying."

She won't ever forget what she saw. "Her whole life was in her face," Terry says. "It just said everything. There are no words that could ever describe that look. I tried to, myself. I even tried to write it down, but I couldn't.

"It wasn't even just her face. It was her whole self, the way she walked and moved. You could see she was steeling herself."

The former President spoke for nineteen minutes, but Pat couldn't bring herself even to say a word of goodbye to her own personal staff of press aides and secretaries. Eyes dead ahead, she walked toward the olive-drab helicopter which would take them to Andrews Air Force Base where the great silver and blue presidential plane waited.

Helen Smith caught up with her, took her hand and squeezed it. Mrs. Nixon turned her head away and squeezed back. Other aides did the same, and Pat responded the same way to each, not daring to look at any of them.

"She really couldn't say goodbye," declared Mrs. Smith. "It would have been too much of a strain. She couldn't and we couldn't. But taking her hand, we all said we love you and we'll miss you."

On that final day, in that last speech, Richard Nixon began a moving tribute to his late mother. "My mother was a saint," he said. "Yes, she will have no books written about her. But she was a saint."

At this point, Ed Cox, certain he was about to mention Pat, pushed her gently from her position slightly behind him, toward the President's side. But Nixon finished his talk without once referring to the woman who had campaigned with him for twenty-eight years.

Recalling the incident, Wauhillau La Hay, the former Scripps-Howard White House correspondent who had covered Mrs. Nixon for years, bursts out: "By God, that infuriated me." Even Cox's face, she says, registered astonishment.

It was not the only time Nixon had ignored his wife in public. Since the Nixons left Washington, a clearer picture has emerged about the former First Lady and her relationship with the driven man who failed to mention her name as he was leaving the office she helped him win.

15

Private Lives

HUSBAND AND WIFE

Bob Pierpoint, CBS White House correspondent: "For the ten years preceding his resignation, I felt strongly that Nixon and his wife were trapped in a situation where the best she could do was not to hurt him. They tried to play this game of being the perfect husband and wife, but it came through as transparent. It looked so phony, so unrealistic."

On March 16, 1974, returning from her six-day trip to South America, Pat learned en route that the President had decided to celebrate her birthday in Nashville, Tennessee, at the opening of the new home of the Grand Ole Opry. Nixon was not a country and western buff, but the backing of the South was important to him in his fight against impeachment. Instead of proceeding to Washington, her plane was diverted to Nashville. That evening, after a 5,000-mile trip from Brasilia, sick with the flu and running a fever, she went to Opryland, USA, the 369-acre park setting for the new building.

The vast new theater, which cost $15 million, is all tile and glass, unlike the former Opry House, the Ryman Auditorium, which had once been a tabernacle. Many business and political leaders were there, including

218

Tennessee's two senators, Howard H. Baker, Jr., and William E. Brock 3d, and Governor Winfield Dunn. The Opry radio program had been on for some time when the Nixons were announced; Pat and the President entered the balcony, took their seats, and the show continued. After a while, Roy Acuff, a famous Country and Western performer, went to the microphone and announced that a President of the United States was visiting the Opry for the first time in its forty-eight years and would the Nixons honor them all by coming down.

The orchestra twanged out a bluegrass version of "Hail to the Chief" as the Nixons came onto the stage and took seats with the performers in front of a large backdrop in which a large red barn was painted. Because it was the eve of St. Patrick's Day, Pat wore a bright green dress. At the mike, Acuff suggested that the audience sing "Happy Birthday" to Mrs. Nixon, and would the President play the piano for them? He would and did. The audience bellowed the song and Pat, looking embarrassed, sat and waved.

When the song ended, she rose and came forward, her arms extended to hug him. He turned away from her. Her hands dropped to her sides and she went back to her chair.

Nixon had a yo-yo in his hand. Somehow, he had gotten hold of the gadget which Acuff uses as a performing "schtick," a mark of professional identification. Nixon tried to spin the yo-yo but failed. He told Acuff: "I'll stay here and try to learn how to use the yo-yo and you go up and be President." For ten minutes, the President of the United States stood behind the Country and Western star, before 4,400 people, trying to make a yo-yo spin up and down a string. Pat, flushed with fever and perhaps embarrassment, sat and watched him.

At best, it was a silly display but the women reporters who traveled with Pat, the East Wingers who were there, and even some of Nixon's own aides were shocked. For the President had not said one word to his wife all evening long.

Terry Ivey watched aghast. Several years later, looking back, she was still blazing: "He absolutely, in front of thousands of people, turned his back on her, totally ignored her. He turned his back! It was simply incredible.'' Helen Smith, too, remembers the incident. "I shall never forget the expression on her face when he ignored her outstretched arms," she says. "It was one of the times some of us winced."

The trouble was that this was not an isolated incident. Nixon's public treatment of his wife during his presidency was so indifferent that close observers, especially the astute women's press corps, were outraged.

He usually spoke *about* her to audiences: "Pat, my wonderful wife"; "Pat, who's such a great help"; "Pat, who does so much, and I know you'll love her." But rarely did he speak *to* her, and certainly he did not treat her with the warm affection and solicitude that other Presidents have shown for their wives. Gerald Ford would always reach out for Betty; almost unconsciously, in public, his hand would go around her waist and he would draw her to him. Lyndon Johnson sometimes almost cooed to Lady Bird in public; Eisenhower and Mamie held hands. The Trumans' affection for each other was apparent, legendary, and touching.

But Nixon was strangely aloof, never tender, often cold. Myra MacPherson, the *Washington Post* correspondent, wrote: "The press corps used to look in vain for some sort of emotion to pass between Pat and Dick Nixon; observers looked for anything that spoke of warmth."

Not long after the yo-yo incident, the Nixons attended a $1,000-a-plate fund-raising dinner in the capital. She sat behind him and never once did he turn to acknowledge her presence. Worse, he spoke for a long while on Latin American relationships, stressing the need for close neighborly ties. The First Lady had just returned from a triumphant visit to the country where, sixteen years before, she and her husband had been stoned and spat upon; she had led his delegation and at countless functions conveyed her husband's best wishes. She told her hosts in Venezuela that her husband had not been able to come but had sent "the closest thing to his heart—me."

That evening in Washington, it did not look as though she was. He never mentioned her name or called her to the rostrum.

He not only ignored her in public much of the time but spent little time with her in private. A President's free hours are limited, but he cannot be occupied constantly and he isn't. But on many of his weekends, Nixon was either alone or in the company of male companions, particularly his best friend, Bebe Rebozo. Time and again announcements from the White House stated that the President would be spending the weekend at Camp David alone—Pat would remain in Washington. When he vacationed at Key Biscayne or San Clemente, the pattern often was the same.

Once at a dinner for representatives of black African nations at the Sheraton Park Hotel, he arrived with Pat, made his customary "V" sign, delivered a brief address, and walked out of the ballroom.

"He left her standing there, right in the middle of the huge room," says Kandy Stroud, at the time Washington correspondent for *Women's Wear Daily*. "He didn't touch her or say goodbye, there was no 'see you later,' no kiss, not even instructions of where to sit or where to go. He just dropped her in the middle of the floor in front of two thousand people. If it had been my husband, I would have wept, or been furious, or both. Pat just smiled as she stood there and finally, after a long embarrassing few minutes, someone came up and got her seated."

In an incident that was almost funny, they flew to San Antonio in separate planes for a party at the then Treasury Secretary John B. Connally's ranch. Nixon came down the ramp with Texas Senator John G. Tower, who had flown down with him. Pat, who had landed first, began walking across the field to greet her husband. Tower reached her first and kissed her. Then Nixon came up—and shook her hand.

Once, but only once, Pat ignored the outstretched

hand. She had concluded her arduous nine-day trip to three African nations and an elaborate official welcome had been arranged at Andrews Air Force Base. When the plane door opened and Pat emerged, President Nixon was at the top of the ramp to greet her. He extended his hand and touched hers, but she reached up and kissed him instead of shaking it, her left arm around his waist.

The catalogue of such behavior of Nixon toward Pat is distressingly long. A few more examples:

• One of Nixon's aides who conferred with him daily over an entire decade says something one finds almost impossible to believe: "In all that time, Pat's name never once came up in conversation."

• In June of 1970, a state dinner was held at the White House for Venezuelan President and Mrs. Rafael Caldera. At the end of the evening, the Nixons stood at the North Portico, bidding goodbye to their guests. After they had gone, and while some of the other guests were still dancing, Nixon and Pat went toward their private elevator leading to the upstairs quarters. He had his hand on her arm and he seemed to be leaning attentively toward her as other guests watched them depart. Then, as they moved down the hall out of sight of most of the remaining guests, they separated, moving apart as though they had concluded a little game. Writer Judith Viorst, who tells the story, concludes it thus: "Untouching and in silence, each walked on alone."

• The night before he quit the White House, Nixon summoned a delegation of five congressmen to whom he read the letter of resignation he had written to Secretary of State Kissinger. Afterward, he talked to them about the crisis, saying that it had been his own inclination to fight on. "After all," he said, "I have a wonderful family and a pretty good wife."

Could Nixon have been joking? Hardly, at a time like that. Was he too befuddled to realize how the phrase could be interpreted? Or was he simply saying what he felt?

Nixon's friends point out that he has always been a reserved, undemonstrative man, decorous perhaps to a major fault in that he was unable to unbend with the eyes of the world upon him. At home, they say, he was considerate and tender, that he never intended to ignore her, that the family was warm, compact, and affectionate. Julie, indeed, always found him loving, kind, even impulsive as he would exclaim: "Let's do something special tonight!" Or, on the spur of the moment, take them all out for a birthday or anniversary celebration.

Of course, Julie was seeing her father from a daughter's-eye view, which is hardly the same as the view from a mate. Pat, for example, would never intrude upon his work but Julie would not hesitate. She would call often, no matter how pressing the business at the moment; and he would listen. Late one day in 1969, when she was twenty-one, Nixon was working with William Safire on a foreign policy speech when his private phone rang. Answering, he launched into an elaborate discussion of this country's relations with its South American neighbors. Safire, sitting patiently, thought that Henry Kissinger, then National Security adviser, or Secretary of State Rogers was at the other end. It was Julie. The following morning, she was scheduled for an interview-discussion with people from the United States Information Agency on Latin America and wanted a briefing.

But there are just too many documented incidents of Nixon's cold behavior toward his wife to pass them off as shyness or forgetfulness or even total involvement with politics and the business of government. Nixon could be so wrapped up in his own thoughts that he did not notice people around him. But why was Pat so often the object of inattention unless there was a reason?

The question is valid and prompts another: What was their true relationship as husband and wife? On the basis of evidence that has presented itself in the course of my research, I have reached two conclusions:

First, that the warmth and affection that existed between them in the early years of their marriage cooled as the years passed. And second, that the coolness came from his side, not hers.

"She loved him very much," correspondent Helen Thomas says. "That was genuine." And all of Pat's close friends and staff aides to whom I spoke echoed the statement. I heard too many stories of her attitude toward him from too many people to believe otherwise.

But what about him?

He was not unlike other authoritative husbands who place their work and home lives in separate compartments. As we have noted, he told his wife little about his outside life, accepting—and expecting—her support of his decisions but not asking her to share in making them. As time passed and his career advanced, he communicated with her less and less. Pat admitted he had not asked her opinion about running for a second term in 1972. He never talked matters over with her as President Johnson did with Lady Bird, as Jimmy Carter does with Rosalynn. One former staff assistant once observed: "I can't see Dick saying, 'An awful thing happened in Cambodia today, Pat.' " He did not ask what she thought of his State of the Union speeches. Once Pat was asked if her husband had tried out any of these important speeches on her. Her reply: "He never tries anything out." Not until the Watergate crisis did he "try anything out" on his family.

He was, in this sense, cut from the same traditional cloth as Joseph P. Kennedy, whose wife, Rose, knew he was successful but had little notion of what he was doing and was certainly not consulted about any of his ventures. Once Rose read in a newspaper that Joe Kennedy was worth $300 million. Amazed, she said to him: "I didn't know we had that much money." His reply was: "You never asked."

"She gave so much and got so little of what was really meaningful to a woman—attention, companionship, consideration," says Ms. Stroud of Pat Nixon. "Sometimes he was so brutally indifferent I wept for her."

Ms. La Hay puts it this way: "She is a wonderful person whom most of us love deeply, a person of incredible courage and dedication. But she was married to a man who didn't appreciate her and this can be devastating to a woman.

"She's the one we worry about," Ms. La Hay told me just about the time the Nixons left. "The hell with him.

"Let's understand something. This man was the biggest male chauvinist pig of all time."

THE NIXONS AND SEX

When it came to sex, Richard Nixon was unlike many of his predecessors in office and, indeed, much of the Washington establishment. Whatever historians may eventually conclude about him, one can say with considerable assurance that the 37th President was no swinger.

The Washington sex scandals of the mid-1970s caused a lot of skeletons to come tumbling out of capital closets. It all began when former Representative Wilbur D. Mills of Arkansas was stopped by Washington police after a night on the town with Argentine stripper Fanne Foxe, and then when it was revealed that former Representative Wayne Hays of Ohio apparently paid blond, thirty-three-year-old Elizabeth Ray $14,000 a year of the government's money to act not as a congressional committee clerk but as a mistress.

Tales of sex and politicians came pouring out of Washington. Yet the funny part was that it had been going on all along, but the capital's press corps, the insiders, and certainly the principals themselves weren't talking about it—in print or on the air. Women have always been plentiful in Washington and legislators are important people. And as Henry Kissinger said, "Power is the ultimate aphrodisiac."

Presidents, certainly the most powerful people in the country, have recognized and sometimes operated on Henry Kissinger's great principle.

Some irreverent White House watchers called John F.

Kennedy Jack the Zipper. As President, he is said to have had liaisons in the White House and in hotels in New York, Palm Beach, Chicago, and Los Angeles. According to rumors, a staff aide would get in touch with the lady he chose, often an important film star, and then, when he visited the city, he would slip into the suite and join her for the night. When a reporter once asked a publisher friend of Kennedy if it was true that Robert was on intimate terms with Marilyn Monroe, the publisher answered that if Bobby wasn't, "he's not Jack Kennedy's brother." Once Kennedy reportedly tried to seduce an attractive woman educator and author on their third meeting. She refused and asked him: "Do you do this to all the women you meet?" He is said to have answered: "My God, no, I don't have the strength."

Lyndon Johnson was a toucher, a kisser, and an outrageous flirt. He would sit on the deck of the *Sequoia* between two attractive women, holding their hands as he watched the TV news. He would stroke the hand of a pretty woman who sat beside him in the basement theater in the White House as a movie unrolled. He would dance at White House receptions, his body glued to his partner's, and the prettier and more youthful she was, the closer he was stuck. Barbara Howar, one Washington personality whose hand he stroked at the movies, says that Lady Bird had "been forced to deal politely with several female employees whom Johnson fancied." Ms. Howar, who worked in the 1964 campaign and came to know the Johnsons well, wrote in her memoirs of those years: ". . . while I am not suggesting that the thirty-sixth President of the United States was a dirty old man, I would not bet the rent money that he was not."

Warren G. Harding's sex life was, of course, notorious. He had an illegitimate daughter who was conceived, as her mother, Nan Britton, recounted the story, in the Senate Office Building while Harding was a senator. Later, after he was elected to the presidency, Nan said they made love in a White House closet. Harding also carried on a lengthy extramarital affair with a woman named Carrie Phillips. Franklin D. Roosevelt's affair with Lucy Mercer Rutherford and possibly another with Missy Le Hand, his secretary, have been duly recorded by his son Elliott. Eisenhower's much-discussed wartime relationship with his female driver, Kay Summersby, has been commented on by the late President Truman and, most recently, described by the lady herself in a posthumously published book.

And Nixon? There were some ugly rumors about him and his close friend Bebe Rebozo, none of which have been shown to have the least basis in truth. They are noted here only for the fact that the White House itself buzzed with them because Nixon and Rebozo spent so much time together at Camp David and Key Biscayne. The two were close friends and Nixon probably needed a confidant. That he apparently chose Bebe Rebozo and not his wife may be significant in terms of his relationship with Pat, but allegations that the friendship went any further have no foundation at all.

What, then, can be said about Nixon's sexuality?

As we have already discovered, from the testimony of his first serious girlfriend, Nixon had been a "perfectly normal young man," as sexually aggressive as young men generally are in their teens and early twenties. Though he was hardly a swinger even then, with little time for dates, his college classmate, Wood Glover, Jr., now retired in San Clemente, says he "definitely had an eye for the girls." At law school, though still too poor and too busy to have many dates, he eyed the girls even more closely and spoke appreciatively about their attributes. Dr. David Abrahamsen, in his psychobiography of Nixon, suggests that Nixon "shared Frank's [his father's] strong sexual drive."

Once, soon after he was married, Nixon and Jack Drown took their young wives to a Los Angeles cabaret. A master of ceremonies handed the two men a fistful of gaudy garters with instructions to toss them at the high-kicking legs of the chorus girls who were dancing on stage. Richard rose happily to the challenge, aiming carefully and scoring a ringer. So did Drown and each won a bottle of champagne.

But if sex and girls' legs held interest for Richard Nixon as a younger man, and if Dr. Abrahamsen is correct in his analysis that he had "powerful amorous inclinations," did the passions wane as the young man grew older?

Friends say no. One visitor to San Clemente told me: "The old man was furious about that stuff in *The Final Days* about their sex lives." (Woodward and Bernstein had written that Pat had rejected his advances since 1962.)

Still, on the basis of his apparent excessive coldness in public and the observations of many who were close to him, one may speculate that Nixon's power drive may have claimed still another victim—his own sexual impulses.

A common psychological process, more widespread in our sex-ridden society than many realize, may have been at work. Declares Dr. Herbert M. Adler, associate professor of psychiatry at Hahnemann Medical School in Philadelphia and a practicing psychiatrist: "In persons who are preoccupied with the issues of survival—and one can interpret what one does in any arena, whether political, business, professional or whatever, as survival—the sex drive will be relegated to a relatively minor position."

Making it clear that he was speaking in general terms and not "analyzing" Richard Nixon, Dr. Adler explains further: "Individuals who become totally engrossed in other matters pour all their mental and physical energies into them and sex has a low priority in their lives. In the current phrase, for them sex is not 'where it's at.' "

Casebooks of psychiatrists and marriage counselors are filled with complaints of corporate wives, the wives of busy doctors and others who have immersed themselves in work and have little time, energy, or interest for the marriage bed.

Dr. Abrahamsen suggests that Nixon's strong sexual impulses became inhibited quite early in his development. "Having been taught by his mother to curb them," he writes in *Nixon vs. Nixon*, "he consciously set out to do so." The secretiveness that characterized his later years, Dr. Abrahamsen believes, stems from the repression of his sexual wishes. "Those who repress sexual desires are unable or find it very difficult to tell anyone anything about themselves because this would be the same as betraying their inner selves and their deep sexual needs."

Writing in the British publication *The Listener*, Elaine Morgan asserts:

We can be pretty certain that there is now, as there has always been, a minority of men who find that after a brief flareup in adolescence, the interest in sexual activity becomes rapidly less obsessive. . . . They usually retain a keen interest in sex as a spectator sport—in the sense that they will eagerly turn to page three of the tabloids to look at the nude*—but if they were given a choice between a night of love and tickets to the cup final, it would have to be Raquel Welch to make it anything of a contest—and even then, they would ask her for time off to view the Match of the Day.

While nobody has ever claimed that Nixon peeped at *Playboy* or *Penthouse*, the description otherwise appears to be an accurate fit. In his public years, he exhibited an avid interest in sports, especially football; he knew the names of the players, the standings of the teams, and was a TV quarterback in good standing as he commented on the braininess, or lack of it, of the coaches. But a keen interest in sex was either one of the many secrets of this very secretive President, or it did not exist.

There were even jokes in the Nixon White House about his relationship with Pat. Because they appeared so austere, removed, and unloving, the aides buzzed constantly about their sex lives. One stale quip, revived from time to time, went: "They must have done it twice."

Only twice in his long political career has a story been

*The flashier British papers feature bare-breasted young women, often unrelated to any news development, in that prominent spot.

whispered about Richard Nixon and another woman. Before the resignation, rumors flew around the mansion that the President was having an affair with an attractive Far Eastern woman. Gossip about it later seeped into the newspapers.

Members of the press corps were startled, disbelieving, and highly amused. One correspondent grinned when he heard it and shouted: *"Halevai,"* a Yiddish word meaning "I wish it were so." He told me: "That would have been the best thing that ever happened. It would have humanized the guy. But it wasn't true. Nixon? An affair? No way."

In June of 1976, an anonymous tip came to a New York literary agent from a man who claimed to have twenty-two love letters Nixon had allegedly written to the wife of a Spanish diplomat. The Western White House branded the incident a "sordid hoax."

Terry Ivey contributes a fascinating woman's-eye view: "A woman can tell if a male is a ladies' man. Perhaps it's an instinct but she senses it instantly, by the way he looks, talks, acts. It has nothing to do with intelligence or training; she simply *knows*. At a party, I can always tell. There were plenty of men in the White House who certainly were interested; it didn't take very long for the girls to find out.

"But Nixon wasn't. He just cared about the presidency."

The question arises: Why do some high Washington officials and other individuals with soaring ambitions, whose lives are stressful and problems burdensome, lead such sexually active lives, while the drive wanes in others who are like them?

"The effect," declares Dr. Adler, "may be similar to the hunger drive. It is well known that many people under considerable stress will lose their appetites while others, under similar tension, will derive emotional comfort from food, eating more than usual. Tension, then, affects the appetite but it is an individual matter which way the appetite will go.

"Possibly the same process may operate in the sexual sphere, where stress produces a dysfunction of the drive. It will go out of kilter and go either way, either positively or negatively.

"We may also say that those with a tendency to be thin will tend to lose their desire for food under stress, while persons who tend toward being stout may find their appetites increasing.

"Similarly, persons who tend to be extroverts, hail-fellow-well-met, so to speak, may find their sexual appetites increasing under stress. But the sex drives of persons who tend to be asocial, withdrawn, and introverted are likely to be decreased under pressure.

"In other words, there is a style or bent of the personality which becomes exaggerated in the direction that it was already skewed."

16

Full Circle

HEALING NIXON

They were sitting apart—he in the presidential compartment of the big airplane and she in the First Lady's quarters just behind—when they officially ceased being the President of the United States and the First Lady.

Nixon's resignation was to take effect at noon. Three minutes later, Gerald Ford was sworn in by Chief Justice Burger in the East Room. At the time, Air Force One was 39,000 feet above Missouri, halfway between St. Louis and Kansas City.

Tricia and Ed Cox had gone toward the rear to listen by radio to the new President's inaugural address. (Julie and David had remained in Washington.) Richard Nixon was in his closet-size office which adjoined the presidential compartment and his wife was in the VIP reception lounge, directly behind, which she occupied when she traveled with him. Neither left to hear the broadcast or to talk to the other.

Four hours and forty-four minutes after the big silver, blue and white Boeing 2700 took off from Andrews Air Force Base, it landed at the El Toro Marine Base, fourteen miles from San Clemente. Some five thousand persons, sitting on bleachers built by the Marines, were there to welcome them. Pat, the mask with the tight smile affixed, emerged and followed her citizen-husband to a microphone. "We're home," he said, and the crowd cheered. "Having completed one task," he said, "does not mean that we will just sit and enjoy this marvelous California climate and do nothing." Pat, at his right, stood stiffly, hands at her sides. The family boarded a helicopter which lurched up and flew off to La Casa Pacifica, where it landed on the helipad adjacent to the office complex. There, golf carts took them a quarter-mile to the house. About three hundred persons were outside the gates but they could not see them arrive.

Security was drum-tight. No reporters were allowed inside and even a pool TV cameraman was permitted no closer than a half-mile from the gate, where all he could shoot were the walls, trees, and shrubs. Even the welcoming mayor of San Clemente, Thomas O'Keefe, was kept out, though his wife, with a large bouquet of yellow roses for Pat, was admitted.

It was the first of a floral flood to arrive that same day. Pat was amazed and delighted. "Imagine," she told Helen Smith, who had telephoned, "I got four hundred flower arrangements."

There was little time for thinking during those first few weeks. Crates had to be unpacked, their contents sorted and rearranged; the furniture had to be placed, and repaired where necessary. And her husband had to be watched carefully. As events were to turn out, this would be the most important of her concerns.

After the unpacking and settling-in, she began a garden and spent hours planting and cultivating flowers and vegetables. How was she feeling? "Saddened by it all," Julie told me then. "In her heart she knows that my father has done more for his country than any President. He is known as the peacemaker. No, she's not happy over what happened, but she's a fighter to the end."

They were in almost total isolation. The big gates were guarded closely. All phone calls were carefully screened and only a very few got through. Bebe Rebozo and Bob Abplanalp were the only visitors permitted.

One observer stated that it was as though Nixon had pulled the ladder up behind him after a few greetings and handshakes.

There was a secluded area near Oceanside, south of the estate, called Red Beach. It was Camp Pendleton property and the public was barred. They went there once, since they could no longer have the exclusive use of the beach outside their enclave. A month later, they slipped out in the darkness and drove to the baronial Palm Springs estate of Walter Annenberg, former ambassador to England, where they stayed five days.

That was all.

Julie denied heatedly that her mother was "hiding." She told me at the time: "She's trapped there. The press is keeping a deathwatch on the house and the moment she steps out, they'll pounce on her. What do you expect her to do, stand at the checkout line at the Alpha Beta supermarket? She'd be mobbed."

Nevertheless, her friends were becoming worried about her. Victor Lasky, one of the few journalists whom the Nixons trusted, says she was "numb." Earl Mazo uses the same word and adds: "Hurt beyond words." Helen Smith recalls that those early days were "hard for her, so very hard." Helene Drown says it was "a miserably awful time . . . the worst period in their lives." Patricia Reilly Hitt, a longtime friend, said a month after the Nixons left: "She would be something less than human if she were her usual ebullient self. She was undergoing an enormous adjustment." *Time* magazine reported that her despair was so deep "she did not even communicate with her closest friends."

A pathetic little birthday party was held at La Casa Pacifica on January 9, five months later. Nixon had almost died following surgery. He was pale and shrunken, and he was emerging from the deepest depression of his life.

He was sixty-two years old. He sat at one end of the long table and Pat, watching him carefully, sat opposite. Between them were only five guests.

The party was a surprise. He had told Pat the day

before that they would have a quiet little celebration by themselves. "We'll have dinner and then we'll open a bottle of wine," he said. Then she received a telephone call from Victor Lasky in Washington, who told her that old friends were cooking up something.

Bob Abplanalp in Florida had called Bebe Rebozo, who had phoned Lasky. "Let's go out to San Clemente," Bob had said, "and surprise the Old Man on his birthday." They would bring along some big steaks and some of those king crab claws, with the special sauce he liked; and they'd load up with lots of gag presents and, of course, a large birthday cake. Pat quickly agreed and promised not to tell him.

She arranged for the five men to be picked up at the airport the next day and driven to the office complex. Besides Bebe, Lasky, and Abplanalp, the party consisted of a restaurateur from Miami and Abplanalp's lawyer.

Nixon was astounded to see them. He stood outside in the cold, greeting them effusively. On the walk from the office complex to the main house, Lasky noted that the grounds had already begun to look seedy. They went inside the house and Nixon kept exclaiming that he couldn't get over the surprise. Pat was almost childishly delighted that she had pulled it off successfully.

"Well," she said at last, "I guess I'd better go up and get dressed." Fifteen minutes later a fire had been started in the living room and Nixon mixed drinks; he and Pat had wine. Foreign governments had sent gifts on his birthday, among them a two-pound jar of caviar from the Shah of Iran. Pat brought out some crackers and the caviar to serve with the drinks. "He kept urging us to eat the stuff, like a Jewish mother," Lasky says. " 'Eat it, eat it, or the Shah will be angry.' " Pat laughed at this. Israel had sent a scroll which Nixon had placed on the mantel. He went to get it to show it to his guests, reached up, and almost fell. Lasky, behind him, grabbed him and was shocked at how frail he was. ("He was nothing, just bones. He was so weak. He was at the weakest point in his life.")

Afterward, in the living room, he opened his gifts.

Abplanalp had brought an apron inscribed: "I got my job through *The New York Times*." It gave Nixon his biggest laugh of the evening. There were some ties, a few books, and some raunchy presents the men decided not to give him because Pat was there.

The dinner followed. Nixon exclaimed over the crab claws; he hadn't had them for ages, he said. The talk was light. Afterward, the birthday cake was brought in and they all sang "Happy Birthday" as Nixon blew out the candles.

Pat kept watching him. After five hours, she saw he was tiring and said it was time for the company to leave. They stood but Nixon didn't want them to go. Finally, a few minutes later, they left. Nixon stood outside, saying goodbye, chiding Lasky for having put on weight. "You've got to lose it, get it down, it's not good for you," he said.

The company departed. Nixon and Pat stood in the doorway watching them, waving goodbye. Then they went inside and shut the door.

Nixon was recovering from the illness that had almost killed him and the depression that had brought him to the brink of total collapse.

On the airplane heading westward, the depression was already setting in. Compounding his emotional problem was the phlebitis which had eased somewhat during the crisis month but had flared up again. It was not a new problem. Ever since the mid-1960s, he had been bothered by an inflammation of a wall in a vein of his left leg; it had come and gone, giving no serious trouble until June, 1974, when it began to worsen. In the midst of Nixon's journey to the Middle East, the leg had bothered him. He was examined by Dr. Walter Tkach, the White House doctor, who discovered that a thrombus, or clot, had developed high on the left leg, which felt hot and was painfully swollen. It was risky business, Tkach knew. A piece of the clotted blood could break off, move through the bloodstream, and lodge in some far-off part of the body where it could obstruct the blood flow. If a major blood vessel in the heart or lungs were blocked, Nixon would die in seconds. Tkach warned his patient against continuing the trip but Nixon would not listen.

After the resignation, Dr. Tkach was at San Clemente for three weeks. By mid-September, despite President Ford's unconditional pardon, the physician found Nixon in deplorable emotional shape, "a ravaged man who had lost the will to fight." Quickly, Nixon's staff denied that this was so. But it was. The staff gave out stories that he was in "good spirits" and "very comfortable" with his decision to resign. Friends able to get through put a similar gloss on what was really happening.

The stories were pure bunk. Nixon was gripped by deep melancholia. He would sit for hours in his study, unable or unwilling to move, eating little. He suffered from severe insomnia, which had always afflicted him during bad times. Lasky says: "He was going through a horrible agony. Nobody will know what he suffered, nobody can know."*

Ed Cox knew because he saw what was happening. The "full, free and absolute pardon" hadn't helped his father-in-law, he realized. "He's still way down, very depressed," he reported a few days after the pardon. "He is in a deep depression. I would hope the pardon would eventually lift that but I just haven't noticed that."

Richard Nixon was no stranger to bouts of despondency when his fortunes ebbed or responsibilities mounted. "He takes his falls hard," Garry Wills wrote in *Nixon Agonistes.* "People forget that he is Irish, both sides of his family—a black Irishman, melancholy, prone to despondency." Father John Cronin, an adviser to Nixon during the 1950s, discloses that he was gripped by a severe depression in the early months of 1960 when he realized that Nelson Rockefeller would not be a can-

---

*Nixon later was to confirm, during his TV interviews with David Frost, that life had become "almost unbearable" at that point and that it had lost its purpose for him.

didate for the presidency and that he, Nixon, would probably lead the field. "He brooded on the responsibility," says Father Cronin. "I think he was overcome by the thought of it. Dick has great physical and moral courage but there is an element of self-doubt very deep in him."

But this depression was the worst, especially since it was compounded by a serious physical illness which was draining the strength he needed to cope with his emotional debility. Dr. Tkach, now surgeon general at Andrews Air Force Base, recalls that neither Pat nor Richard talked about the resignation. Pat would talk of other things—the flower beds she was putting into shape, the house, everything but the crisis they had gone through. But he could see her concern. Even more clearly, he saw that Nixon's condition was deteriorating. He urged him to go to a hospital but Nixon stubbornly refused. "I can't get him near one," Dr. Tkach said at the time, and quoted Nixon as saying: "If I go into a hospital, I'll never come out alive."

On September 23, Nixon finally entered Memorial Hospital Medical Center in Long Beach where Dr. John C. Lungren, his personal doctor, found no need for surgery at the time. A clot had been discovered in his right lung but that and the phlebitis were responding to treatment. He remained twelve days and was discharged on October 4 with instructions to rest. Later that month he was readmitted when his condition worsened and surgery was performed after tests had shown the presence of new and dangerous clots. During surgery, he suffered intensive bleeding and was in shock for five hours. Pat was staying at the Drowns' home in Rolling Hills so that she could be closer to the hospital. During the days Nixon was on the critical list, she never left the hospital. She sat outside his room constantly, coming in to see him, when the doctor permitted her, for a few minutes. When he opened his eyes after coming out of shock, she was the first person he saw. Later, the doctor told him he had been "more dead than alive." On November 3, he was removed from the critical list. Ten days later he was allowed to go home.

There is reason to speculate that if it were not for Pat Nixon's constant attention and encouragement during the low points in his life from August until past Thanksgiving, Richard Nixon might have gone over the brink into a total mental breakdown.

He had come close. He admits that he had been in "the depths." Helen Smith is one of their intimate friends who will say on the record that Pat helped bring him out of the darkness. "During those critical days and weeks," she told me, "Mrs. Nixon gave him strength, was right behind him, encouraging him."

Q. "What, actually, did she do to help him?"

A. "She told him to look forward to new accomplishments, and then to look back on all his great positive accomplishments, which she enumerated. In the hospital during his illness, she was there every day. When he awoke, she would be at his side, holding his hand. At home, she rarely left him. If she had not been there, and if he didn't have the devotion of his family at that critical juncture, he would have suffered a real emotional collapse because he thought that everyone had turned against him at that point."

Ethel Kennedy played the same role with her husband, Robert F. Kennedy, after the assassination of John Kennedy in 1963. Bobby slipped into a depression several weeks after the murder. He would not return to his job as Attorney General for a while and when he did, he would spend hours staring or go suddenly for long walks. Home at Hickory Hill he would sit unmoving and silent. At the time, a close friend admitted that, were it not for Ethel, Bobby "might have gone off the deep end." Ethel made certain that the household routine was not disrupted, that there would be no show of sadness in the house, that friends would be present to distract Bobby from his gloom and, most important of all, she communicated to him her own deep religious faith, hoping that he would derive comfort and strength from God. By mid-summer, Bobby's depression lifted.

But now, as Nixon began to emerge from his illness and depression, Pat's own personal problems were just beginning.

STROKE

On July 6, 1976, two years after the resignation, Pat and Richard Nixon left San Clemente for one of the few social occasions they shared. A few miles to the north was the Marriott Hotel in Newport Beach where some two hundred friends had gathered for a party in their honor. Guests included many old-time Republicans of the area, as well as close friends from Whittier. The dinner was excellent and the speeches complimentary. Nixon felt good. He smiled, shook hands, and signed autographs.

Pat, however, seemed quiet. One woman commented that her eyes had a strange glaze and she had turned pale. "This isn't like Pat," another whispered.

She said little, sitting quietly until they finally left the party long past midnight. She gave no hint that anything was amiss.

The next day, Wednesday, July 7, Pat followed her customary routine. In the late afternoon she settled down on the patio to read. Sometime about four P.M. the former First Lady apparently suffered a stroke.

She said nothing and retired for the night, although later her doctor said she suspected what was happening. She had always been in robust health and it may be that she was not accepting any measure of physical weakness. While she was First Lady, she had never had a full physical examination, refusing Dr. Tkach's requests to come down to the fully equipped clinic he supervised on the ground floor of the White House.

In the morning, she had difficulty getting out of bed. Nixon was told and a local San Clemente doctor was summoned. After a quick examination, he called Dr. Jack Mosier, a neurologist, who diagnosed an apparent stroke. Arrangements were made at once to transfer her to Long Beach Memorial.

At noon on Thursday, hospital personnel were notified that Mrs. Nixon was on her way. Shortly after two P.M., an ambulance carrying Pat, accompanied by Nixon and Julie, pulled up at the Columbia Street emergency entrance.

Memorial Hospital Medical Center of Long Beach is a modern stone and glass structure which provides hospital and outpatient care to more than 150,000 persons annually. The seven-story facility, whose lush foliage and landscaping shield it from the busy city, is an outgrowth of the eighteen-room Seaside Hospital started in 1907 in Long Beach by a group of doctors and greeted as "America's first space-age hospital" when it was opened in 1960. It is one of the largest and most advanced medical centers in the West, giving comprehensive medical, surgical, and psychiatric care to Long Beach residents and those from other communities.

The electronically controlled double glass doors swung open as Pat's stretcher was borne through the lobby, past the waiting room to an elevator which rushed her to the seventh-floor Critical Care Center. Nixon and Julie, looking anxious, followed closely.

Memorial Medical Center is decorated in carefully selected soothing colors, with shining glass doors and wide windows, recessed lighting, and matching drapes and carpets. The emergency lobby has gleaming beige vinyl floors and cream walls splashed with green and blue. A nurse intercepts visitors and directs traffic from a desk in the waiting room off the corridor. Since each of Memorial's floors has its own admitting office, Pat was taken directly upstairs to the cardiac care unit, staffed by specially trained nurses, round-the-clock physician coverage, and complete life-support and monitoring systems.

Pat's stretcher was met at the seventh-floor central nursing station by Connie Hamilton, Associate Director of Nursing-Critical Care. Hamilton had supervised Nixon's care when he was hospitalized and had become friendly with the family at that time. She immediately took charge.

Pat was transferred to a large room in cardiac care and attached to a heart monitor. Almost immediately, Dr. Lungren, the Nixon family physician, arrived to see Pat for the first time since she had become ill. Dr. Mosier, a staff neurologist, was also called.

Nixon and Julie were a few steps away in a small, well-furnished waiting room. He signed the hospital release papers brought up by public relations director Jeffrey Gerew. A Secret Serviceman was stationed outside Pat's room, another in the waiting room.

That afternoon and evening she underwent a battery of diagnostic tests, including an electroencephalogram, a brain scan, and examination of spinal fluid.

Press facilities had been hastily set up on the first floor of the adjacent Children's Hospital, where fifty newspeople remained day and night. Dr. Mosier came down and told them Pat was in serious condition but "conscious, communicating, and resting comfortably." He explained that the stroke had caused some slurring of words (dysarthria) and some motor weakness and loss of sensation in her left arm, leg, and side of her face. "The next thirty-six to forty-eight hours are crucial," he said. There had been a small hemorrhage in a pea-sized area of the right cerebral cortex of the brain, which controls the functions on the left side of the body, and this had caused the partial paralysis.

Answering reporters' queries, the doctor said Mrs. Nixon would undergo further testing with the EMI brain X-ray machine when she was "a little more stable." In this test, he explained, small sections of the brain are examined one at a time. This can disclose any possible abnormality or distortion. While Mrs. Nixon's condition would remain serious for the next two or three days, Dr. Lungren was feeling increasingly optimistic. "We've got another twenty-four hours behind us and there's no great evidence of increasing bleeding," he said.

The doctors said Mrs. Nixon was able to walk "with assistance" and she would be permitted to move around for ten minutes twice a day.

Pat was surprising her doctors. Many stroke patients, Dr. Mosier knew, become despondent. "They think life is over, they give up the fight," he said. But Pat Nixon wasn't of that breed. Her mental attitude, the doctor found, was "excellent."

Tricia, who flew in from New York, arrived at the hospital Thursday night, having caught the first plane she could. "I'm just trying to see my mother," she told reporters. "I know you'll understand." Julie and David and Richard Nixon were at the hospital much of the time the first few days but were permitted to see Pat only for a few moments to avoid tiring her. On Friday, July 9, Nixon told the press: "One characteristic she has is self-reliance." Pat's spirits, he said, were "indomitable" and she "would see this thing through." During the entire period of her hospitalization, only Julie, David, Tricia, and the former President visited Mrs. Nixon; Tricia's husband was not there.

The first few days, Pat rested quietly. She was permitted to take a few steps around the room, aided by a nurse, several times daily. She had no private nurses—the ratio in the cardiac care unit was one patient to one nurse. Nurse Hamilton remained close and in charge.

On Saturday, two days after she was hospitalized, Mosier told reporters that the doctors were "quite satisfied" with Pat's progress. Nixon, who appeared tense and tired when he arrived at the hospital with Tricia and Julie, was smiling and cheerful when he left two hours later.

"The determination and fire in her eyes I've seen so often in difficult times in the past is coming back and I think this is going to be the determining factor," he said. "This determination and will is as important, or more important, as her physical condition. In this case, the doctors believe her remarkable spirit to get well is working with them and gives them an opportunity to make a more favorable prognosis as to the time and extent of recovery."

On Sunday, July 11, Dr. Lungren declared that the critical stage was over. He warned, however, that Pat was not yet out of the woods. Her condition had stabilized, he said, but there was always a chance of sudden deterioration of condition in stroke patients. That afternoon she was moved from the critical care unit to Room 660 on the sixth floor, the same room where

Nixon had been treated for phlebitis twenty-one months earlier.

Pat's room was at the end of a long corridor to the left of the elevator. It was small—about 12 feet by 15 feet—with a large window facing south toward Palos Verdes. Adjoining it was a patients' lounge which was taken over for Pat's physical therapy because hospital officials felt that her use of the regular rehabilitation center would disrupt other patients too much.

Patient-to-nurse ratio on the sixth floor is about four to one. Pat didn't have private nurses but Hamilton did send down two of the seventh-floor nurses to replace two on the sixth floor. They were assigned to Pat—and others. After a few days, however, this was discontinued.

The staff had, of course, gotten to know the Nixons during Dick's illnesses and treated them with a minimum of fuss. Although the hospital permits families to spend the night in patients' rooms and eat meals with them, the Nixons did neither. Only the presence of the Secret Servicemen, one at the head of the corridor and others in the waiting room, hinted that the patient was somewhat special.

On Tuesday, July 13, Pat began a program of restricted physical exercise. Twice a day, at 11 A.M. and at 2 P.M., she and a therapist worked at a program developed by Dr. Bernard J. Michela, director of the Department of Rehabilitation and Physical Medicine. The exercises were aimed at strengthening her left side. In one, Pat would hold out her left hand and the therapist would push against it. Pat, aided by the therapist, would also walk back and forth on the carpeted floor.

The sessions began with twenty-minute periods and were lengthened as Pat became stronger. Later, occupational therapy exercises directly related to daily activities were added. On July 15, Dr. Michela said Pat was walking independently with only standby assistance by a therapist or nurse.

On Friday afternoon, July 23, two weeks after she had entered, Pat Nixon left Long Beach Memorial

Medical Center. Wearing a bright yellow pants outfit, a smiling and waving Pat was wheeled through the hospital lobby by an equally smiling Richard. Daughters Julie and Tricia and Dr. Lungren followed.

"I feel fine, but I'm a little frightened about the driver," Pat joked, motioning over her shoulder.

Some fifty persons—staff, patients, and visitors —cheered and clapped as the group posed briefly for photographers. Then Nixon helped Pat out of the wheelchair and she walked a few steps to the waiting limousine, driven by agent Bill Granger, which took her back to San Clemente and a life of increasing reclusiveness.

More than a year and a half later, she was still secluded. She had improved so much since her stroke that even her doctors were amazed. A close friend admits: "Only God knows whether she will or will not get back to her former self."

Nixon once said that his wife, like his mother, was a "sundowner," a woman of great strength and resilience. She will never cease trying.

Epilogue

They bore within their breasts the grief
That fame can never heal—
The deep, unutterable woe
Which none save exiles feel.
—William Edmonstoune Aytoun,
"The Island of the Scots"

She has come full circle.

Pat met Richard Nixon in California, married him there, and began with him there his political career that was to bring them both great fame and prestige. Now she has returned with him, not far from where they started, to be sequestered inside their mansion amid the wreckage of his presidency and the hollowness of her infinitely sad life.

She allowed herself to be forced into a role that she would not have chosen for herself. She played that role with rare magnificence, fully supporting the man who wanted what she did not. In the process she yielded up her personal independence, but that did not matter to her. She loved Richard Nixon and devoted her life to him. She will undoubtedly continue to do precisely that for the remainder of her life.

She has had times of glory and now there is sorrow. She wanted peace and privacy, but she wanted them with grace, dignity, and honor, not with the legacy of shame that, barring a miracle none can foresee, must be left to their descendants.

She was a vibrant young girl, tall and beautiful, life-loving and hard-working. She chose to link her life to Richard Nixon and this is the way it turned out.

Appendix A

A FIRST LADY'S TRAVELS

The following is a list of the 74 countries, and Hong Kong, visited by Mrs. Nixon since 1953, including the years she traveled to each country:

Afghanistan 1953
Argentina 1958
Australia 1953
Belgium 1974
Bolivia 1958
Brazil 1956
Burma 1953
Cambodia 1953
Canada 1959, 1972
Ceylon 1953
Colombia 1958
Costa Rica 1955
Cuba 1955
Denmark 1961, 1964
Dominican Republic 1955
Ecuador 1958
Egypt 1963
El Salvador 1955
Ethiopia 1957
France 1963, 1966
Germany 1963, 1966
Ghana 1957, 1972
Great Britain 1958, 1963, 1964, 1966, 1969, 1970

Greece 1963, 1966
Guatemala 1955
Haiti 1955
Honduras 1955
Hong Kong 1953
Hungary 1963
Iceland 1956
India 1953, 1969
Indonesia 1953, 1969
Iran 1953, 1972
Ireland 1964, 1970
Israel 1966
Italy 1957, 1963, 1970
Ivory Coast 1972
Japan 1953
Jordan 1966
Korea 1953
Laos 1953
Lebanon 1963
Liberia 1957, 1972
Libya 1953, 1957
Malaya 1953
Mexico 1940, 1952, 1955, 1965, 1970

Morocco 1957
New Zealand 1953
Nicaragua 1955
Norway 1964
Pakistan 1953, 1956, 1969
Panama 1955
Paraguay 1958
People's Republic of China 1972
Peru 1958, 1970
Philippine Islands 1953, 1956, 1969
Poland 1959, 1972
Portugal 1963
Romania 1969

Singapore 1953
Spain 1963, 1970
Sudan 1957
Sweden 1964
Switzerland 1963, 1966
Taiwan 1953, 1956
Thailand 1953, 1956, 1969
Tunisia 1957
Turkey 1956, 1966
Uganda 1957
Uruguay 1958
USSR 1959, 1972
Venezuela 1958
Vietnam 1953, 1956, 1969
Yugoslavia 1970

Appendix B

A FIRST LADY'S SCHEDULE OF ACTIVITIES

In addition to foreign travel, Mrs. Nixon's schedule was divided into three sections: "In-House"—activities in the White House and its grounds; "Area"—activities in the Washington district; and "Domestic"—activities around the nation. Here, from official White House sources, is Pat Nixon's schedule for 1973, her last full year as First Lady.

In-House

JANUARY

5   Reception for freshmen Congressmen
8   Photo opportunity of Inaugural display cases
9   The President's birthday—dinner for 15
12 Reception for Shenyang Acrobatic Troupe of China
21 Worship Service at the White House
    Nixon-Ryan families reception
    Republican National Committee Reception

FEBRUARY

1   Arrival ceremony for Prime Minister Heath
    State dinner for the Prime Minister
2   Swearing-in ceremony for Cabinet members
6   Presented with Gift of Life Certificate by Hadassah

251

	State dinner for King Hussein
7	Tea for the Continental Society of Washington, D.C.
13	Reception for the Women's Committee of the National Symphony
14	Tea for the winners of the National Center for Voluntary Action Contest
22	Tea for the American Registry of Radiologic Technicians
	Tea for the wives of the Board of Directors of the United States Chamber of Commerce
25	Worship Service—Dr. Norman Vincent Peale
28	Governors' Dinner

MARCH

1	State dinner for Mrs. Golda Meir
2	Reception for American Bandmasters' wives
6	Presentation of the White House Guidebook
11	Worship Service—Monsignor John Kuhn
13	Presentation of a quilt from two ladies of Appalachia
	Reception for the Association of American Foreign Service Women
14	Greeting of the National Easter Seal Child Ambassadors' wives for tea
20	Reception to present the White House recording library

APRIL

12	Presented awards for landscaping on behalf of the American Association of Nurserymen
14,15	Tour of the White House grounds with Mrs. Nixon
15	Worship service—Rev. Edward V. Hill
17	Arrival ceremony for Italian Prime Minister Andreotti
	State dinner for the Prime Minister
18	Awarded Queen Olha medal by the Women's Association for the Defense of the Four Freedoms for Ukraine, Inc.
	Presented the Teacher of the Year Award

*   *   *

MAY
- 1   State dinner for Chancellor Willy Brandt
- 2   Greeting of the Hearing and Speech Poster child
- 7   Luncheon for the Senate ladies
- 8   National Trust Historic Preservation Luncheon
- 9   Greeting for the D.C. Chapter of the American Red Cross Volunteers
Greeted the Goodwill Worker of the Year
- 11   Greeted Argentine Ambassador Muniz and received gift
- 16   Reception for the winners of the Wheelchair Decorating Contest
Reception for the Military Wife of the Year finalists
- 17   Greeted members of the Arthritis Board for Arthritis Month
Greeted wives of the Presidential Executive Interchange Program
- 24   Dinner for the POW's
- 25   Swearing in Ceremony, Attorney General Richardson

JUNE
- 4   Luncheon for Committee for the Preservation of the White House
- 6   Greeted and photographed with Multiple Sclerosis Mother and Father of the Year
Tea for Mrs. Tolbert of Liberia
- 7   Private visit with Mr. Goodwin N. Anim from Ghana
- 12   Greeted students from Maimonides Institute
- 13   Launched presidential cruise program—first of a series on the *Sequoia*
- 14   Received members of the American Symphony Orchestra League at a tea
- 18   Attended arrival ceremony for Secretary Leonid I. Brezhnev
- 22   Attended signing ceremony U.S.-U.S.S.R. agreement with Julie and Tricia

*   *   *

JULY
24	Arrival ceremony for Shah of Iran
26	Greeted wives of White House Fellows and Independent Agency Wives
31	Attended arrival ceremony of Prime Minister Tanaka

AUGUST
2	Tea for Mrs. Bongo of Gabon
3	Tea and reception for members of the Bolshoi Ballet

SEPTEMBER
10	Republican National Committee Reception with the President
18	Arrival ceremony for His Excellency Ali Bhutto of Pakistan
19	Greeted members of "Inter-Tribal Council of the Five Civilized Tribes"
22	Swearing-in Ceremony of Dr. Kissinger in the East Room
25	Reception for wives of members of the National Defense Transportation Association
27	Greeted Freedom Foundation of Valley Forge
28	Received members of Zonta International at reception in Blue Room

OCTOBER
2	Greeted Whittier Senior Citizens in Yellow Oval Room
	Reception for National Recreation and Park Association—East Garden
3	Gave reception for the Capital Speakers Club—State Floor
8	Photographed with Mr. and Mrs. James Welles of the National Carousel Roundtable Club—Map Room
	Accepted copy of White House Gardens Book from Mr. and Mrs. James Welles—East Garden
9	Joined the President at arrival ceremony for His Excellency Houphouët-Boigny, President of Ivory Coast

10   Accompanied the President to the National Medals of Science Presentations in the East Room
Coffee with Mrs. Mobutu of the Zaire Republic—Yellow Oval Room
Tea for Mrs. Houphouët-Boigny—Blue Room

12   Reception—President announced new Vice President

15   Accompanied the President to Medal of Honor Ceremony—East Room

18   Reception for Salvation Army Auxiliary of Washington, D.C.—Blue Room and State Dining Room

20,21   White House Grounds Fall Garden Tour
Gave Beautification Awards

23   Reception for American Association of Medical Assistants—State Floor

24   Photographed with Muscular Dystrophy Poster Child, Michael Newsome—Map Room

26   Greeted members of the American Association of University Women. Exchange Participants from Soviet Women's Committee—Map Room

NOVEMBER

2   Reception—Volunteer Committees of Art Museums—State Dining Room

13   Accepted First Christmas Seals in the Library
Sahel Area Ambassador Wives Tea in Blue Room

14   Photographed with poster children of the National Hemophilia Foundation in the Library
Accepted Thanksgiving Turkey from National Turkey Federation
Reception for National Association of Realtors Wives in the Blue Room

DECEMBER

4   Arrival ceremony for His Excellency Nicolae Ceausescu of Romania
Attended dinner with President for Ceausescu

5   Reception for International Conference on the

	Role of Women in the Economy and Advisory Committee on Economic Role of Women in the State Dining Room
10	Accepted White House Christmas Tree from North Carolina Christmas Tree Growers
14	Press Preview Tour of Decorations of White House
16	White House Worship Service conducted by Reverend Billy Graham
17	Diplomatic Children's Party

Area

JANUARY

18	Reception honoring the Vice-President Salute to the States
19	Salute to America's Heritage American Music Concert Youth Concert Symphonic Concert
20	Inaugural Ceremony Inaugural Parade Inaugural Balls
25	Final tribute to former President Johnson

FEBRUARY

1	The Presidential Prayer Breakfast at the Washington Hilton
7	Visit to Alice Roosevelt Longworth at her home
20	Received the Molly Pitcher Award from the Women's Forum on National Security at the Washington Hilton
22	Attended performance of *Irene*
27	Attended briefing on the National Center for Voluntary Action at the State Department

MARCH

15	Attended dinner for the National Cystic Fibrosis Foundation
16	National Wildlife Federation dedication at Tyson's Corner, Va.

*   *   *

APRIL
10 Attended Senate ladies' luncheon in the Caucus Room, Senate Office Building
11 Presented courage award to Jack Pardee on behalf of the American Cancer Society
Attended the Cherry Blossom Luncheon at the Sheraton Park
14 Attended White House Correspondents' Dinner
18 Attended "An Evening with Sandra Fortune"—outstanding black ballerina

MAY
9 Accompanied President to New Majority at Washington Hilton
11 Attended St. John's College Father-Son Banquet
23 Attended Congressional Breakfast at Shoreham

JUNE
14 Attended Lions Club luncheon at the Sheraton Park
21 Accompanied President to dinner at Soviet Embassy celebrating their 33rd Anniversary

JULY
26 Attended luncheon given by Mrs. Talmadge for senate wives in Senate dining room

AUGUST
1 Accepted Georgetown Post Office commemoration medal

SEPTEMBER
19 Installed Wauhillau La Hay as president of Washington Press Club at L'Enfant Plaza Hotel
20 Dedicated Glen Burnie Maryland Park

OCTOBER
17 Attended ground-breaking ceremonies for

Model Secondary School for the Deaf at Gallaudet College

NOVEMBER

8   Reception and dinner of Nevada State Society at Sheraton Park Hotel; received "Outstanding Women of the Century" award; surprise visit by President

13   Accompanied President to drop-by for Senator Wallace F. Bennett, Happy Birthday party in the Congressional Club

27   Visited Model Home to conserve energy at the Bureau of Standards, Gaithersburg, Maryland

30   Attended SOS Desert Ball with President at the Sheraton Park Hotel

DECEMBER

5   Attended reception with President at the Romanian Embassy

6   Gerald R. Ford Swearing-in, at U.S. Capitol, with President

11   Attended Meeting of Foreign Service Women at the State Department

12   Attended Presidential Appointees Dinner Drop-By with President

14   Lighting of National Christmas Tree at Ellipse

Domestic

JANUARY

1   Attended Rose Bowl Game and Parade —Pasadena, Calif.

4   Attended Memorial services for Hale Boggs

FEBRUARY

MARCH

29   Attended Town and Gown Luncheon at USC Pasadena, Calif.

30   Attended L.A. Medical Association Luncheon

*   *   *

APRIL
2 Visit of Nguyen Van Thieu at Western White House
19 Visit to Norfolk
27 Accompanied President to Stennis Center

MAY
30 Attended funeral of Secret Service agent in Greenwich, Conn.

JUNE
8 Accompanied President to Orlando, Florida—Florida Technological Fair
15 Accompanied President to Pekin Library and Dirksen Research Center—Unveiling of Cornerstone
28 Gave poolside reception at San Clemente for Secretary Brezhnev

JULY
9 Kelley Swearing-in at Kansas City with the President
18 Attended funeral of brother
25 Reciprocal Dinner at Embassy of Iran

AUGUST
20 Accompanied President to 74th Annual VFW Convention—New Orleans

SEPTEMBER
none

OCTOBER
11 Attended 75th Anniversary Dinner of the American Irish Historical Society in New York at Waldorf-Astoria

NOVEMBER
18 Accompanied President to Georgia and Memphis, Tennessee

Acknowledgments

I want to express my deep gratitude to all the persons who, as individuals or representatives of organizations, helped me reconstruct the life of my subject. Many are specifically named in the text in appropriate places but some I must single out for special thanks.

I owe a great debt to Helen Smith, Terry Ivey, and others of the East Wing, former members of Mrs. Nixon's staff, who patiently tolerated my persistent questioning and shared with me their knowledge and insights. High on my list, too, are Earl and Rita Mazo and Victor Lasky; Earl and Victor were follow journalists with me on *The Stars and Stripes* during World War II. Thanks, also, to Julie Nixon Eisenhower, who, doubtless unwittingly, started me off on this project when she told me in Washington two months after her father's resignation that her mother had been one of the greatest yet least appreciated First Ladies in our history. And to Helene Drown and Virginia Counts, both old and dear friends of Mrs. Nixon. Clement E. Conger, the White House curator who worked with Mrs. Nixon on redecorating the mansion, was also immeasurably helpful. I thank, too, Dr. Walter Tkach, the President's physician, who was interviewed at the White House during Nixon's administration.

I am indebted to the dozens of persons who grew up or worked with or knew the youthful Pat and Richard and graciously took the time to open their storehouse of memories: especially Roy O. Day, Nixon's first campaign manager; Jerry Voorhis, his first opponent; Evelyn Dorn, who worked with Pat and Nixon on many of their campaigns; Marion Nichols, who, as Marion Murray, was a fellow teacher; and Robert C. Pierpoint (now a TV newsman), who remembered Pat so well from his student days. Most helpful and informative, too, were Ola-Florence Welch, Lucy Winchester, Professor Flora Rheta Schreiber, and many members of the Whittier College Class of 1934. I offer a salute to the journalists who covered Pat Nixon over the years and who graciously let the tables be turned and allowed themselves to be interviewed. In a work of this kind, where sensitivities are involved, it is understandable that a number of people gave information but asked for anonymity. Their request, of course, was honored; I extend to them my thanks and appreciation.

I wish also to express my gratitude to individuals and officials of the cities and neighborhoods in California, Washington, D. C., and New York where Mrs. Nixon lived and worked for opening doors and guiding and informing me. They are too numerous to list, so an umbrella thank-you to all. I appreciate the kindness of the Queens Borough Public Library for permission to browse among and publish photographs from the *New York Herald-Tribune* morgue. I gratefully acknowledge the assistance provided by Renée Schulte, director of the Richard M. Nixon Oral History Program of the Department of History of California State University, Fullerton. A more detailed listing of sources from the Oral History Program appears in the bibliography. Thanks also to Dorothea Lobsenz for valuable research assistance.

Finally, and most especially, my gratitude and my love to my wife, Irene, for her expert judgment and for her unalloyed patience during the long gestation period of this book.

Selected Bibliography

Abrahamsen, David, M. D. *Nixon vs. Nixon: An Emotional Tragedy.* New York: Farrar, Straus and Giroux, 1977.

Bradlee, Benjamin C. *Conversations with Kennedy.* New York: W. W. Norton, 1975.

Chesen, Eli S., M. D. *President Nixon's Psychiatric Problem.* New York: Peter H. Wyden, 1973.

Costello, William. *The Facts About Nixon.* New York: Viking Press, 1960.

de Toledano, Ralph. *One Man Alone: Richard Nixon.* New York: Funk & Wagnalls, 1969.

Drury, Allen. *Courage and Hesitation.* New York: Doubleday, 1971.

Edmondson, Madeleine and Alden Duer Cohen. *The Women of Watergate.* New York: Stein and Day, 1975.

Felknor, Bruce L. *Dirty Politics.* New York: W. W. Norton, 1966.

From Fishcarts to Fiestas: The Story of San Clemente. Members of the San Clemente Historical Society, ed. Blythe Walton, 1974.

Howar, Barbara. *Laughing All the Way.* New York: Stein and Day, 1973.

Hoyt, Edwin P. *The Nixons: An American Family.* New York: Random House, 1972.

Lukas, J. Anthony. *Nightmare: The Underside of the Nixon Years.* New York: Viking Press, 1976.

MacPherson, Myra. *The Powers Lovers.* New York: G. P. Putnam's Sons, 1975.

Mazlish, Bruce. *In Search of Nixon: A Psychohistorical Inquiry.* New York: Basic Books, 1972.

Mazo, Earl. *Richard Nixon: A Political and Personal Portrait.* New York: Harper and Brothers, 1959.

Nixon, Richard M. *Six Crises.* Garden City, N. Y.: Doubleday, 1962.

Safire, William. *Before the Fall: An Inside View of the Pre-Watergate White House.* Garden City, N. Y.: Doubleday, 1975.

Spalding, Henry D. *The Nixon Nobody Knows.* Middle Village, N. Y.: Jonathan David Publications, 1972.

Thayer, Mary Van Rensselaer. *Jacqueline Kennedy, The White House Years.* Boston: Little, Brown, 1967.

West, J. B. *Upstairs at the White House.* New York: Coward, McCann & Geoghegan, 1973.

White, Theodore H. *Breach of Faith: The Fall of Richard Nixon.* New York: Atheneum, Reader's Digest Press, 1975.

Wills, Garry. *Nixon Agonistes: The Crisis of the Self-Made Man.* Boston: Houghton Mifflin, 1969, 1970.

Woodward, Bob and Carl Bernstein. *The Final Days.* New York: Simon and Schuster, 1976.

UNPUBLISHED SOURCES

Richard M. Nixon Oral History Project, Department of History, California State University, Fullerton: O. H. 834 (Elizabeth A. Cloes, May 29, 1970); O. H. 813 (Myrtle Raine Borden, April 21, 1970); O. H. 877 (Marian Wilson Hodge, May 15, 1970); O. H. 866 (George Gortikov, May 12, 1971); O. H. 988 (Marcia Elliott Wray, June 10, 1970); O. H. 965 (Madeline Thomas, April 27, 1970); O. H. 855 (Howard Frampton, January 14, 1971).

About the Author

LESTER DAVID'S more than thirty-year career as a journalist has included stints as an editor on the old *Brooklyn Eagle* and as Managing Editor of *Stars and Stripes Europe* during World War II. A graduate of New York University, he also holds an MA from Columbia University. He has won a number of journalism awards and frequently lectures on the art and techniques of his profession. His other books include: *Ethel: The Story of Mrs. Robert F. Kennedy; Ted Kennedy: Triumphs and Tragedies; Joan the Reluctant Kennedy;* and *Jackie and Ari* and *Richard and Elizabeth* (both with Jhan Robbins).

Mr. David lives in Woodmere, New York, with his wife. His two daughters and one son-in-law all work in publishing.

Index

267